THE PRECIOUS THINGS OF GOD

Octavius Winslow

GLH PUBLISHING
Louisville, Kentucky

GLH Publishing Reprint, 2015

ISBN: 978-1-941129-16-6

Contents

PREFACE.

A slight glance at the contents of this volume will convey an idea of its character and design. It is intended to be, not so much a systematic treatise of theology, as the companion, in his hours of devotional, meditative retirement, of the experienced and spiritual Christian. The truths which it contains, and the style in which they are presented, are perhaps more adapted to those peculiar seasons in the Christian experience of the believer, in which, profound discussion and laboured thought would not only be distasteful, but out of place. Bearing with him the volume in his sequestered walks with God, or making it the sharer of his temporary seclusion from the active engagements of life, the "precious things of God" which it unfolds may serve to shed the perfume and the lustre of Jesus' name and work around his lone and pensive path—cheering solitude, soothing grief, and dissolving doubt, depression, and gloom. Many and costly are the precious things of God not enumerated in this work; blessed are they who, from the volume of their personal and spiritual experience, can complete the catalogue, and supply the Author's lack. These pages address themselves pointedly and strongly to that essential principle of vital religion—the experimental. We really know as much of the gospel of Christ, and of the Christ of the gospel, as by the power of the Holy Ghost we have the experience of it in our souls. All other acquaintance with Divine truth must be regarded as merely intellectual, theoretical, speculative, and of little worth. But, to apprehend, in some measure, the value, the glory, and the preciousness of the Lord Jesus, and, as a consequence, to esteem Him above all good, to reflect His image, to labour in His service, and to be found preparing and waiting for the happy moment described with such exquisite beauty by Doddridge, and as he only could portray it,—

> "That blessed interview, how sweet!
> To fall transported at His feet;
> Raised in His arms, to see His face
> Through the full beamings of His grace!"

—this, this is spiritual life. And, compared with the heart-experience of this, when we take a close, realising survey of eternity, all other subjects of study and employments of time appear but solemn trifling with our destiny.

The Author regrets, that to the discussion of themes so transcendently important and precious he should have brought so much human feebleness and infirmity. His work, planned amid the happy tranquility and repose of a long and warmly-attached pastorate, and finished amidst the scenes of anxiety, excitement, and toil incident to a new and more extended sphere of ministerial labour, has necessarily been exposed to much that was unfavourable to that matured thought, careful composition, and literary finish which he considers efforts of this kind should possess. His hope, however, is, that, imperfect as is his production, the Divine Spirit may yet deign to bless it to the saving of precious souls, give it acceptance with the Church of Christ, and use it for the advancement of the cause of God and truth in the world,—and the glory shall be to the Father, and to the Son, and to the Holy Ghost, three Persons in the One God, world without end. Amen.

Bath, *September* 1859.

Chapter I.
THE PRECIOUSNESS OF CHRIST.

"Unto you therefore which believe He is precious."—1 Peter ii. 7.

A felt conviction of the preciousness of the Saviour has ever been regarded by enlightened ministers of the gospel as constituting a scriptural and unmistakeable evidence of the existence of divine life in the soul; and in moments when neither time nor circumstance would admit of the close scrutiny of a theological creed, or a nice analysis of spiritual feelings and emotions, the one and simple inquiry upon which the whole matter is made to hinge has been—"What is your experience of the worth of the Saviour? is Christ precious to your heart?" And the answer to this question has been to the examiner the test and the measure of the soul's spiritual and vital change. And how proper that it should be so. In proportion as the Holy Spirit imparts a real, intelligent sense of personal sinfulness, there will be the heart's appreciation of the value, sufficiency, and preciousness of the Lord Jesus. An enlightened and thorough conviction of the nature and aggravation of the disease, will enable a physician to form a just conception of the remedial process by which it may be arrested and cured. We estimate the force of a motive power by the strength of the body it propels. Thus, as the conviction of our lost and undone condition deepens, as sin's "exceeding sinfulness" unveils, as the purity and extent of God's law opens, as the utter helplessness and impotence of self is forced upon the mind, the glory, the worth, the suitableness, and the preciousness of Jesus will, through the teaching of the Spirit, present itself vividly to the mind and heart, as constituting the one only foundation and hope of the soul. The Bible recognises but two specific and distinctive characters— the SINNER—the SAVIOUR; and all others are but modifications of these. The saint is but the sinner converted, justified, pardoned, adopted, sanctified, saved, glorified. And all the official relations sustained by Christ in the economy of salvation are but so many varied and beautiful forms of the one Saviour, of whom it is said, "Neither is there salvation in any other: for there is none other name under heaven given among men whereby we must be saved." Thus, then, as you feel your sinfulness, you will estimate the fitness and suitableness of the Lord Jesus Christ as your Saviour. There will be a perfect agreement between your consciousness of guilt and your believing apprehension of the excellence of the Atonement to meet your case. Your sinnership and Christ's Saviourship will harmonise and dovetail in exact and beautiful fitness and proportion. Oh, what a divine and blessed arrangement is this! With what grandeur, yet with what simplicity, does it invest the scheme of salvation! What solemnity, yet what hope, does it throw around the present and the future of the soul! It seems to fathom the lowest depth of my sinfulness, while it lifts me to the loftiest height of God's grace.

In a volume designed to place before its readers a few of the precious things of God's revealed word, we commence, as is most proper, with the foundation and source of them all—the dignity, worth, suitability, and preciousness of Christ. The great truth upon which we are about to expatiate is announced in the words placed at the head of this chapter—"Unto you therefore which believe He is precious." In the unfolding of this subject may there rest upon the writer and the reader the fresh anointing of the Holy Ghost, even Him of whom Jesus said, "He shall glorify Me: for He shall receive of Mine, and shall show it unto you;" that, while we treat of a precious Saviour, His preciousness may be felt in our hearts, filling the whole soul with penitence, faith, and love. We propose, in the present chapter, to group our thoughts around two specific views of the subject—the preciousness of Christ—and the character of those to whom He is precious.

We commence with a consideration of Christ's personal preciousness—His preciousness in Himself. It is the conviction of Christ's personal dignity and worth that gives to faith such a substantial realisation of the greatness and preciousness of His work. We have need, beloved, to be cautioned against an error into which some have fallen—of exalting the work of Christ above the person of Christ—in other words, not tracing the efficacy of Christ's sacrifice to the essential dignity of Christ's person. The Godhead of the Saviour admitted—His atoning death becomes a fact of easy belief. Once concede that He who died upon the cross was "GOD manifest in the flesh," and the mind will experience no difficulty in admitting that that death was sacrificial and expiatory. The sufferings and death of a Being so illustrious must be in harmony with an object and in connection with a result of equal dignity and momentousness; and where will there be found such an object and such a result as the salvation of man? The brilliant achievements of a general rushing to the rescue of a beleaguered garrison may so exalt his personal genius and valour as to invest his name with a glory peerless and immortal; but the reverse of this holds good with Christ. There had been no glory in His achievements, no significance in His work, no efficacy in His blood, had there been no divine dignity and worth in His person. And, had He not taken a single step in working out the salvation of man—had He repaired no breach, wept no tear, endured no agony, shed no blood in the redemption of His Church,—had He, in a word, conferred not a solitary blessing upon our race—He still had been the ETERNAL SON of God, divine, peerless, glorious—the object of supreme love, adoration, and worship by all celestial beings and through all eternal ages. While, then, His sacrificial work illustrates His marvellous grace and love to sinners, that work owes all its acceptance and efficacy to the value imparted to it by the essential Deity of His person. Thus, it is the personal preciousness of Christ that imparts an official preciousness to His work.

Who, then, is the Lord Jesus Christ? In common parlance, men term

Him, "our Saviour." But do the great body pause and reflect who Christ really is? Do they regard Him as the Creator of this world—of all worlds? of their being—of all beings? Do they consider that "all things were made by Him; and without Him was not anything made that was made?" If so, would they not give Him divine homage, since that which creates must be antecedent to and above the thing created, and therefore must be pre-existent and divine? But what a grand and glorious truth is this to the believing soul—the absolute Deity of the Saviour—the essential Godhead of Christ! How it endears Him to the heart as the Rock of ages upon which its hope is built! How precious must be every evidence of the divine strength, stability, and durability of that basis upon which the believing sinner reposes his whole salvation. Precious, then, is Christ as God. Precious in His Deity—precious as a distinct person in the adorable Godhead—precious as "God over all, blessed for evermore." But pause, Christian reader, for a moment, in wonder and praise before this august truth. If there be a spot where we should put off the shoes from our feet, surely it is this. With what profound reverence, with what silent awe, yet with what adoring love should we contemplate theGodhead of our Redeemer! But for that Godhead we had been for ever lost! His obedience to the law, His satisfaction to the justice of Jehovah, had been of no efficacy or avail, save only as it partook of the authority, dignity, and virtue of His higher nature. Do not question the existence of the fact because of the mystery of its mode. How Jehovah could become incarnate is a wonder we shall never, in this state of limited knowledge, fully understand; enough that it is so. Let reason reverently adore and faith implicitly trust.

> "The more of wonderful
> Is heard in Him, the more we should assent;
> Could we conceive Him, God He could not be,
> Or He not God, or we could not be men."

Hesitate not, then, to give full credence to all the glorious truths of the gospel, and to place the entire weight of your soul upon the Atonement of Jesus, and to believe that, sinner though you are, be it the very chief, such is the divine worth and sovereign efficacy of His sacrifice, you will, you must, you shall be saved to the uttermost, because your Creator is your Saviour, and your Judge is your Justifier.

But this personal representation of the Lord Jesus involves also the preciousness of His manhood. His personal alliance with our nature, His condescending stoop to our humanity, is not the least endearing feature to the heart of His believing saints. We have claimed for the Son of God absolute Deity; we now claim for Him perfect humanity. "Flesh" real and substantial, yet, "harmless, undefiled, and separate from sinners," was He "made." A humanity identical with His people in all but its original and actual sinfulness. "He knew no sin" And yet, what a sin-bearer was He! All the transgressions of His elect met upon Him! But He could only bear sin, as He himself was essentially free from its taint. Had there been the remotest breath of pollution adhering to Him—had one drop of the moral virus circulated through His veins, it had rendered Him utterly and for ever incapable of presenting to the justice of God an atonement for sin. He then had needed, like the high priest of old, to have offered for sins "first for Himself then for the people." How precious, then, beloved, is our Lord Jesus as "bone of our bone and flesh of our flesh." Think of His perfect humanity—a humanity free from sin, and therefore capable of dying for the ungodly,—a humanity laden with sorrow, and therefore capable of sympathising with the afflicted. Precious to our hearts as God—precious as Man—precious as both united in one—inconceivably and eternally precious is He, whose name is "Wonderful," to His believing saints. Tell, oh tell, how precious is that humanity of the Son of God that partook, by actual participation, and still bears, by the most perfect sympathy, all the sinless weaknesses, infirmities, temptations, and sorrows of His people. Precious humanity! to which, when other human friendships are changed, and other human love is chilled, and other human sympathy is exhausted, you may repair, and find it an evergreen, a perennial stream, a gushing fountain of unchanged affection, tenderness, and sympathy, meeting and satisfying, to their utmost capacity, your hearts' deep pantings. Precious humanity! that dries each tear, that bears each burden, that is touched with each infirmity, that soothes each sorrow, and that succours each temptation of His people. "In all things it behooved Him to be made like unto His brethren, that He might be a merciful and faithful high priest in things pertaining to God, to make reconciliation for the sins of His people. For in that He himself hath suffered being tempted, He is able to succour them that are tempted." Oh, love the Lord, then, all ye His saints; laud Him, all ye His people; and, in all your deep griefs, your lonely sorrows, your sore trials, your fiery temptations, your pressing wants, your daily infirmities, repair to the succourings, and the sympathies, and the intercessions of His humanity, and learn how precious Jesus can be to the hearts of His suffering and sorrowing ones. Upon this rock of Christ's complex person God has built His Church, and the gates of hell cannot prevail against it.

Precious is the Lord Jesus in His work. That must be a costly and substantial superstructure that reposes upon a basis so divine and perfect. No wise or experienced architect would, at a vast expenditure, lay a deep, broad foundation for the purpose of rearing upon it a mean and fragile fabric. Look at the ground-work of our salvation. "Thus saith the Lord God, Behold, I lay in Zion for a foundation a stone, a tried stone, a precious cornerstone, a sure foundation." Upon such a foundation we look for a superstructure in all respects worthy of its costliness and capability. We find it in the work of Jesus. Oh, what a superstructure is it—nothing less than the salvation of His Church! Such a work was worthy of God, and of all the glory, wisdom, and power embarked in its accomplishment. Nowhere have we such a perfect view of the Divine glory as through the medium of the cross. That magnificent sky that spreads above us, studded and glowing with countless myriads of worlds, pales before the subdued glory, the softened splendour of the cross of Christ. Nowhere does Jehovah-Jesus appear to the spiritual, believing mind so exalted as when He stoops,—so glorious as when in eclipse,—so holy as when bearing sin,—so loving as when enduring its punishment,—so triumphant as when vanquished upon the cross. Oh, study not God in the jewelled heavens—in the sublimity of the mountain—in the beauty of the vale—in the grandeur of the ocean—in the murmurs of the stream—in the music of the winds. God made all this, but all this is not God. Study Him in the cross of Jesus! Look at Him through this wondrous telescope, and although, as through a glass darkly, you behold His glory—the Godhead in awful eclipse, the Sun of His Deity setting in blood—yet that rude and crimsoned cross more fully reveals the mind of God, more harmoniously discloses the perfections of God, and more perfectly unveils the heart of God, and more fully exhibits the glory of God, than the combined power of ten thousand worlds like this, even though sin had never marred, and the curse had never blighted it. Study God in Christ, and Christ on the cross. Oh, the marvels that meet in it—the glory that gathers round it—the streams of blessing that flow from it—the deep, refreshing shadow it casts, in the happy experience of all who look to Jesus and live—who look to Jesus and love—who look to Jesus and obey—who look to Jesus and embrace that blessed "hope of eternal life which God, that cannot lie, promised before the world began."

A worthy structure this of a foundation so divine! What could be more worthy of God, whose essence is "love," than the salvation of His people? In nothing could He appear more like Himself. Upon no platform could He so honourably and completely withdraw the veil from His perfections, and stand forth in His full-orbed majesty, "mighty to save" as this. Humble believer in Christ, you are saved 1 Happy saint of God, you shall be in heaven! Christ has paid your debt, opened your prison, broken your chains, and set you free from the law's curse, from sin's condemnation, and from death's · penalty, and you will be for ever with the Lord! Is not this enough to make your whole life, clouded and chequered though it be, a sweet psalm of praise—thus learning the first notes of the song that will employ your tongue through eternity?

How precious is the righteousness of Christ—a righteousness that fully justifies our person, completely covering all our deformity, and presenting us to God, "comely through His comeliness put upon us;" wherefore the renown of the clothed and adorned Church goeth forth through all the earth, and men inquire, "Who is she that looketh forth as the morning, fair as the moon, clear as the sun, and terrible as an army with banners?" And look at the preciousness of His sacrifice, which is as a "sweet-smelling savour unto God," ascending ever from off the golden altar before the throne, in one continuous cloud of incense, wreathing the persons, perfuming the prayers, accompanying the offerings, and presenting with acceptance every breath of devotion, every accent of praise, and every token of love which His people here below lay at His feet. "By one offering He hath perfected for ever them that are sanctified." That "one offering," offered once for all, was so divine, so holy, so complete, so satisfactory, it has for ever perfected the pardon, perfected the justification, perfected the adoption, and will perfect the sanctification when it perfects the glory of all the elect of Jehovah. Beloved, is not this enough to check every sigh, to quell every fear, to annihilate every doubt, and to fill you with peace and joy in believing? What shouts of praise to Jesus should burst from every lip as each believer contemplates the sacrifice that has secured his eternal salvation! When Titus liberated the imprisoned Greeks, they clustered around his tent, chanting his praises and exclaiming, with impassioned fervour, "A saviour! a saviour! a saviour!" Oh, with what deeper emphasis may every child of God, freed from the chains of sin and of death by the "liberty wherewith Christ hath made him free," extol the person and chant the praises of that glorious Saviour, and exclaim, "Jesus! Jesus! Jesus! He hath saved His people from their sins!" Believer, evince your sense of the preciousness of this great sacrifice by bringing to it daily sins, by drawing from it hourly comfort, and by laying yourself upon it, body, soul, and spirit, a "living sacrifice unto God."

How precious is Christ in all the offices and relations which He sustains to His people. Precious as the Head, the covenant-surety Head, of His people, the source of life, the seat of power, the fountain of all blessing. Reader, hold fast the Headship of Christ. Acknowledge no legislative head, no administrative head, no authoritative head, no reigning head of the Church, but the Lord Jesus Christ. There are under-currents of priestly domination in the Church of God in the present day, subversive of this cardinal truth, against which it behooves us to be on our guard. Acknowledge no spiritual Head and King in Zion but the Lord Jesus; and evince your recognition of, reverence for, and love to, His government, by vindicating His Headship, bowing to His authority, and obeying His laws. Oh, how blessed to be under the holy, benign, and gentle government of Christ, whose sceptre is a sceptre of righteousness, so mild and loving in its sway, that "He will not break the bruised reed, nor quench the smoking flax."

Precious is He as the Husband of His Church, to whom He is united by the closest and most indissoluble ties, pledged to discharge all her obligations, to supply all her need, to soothe, by sympathy, her every sorrow, and to increase, by participation, her every joy. Precious is He as a Friend—the Friend whose love is infinite and boundless, changing not with circumstances, chilling not with indifference, nor wearying with lapse of years—a Friend who showeth himself friendly, who loveth at all times, and who sticketh closer than a brother. Precious as a Brother—our Goel, our next of kin, claiming and exercising, as such, the right of redemption, and proving Himself, by His help and succour in all the calamities of His brethren, to be a "Brother born for adversity." Thus might we travel over all the offices and relations which the Lord Jesus sustains to His saints, and find in each that which endears Him to their souls, enthroning Him upon their hearts as the "chief among ten thousand," and exhibiting Him as "the altogether lovely."

But to whom is Christ precious? This is a most important question. He is not so to all. It is a privileged class, a peculiar people, a little flock, few and scattered, hidden and unknown, who feel the Saviour's preciousness. Only to the believer is Christ precious; the declaration of the Holy Ghost is, "Unto you therefore which believe He is precious." This is philosophically as well as scripturally true. There cannot possibly be a felt conviction of the worth of an object of which we have no intelligent and clear perception. There must be something to create interest, to awaken admiration, to inspire love; the object must be seen, known, and tried. Now, the only spiritual faculty that discerns Christ, and in discerning Christ realises His preciousness, is—faith. Faith is the optical faculty of the regenerate, it is the spiritual eye of the soul. Faith sees Christ, and as Christ is seen His excellence is descried; and as His excellence unfolds, so He becomes an object of endearment to the heart. Oh, how lovely and how glorious is Jesus to the clear, far-seeing eye of faith! Faith beholds Him the matchless, peerless One; His beauty eclipsing, His glory outshining, all other beings. Faith sees majesty in His meanness, dignity in His condescension, honour in His humiliation, beauty in His tears, transcendent, surpassing glory in His cross. In natural things, as the beauty of an object unveils to the eye, it awakens in the mind a corresponding interest. The grey mist of morning slowly rising from off the face of nature, revealing a landscape of rich and varied beauty—the blending of mountain and valley, the green meadows and winding streams—presents an object which, in every mind susceptible of the sublime and the beautiful, inspires the feeling of admiration and delight. Beloved, in proportion as the personal dignity, beauty, and excellence of the Lord Jesus unfolds to the believing eye, He becomes more sensibly and deeply enshrined in the heart's warmest love. We must know the Lord Jesus to admire Him, and must admire Him to love Him, and must love Him to serve Him.

The believer, too, beholds a suitability in Christ, sees Him to be just the Saviour adapted to the necessities of his soul; and this renders Him peculiarly precious. "I see Him," exclaims the believer, "to be exactly the Christ I need—His fulness meets my emptiness—His blood cleanses my guilt—His grace subdues my sin—His patience bears with my infirmities—His gentleness succours my weakness—His love quickens my obedience—His sympathy soothes my sorrows—His beauty charms my eye. He is just the Saviour, just the Christ I need, and no words can describe His preciousness to my soul."

There is thus an appropriation of Christ in the personal experience of every believer which endears Him to the heart. A Christ unappropriated is a Christ whose worth is undervalued, and whose preciousness is unfelt. The believer can say, "Christ is mine, and I have all things in one, even in Christ, who is my all and in all." This simple, trembling faith, sublime in its simplicity, mighty in its tremblings, sweeps all the treasures of the everlasting covenant of grace and all the fulness of the Surety of the covenant into its lap, and exclaims, "All is mine, because Christ is mine, and I am Christ's." Do not shrink, beloved reader, from what the quaint divines of other days, and, perhaps, of a deeper experience and of a sounder creed than ours, were wont to term a "Christ-appropriating faith." If you have fled to Jesus as a poor, empty, believing sinner, there is not a throb of love in His loving heart, nor a drop of blood in His flowing veins, nor a particle of grace in His mediatorial fulness, nor a thought of peace in His divine mind, which is not yours, all yours, inalienably yours, as much yours as if you were its sole possessor. And in proportion as you thus deal with Christ, individually travelling to Him, living upon Him, living out of Him, dealing as personally with Him as He deals personally with you, He will insinuate Himself in your regard, and will become glowingly precious to your soul.

There are peculiar circumstances in the believer's experience when Christ becomes especially precious to the soul. For example: in the deeper ploughings of the heart's hidden sinfulness—when the Holy Ghost reveals more of the innate corruption of our nature, and gives a more spiritual perception of sin's exceeding sinfulness, oh, how precious does the finished work of Christ then become!—how precious the blood that cleanseth from all sin! If God is leading you through this stage of Christian experience, beloved, be not alarmed; it is but to build up His dear Son upon the wreck and ruin of your own merit, strength, and sufficiency. He will have us love His Son with a love like His own—a love of divine, supreme, ineffable affection—and this can only be felt in the region of our own nothingness.

In circumstances of spiritual relapse, how precious does Christ become, as the Restorer of His saints, as the Shepherd that goeth in quest of His stray sheep, and bringeth it back to the fold with rejoicing! How unspeakably dear is the Saviour to the wandering yet restored heart! Our backslidings are perpetual and aggravated, our affections fickle and truant, our faith fluctuating, our love waning, our zeal flagging, our walk often feeble and unsteady; but Jesus withdraws not His eye from His own work in the soul, and never for a moment loses sight of His stray-going sheep. Ah, there are few aspects of the work of Jesus more precious in the experience of the saints of God than His divine and gracious restorings. "He restoreth my soul" is a declaration of David which finds its response in every believer. Precious, then, is that Saviour who breaks the heart, checks its waywardness, restores its wanderings, heals its backslidings, rekindles its love, and once more wakes its languid, silent chords to sweetest harmony.

How precious is Christ in the season of fiery temptation! When the arch-foe comes, robed as an angel of light, with gentle tread, and oily tongue, and soft persuasiveness, seeking to ensnare and beguile the unsuspicious and unwary—levelling his darts at the very foundations of our faith—insinuating his doubts of the truth of the Bible, of the being of God, of the sufficiency of the Saviour, of the reality of a future world—thus seeking to shake the confidence, obscure the hope, and destroy the comfort of the Lord's people—oh, how precious then is Christ as the Conqueror and Spoiler of Satan; as He who enables the trembling believer to quench the fiery dart in His own blood, and to take refuge beneath His outspread, all-sheltering wing! How doubly precious must the Saviour have been to the tempted Peter, when Christ assured him that, by an anticipated intercession, He had blunted the keen edge of the sword by which the subtle enemy sought the downfall of his disciple. Tempted believer, the Tempted One—He who, alone and unaided, battled with Satan those forty days and nights in the solitary wilderness—is He who was "in all points tempted like as we are" and "knoweth how to deliver the godly out of temptation," and will shortly bruise Satan, crushed and conquered, under your feet.

In the hour of adversity, of trial, of sorrow, oh, how precious is Christ in the experience of the believer! It would seem, beloved, as though we had never really known Him until then. Certainly, we never knew from experience that there was so much that was human, tender, and compassionate in His heart until sorrow touched our own. We had no conception what a fount of sympathy was there. A new bend in your path, a new epoch in your history, or a new stage in your journey, has frosted with the snowflake and swept with the storm-blast of winter the entire landscape of life; fortune gone—friends removed—health failing—poverty threatening—want pressing, oh, how dreary and lonely seems the path you tread! But pause—it is not all winter! Jesus approaches! He unveils a bosom once pierced, shows a heart once sad, and drawing you within its blest pavilion, hides you from the wind and covers you from the tempest You never thought Jesus had a heart of such exquisite tenderness until now. I do but give utterance to the experience of many a timid believer, many an afflicted Christian, when I say that, looking back upon all the way the Lord our God has led us, we can thank Him for the swelling surge, can bless Him for the wintry blast, can praise Him for the falling blow that veiled the sky, and draped the landscape, and smote the idol, since that was the last occasion of making the Saviour better known to you, and of endearing, him unutterably to your heart. "Thou hast known my soul in adversities." And that adversity was the time in which you were more fully brought to know Him. Chastening seasons are teaching seasons; suffering times are Christ-endearing times; trying dispensations are purifying processes in the experience of the godly. The whirlwind that swept over you has but cleared your sky and made it all the brighter, but deepened your roots and made them all the firmer. Earth may have lost a tie, but heaven has gained an attraction. The creature has left a blank, but Christ has come and filled it. Reverse has made you poor, but the treasures of divine love have enriched you. In the Lord Jesus you have more than found the loved one you have lost; and if in the world you have encountered tribulation, in Him you have found peace. O sweet sorrow! O sacred grief, that enthrones and enshrines my Saviour more preeminently and deeply in my soul!

There is a supremacy in the feeling of Christ's preciousness to the believer, which is worthy of a remark Christ has the preeminence in the affection of the regenerate. "Whom have I in heaven but thee? and there is none upon earth that I desire beside thee." Listen to His own words, asserting His claim to a single and supreme affection: "Whoso loveth father or mother, brother or sister, wife or children, more than Me, is not worthy of Me." There are natural ties of affection—the parental, the conjugal, the filial; there are ties, too, of human love and friendship, linking heart to heart; but not one word does He who inspired those affections, who formed those ties, breathe, denying their existence or forbidding their exercise. Nay, the religion He came to inculcate distinctly recognises these human relations, and seeks to strengthen and intensify by purifying, elevating, and immortalising them. But mark the emphatic word employed by Christ—"more than Me!" All these affections are to have full play and exercise, but ever to be maintained in profound subordination to Himself, and to be so sanctified and employed as to become auxiliaries and aids to the higher and purer affection of supreme attachment to the Saviour. In a word, Christ should become more supreme and precious to our hearts by all the sweet, sacred relations and affections of life. We should enjoy the creature in Him, and glorify Him in the creature.

Christ is not only supremely, but He is increasingly precious to the believer. It must be so, since a closer intimacy with a perfect being increases our knowledge of His perfection, and, in the same ratio, our admiration and love. The further the believer advances in the divine life, the more he must necessarily become acquainted with Christ; for his re-

ligious progress is the measure of his growing knowledge of the Lord
Jesus. We can only really advance in grace, truth, and holiness, as we have
close relations with Jesus, constant transactions with the Saviour. Christ
is our life; and our growth in spiritual life is Christ increasing within us.
It is as utterly impossible to cherish a holy desire, to conceive a heavenly
thought, to perform a good action, to conquer a single infirmity, or to baf-
fle a solitary temptation, apart from a direct communication with Christ,
as for the lungs to expand without air, or light to exist without the sun.
Oh, yes! Christ is increasingly precious to the believer. The absence from
His beatific presence—distance from His blest abode—the vicissitudes of
life—the fluctuations of time—the advance of infirmities—the increase of
anxieties and cares—and the formation of new friendships, render not the
Saviour less precious to the believing soul. Other objects often lose their
attraction, their desire to interest, or their power to charm us, by the lapse
of years; but Jesus is that glorious object who grows more precious to the
heart in time, as His capacity unfolds of making us supremely happy; and
in eternity will become increasingly the object of our love, and the theme
of our song, and the source of our bliss, as growing ages unveil His loveliness, His glory, and His grace. Beloved reader, is Jesusincreasingly precious to your soul? Each day's history, each day's trial, each day's sin,
each day's want, should endear the Saviour to your heart, because in each
and all of those circumstances you should have direct and close dealings,
daily and personal transactions, with Christ; and you cannot cultivate an
intimacy with Christ and not be enamoured of His beauty, charmed with
His graciousness, and absorbed with His love.

Be cautioned against an eclipse of the Saviour. Let no object come
between your heart and Christ. Be not presumptuous in high spiritual
frames, nor be depressed in low ones. Let not your conscious shortcomings, failures, and stumblings estrange your affections from Jesus. Nor
suffer pride or carelessness to insinuate itself if the Lord confers upon you
some especial favour or proof of His regard. The foot is more apt to slide
in the smooth than in the rough path; and it is more difficult to carry with
a steady hand the brimmed than the empty cup. Walk humbly with God
in all circumstances, especially after seasons of peculiar nearness to Him
in your soul. Forget your spiritual attire, and your ornaments, and think
of and love only Him who clothed you so beautifully and who adorned
you so magnificently. Do not toy with your graces, but look to Him who
gave them. Let all your thoughts, affections, and admiration be concentrated in that precious Saviour, who took all your sins, deformity, and
sorrow upon Himself, and who transferred all His righteousness, beauty,
and blessing upon you. Oh, let your heart and Christ's heart be one heart!

Receive as precious everything that flows from the government of
Jesus. A precious Christ can give you nothing but what is precious. Welcome the rebuke—it may be humiliating; welcome the trial—it may be
painful; welcome the lesson—it may be difficult; welcome the cup—it may
be bitter; welcome everything that comes from Christ in your individual
history. Everything is costly, salutary, and precious that Jesus sends. The
rude tones of Joseph's voice, when he spoke to his brethren, were as much
the echoes of his concealed affection, as the softest, gentlest accents that
breathed from his lips. The most severe disciplinary dispensations in the

government of Christ are as much the fruit of His eternal, redeeming love, as was the tenderest and most touching expression of that love uttered from the cross. All is precious, wise, and salutary in the dealings of Christ. His teachings, His woundings, His withholdings, His withdrawings, His slayings, His changed countenance, His altered tones,—when, in a word, His uplifted hand lights heavily upon us, smiting us seven times, even then, oh, how precious should Christ be to the believing soul! Then it is we learn by experience what a balsam exudes from His pierced heart for the very wound His own hand inflicted!—what a covert from the stormy wind, and what a hiding-place is He from the fierce tempest which His own providence created!—what a succouring, appropriate to our sorrow, springs from the very hand that winged the dart which pierced us through and through! Oh, precious Christ! so divine, so all-sufficient, so indescribably precious, may we not welcome with thankfulness and receive with submission all that Thou dost send—the mingled ingredients of bitter and sweet, the blended tints of light and shade, of all the wise, righteous, and salutary dispensations of Thy wise, loving, and ever watchful providence?

But there is approaching a period—ah, how it speeds!—which will be the most solemn and severe, yet the sweetest and truest test of the sustaining, soothing power of Christ's preciousness in the experience of His saints—the last sickness and the closing scene of life. Imagine that moment to have arrived! All of earth's attraction ceases, all of creature-succour fails. Everything is failing—heart and strength failing—mental power failing—medical skill failing—human affection and sympathy failing; the film of death is on the eye, and the invisible realities of the spirit-world are unveiling to the mental view. Bending over you, the loved one who has accompanied you to the margin of the cold river, asks a sign. You are too weak to conceive a thought, too low to breathe a word, too absorbed to bestow a responsive glance. You cannot now aver your faith in an elaborate creed, and you have no profound experience, or ecstatic emotions, or heavenly visions to describe. One brief, but all-emphatic, all-expressive sentence embodies the amount of all that you now know, and believe, and feel; it is the profession of your faith, the sum of your experience, the ground of your hope—"Christ is precious to my soul!" Enough! The dying Christian can give, and the inquiring friend can wish no more. Dearest Saviour, be Thou close to me in that solemn moment! Tread the valley by my side, pillow my languid head upon Thy bosom, speak these words of heart-cheer to my struggling, panting, departing soul, "Fear not, I am with thee;"—then, it will be happiness for me to die,—death will have no venom—the grave no gloom—eternity no dread; and, from the measured experience of Thy preciousness on earth, I shall pass in triumph through the shadowy portal into the full sunshine and perfect realisation and eternal enjoyment of all that faith believed, and love desired, and hope expected, of Thy full-orbed glory and preciousness in heaven. "In Thy presence is fulness of joy; and at Thy right hand there are pleasures for evermore."

"Precious Jesus! O how lovely art Thou to my longing heart: Never, never let me grieve Thee, ne'er from Thee let me depart. Precious Jesus! all in all to me Thou art."

Chapter II.

THE PRECIOUSNESS OF FAITH.

"Precious faith."—2 Peter i. 1.

The indispensableness of faith as an essential element of salvation, and as an influential instrument in all well-doing for God, is very clearly and impressively set forth in the apostle's declaration, "Without faith it is impossible to please Him." And yet, what crude and superficial views of this eminent grace of the Spirit do the most of us entertain. To believe is by many regarded as a most facile and commonplace thing. They suppose that an individual can believe when he will, and may believe what he will; that faith is the mere assent of the judgment to a certain creed; and that with this intellectual reception of the truth, there requires no other operation of faith to give its mould to the character, and to impart root and acceptableness to the actings of the Christians life. And have not even the most enlightened and spiritual of God's people to mourn over their deficiencies touching their conviction of the nature, worth, and preciousness of this grace of the Holy Ghost, apart from which nothing is well-pleasing to God; but springing from which, the lowliest action, the faintest desire, the· gentlest throb of the spiritual believing soul, is infinitely precious in the view of Jehovah?

Having in the preceding chapter considered the preciousness of the Object of faith, it seems proper that our thoughts should next be directed to a consideration of the preciousness of faith itself. We desire, as God the Holy Ghost shall guide us, so to unfold the nature and operations of this cardinal grace of the Christian character, as that the unbelieving reader may learn the true nature of saving faith, and that the reader who through divine grace does believe, may have his views of faith so cleared, and faith itself so nourished and invigorated, as shall result in a deeper experience of the power and preciousness of the doctrine of faith. The faith of which we are now to speak is described by the apostle in the passage from whence our motto is taken, as being "like precious faith with us." The "faith of God's elect" in all ages of the world, and in all dispensations of the Church, is essentially and identically the same. There is a divine unity in faith which no distance of time, or differences of nation, or standards of theological opinion, or modes of religious worship, or forms of ecclesiastical polity can touch. True faith is essentially and unchangeably the same, in every age, and in every Church, all the world over. Just as the sun that now pours its golden beams by day, and in the moon's soft lustre sheds its reflected silver rays by night, is the same that shone on Eden's bowers, that

14

veiled its face in sackcloth when its Incarnate Creator died, and that illumines all creation, so the "precious faith of God's elect," that now pulsates
in the lowliest breast of the believer, is essentially the same as that which
poured the joy and lustre of a glorious hope upon the trembling spirit of
our primeval parent, when God, in evening's twilight, revealed to Adam
the promise of a Saviour. We propose, in the present chapter, to unfold the
preciousness of faith in two or three particulars.

We have already expatiated upon the preciousness of the Object of
faith; but we revert to it again, for a moment, as illustrating the preciousness of the character of the grace of faith.

The believing soul, while it reposes on the three persons in the ever
adorable Trinity, fixes its eye, in the great matter of salvation, especially upon One—the central Person of the Godhead—embracing whom, it
includes in its faith, and enfolds in its affection, the Father and the Holy
Ghost. There is a unity and simplicity in all Jehovah's works. In nothing
is this more traceable than in the salvation of man, the master-work of
God. The object which the gospel presents for his belief is, the Lord Jesus
Christ. "Believe in the Lord Jesus Christ, and thou shalt he saved." Thus, a
simple and not a complex object is upheld to his eye. There is here nothing
to divide the attention, and thus bewilder the mind. As the pole which
Moses erected in the wilderness was single—no other object commanding
the look of faith—so single and simple is the object of salvation presented in the gospel "Look unto me, and be ye saved"—"Believe in the Lord
Jesus Christ, and thou shalt be saved," is the united voice of the two witnesses for Christ, the Old and the New Testament, touching the one Object
of faith—a crucified Saviour.

Thus, while human religions, be they Romish or Protestant, present
a plurality of objects for belief—false saviours many—to the eye, the Bible presents but One—Christ crucified. It is interesting and instructive to
trace the interweaving of this blessed doctrine—the unity of the Object of
faith—like a thread of gold, throughout the entire Scriptures of truth. In
the Levitical economy, every type however varied, every symbol however
mysterious, every shadow however profound, had Jesus for its object—all
conspired to exalt, and all pointed to, the Lamb of God as the one object of
saving faith. Thus, too, with the prophetical writings of Scripture,—" To
Him gave all the prophets witness." And in the New Testament the agreement is perfect touching this typical and prophetical testimony to the unity of the object of faith—"And I, if I be lifted up from the earth, will draw
all men unto me." In another place, the same Divine Saviour says, "This
is the work of God, that ye believe in Him whom He hath sent." "And,
as Moses lifted up the serpent in the wilderness, even so shall the Son of
man be lifted up, that whosoever believeth in Him should not perish, but
have everlasting life." Oh, rejoice, beloved reader, that in the great matter
of your salvation, your faith has to look to one object only; that, amidst
your own fluctuations of spiritual feeling, and the conflicting judgments
of men, you can—like the roving dove, sweeping with drooping wing
the troubled waters and finding no repose, until, weary and panting, she
behies herself to the ark,—turn to a full and perfect rest in that one, precious object of faith—the Lord Jesus Christ. You find creed contradicting
creed, opinion conflicting with opinion, church opposed to church, and

your heart sickens within you; but, amidst your embarrassment and depression, you bethink yourself of Jesus, and betake yourself to His feet;
and in that one object, for ever blessed and precious, and in this lowly posture, your fluttering, believing heart finds perfect rest. Oh, thank God that
the object of saving faith is one; that, in knowing Jesus, in looking to Jesus,
in trusting in Jesus, in confiding your soul to Jesus, you have no fear, misgiving, or doubt; but, in the confidence of a humble, yet unwavering faith,
can exclaim, "I know in whom I have believed, and am persuaded that He
is able to keep that which I have committed unto Him against that day."

Thus, then, does faith derive a preciousness from the preciousness of
its Object—precious in His person, to which faith looks; precious in His
atonement, to which faith leads; precious in His fulness, from which faith
draws; precious in His intercession, in which faith relies; precious in His
example, by which faith walks. Thus, let faith contemplate the Lord Jesus
in any one of His ten thousand forms of beauty—as the sun unveils the
landscape's loveliness, while the landscape endears the lustre of the sun—
its preciousness is enhanced by contemplating Christ's beauty, while the
loveliness of the Saviour illustrates the costliness of faith. Precious faith
dealing with a precious Christ enriches the believer with the two most
precious things of God.

But faith is not only relatively, it is intrinsically precious—precious
in itself. It is emphatically denominated, "precious faith." And with this
description of its character will correspond the experience of every true
believer in the Lord Jesus. As the universal testimony of men will confirm the value of gold, all evidencing by their earnest, and many by their
covetous, pursuit of the metal, its intrinsic value; so shall each believer,
though possessing but the smallest portion of this divine gift, witness
to its essential and priceless worth. One grain of this precious grace, in
his estimation, hath in it more of real value; more of positive good, than
all the wealth which ever hath been, or which yet may be, dug from the
mines of the earth. Glance at some of those essential features which stamp
the preciousness of faith.

Faith is a divine grace, consequently precious. It has not its origin
here. It is a plant indigenous not to our fallen humanity. Faith in that
which is created, springs from the creature; faith in that which is human,
is human; but the faith which deals with God, believes His word, trusts in
His Son, beholds the invisible, and is the "substance of things hoped for,
the evidence of things not seen," must be divine. It deals with the spiritual, and itself is spiritual; it has to do with the divine, and itself is divine.
We are not born believers. A parent, as Cecil did, may explain to his child
by a simple and ingenious illustration the nature of faith, but the faith itself he cannot give. A minister may enforce upon his hearers the necessity
of faith (and it is his duty so to do), but he forgets not that the Holy Ghost
has written, "Faith is the gift of God." Thus, then, faith is a superhuman
grace. It cometh from God, it descendeth from above; and because it is a
supernatural and heavenly grace—proceeding from heaven, and leading
to heaven—it is of itself inconceivably precious. Think not lightly, then,
beloved reader, of the faith which you may have, measured though it may
be in its degree and feeble in its exercise—it is divine and precious; and
although of this gold from God's mint you may possess but the smallest

coin, yet that coin, bearing the superscription of God, will secure your admission into glory, and will put you into the full and eternal possession of that "inheritance which is incorruptible, undefiled, and which fadeth not away, reserved in heaven for you who are kept by the power of God through faith unto salvation."

But faith is precious being the product of the Holy Ghost. As a fruit of the Spirit, it is preeminently costly. "The fruit of the Spirit is—faith." As He is the Author of all that is divine, and holy, and sanctifying, He is, and must be, the Author of that divine root of all holiness in the heart—the grace of faith. The lowliest fruit of the Spirit in the regenerate soul is of priceless worth. And how low and feeble that work may be, who can tell? How hidden—how unsuspected—how faint? Yet, be it but a tear of godly sorrow falling in secret—a sigh soft as an infant's, and breathed to the lone winds of heaven—the eye smiting the earth with its downcast glance of conscious sin—it is truly an emanation of the Spirit, and is as essentially the offspring of faith as is the 'abundant entrance' into the kingdom of grace with which, when in full sail, faith wafts the believing soul. How full is God's word of this! The imagery of the Bible, illustrative of this truth, is exquisitely beautiful. We read of the lily springing amongst thorns—of the lamb browsing amongst wolves—of the tremulous touch of the hem—of the dim look—of the bruised reed—of the smoking flax—of the faith that doubts Christ's power while it believes His willingness—of the faith that disbelieves His willingness, yet reposes in His power. Why these varied and expressive images, but to teach us that grace in the soul may be limited in its degree, and yet real in its character,—that faith may be weak in its actings, yet divine in its nature,—that God despiseth not the day of small things in the spiritual experience and exercises of a gracious soul? Is there a single product of God in nature upon which He looketh down with disdain? Is there a spire of grass—a shaded flower—a buzzing insect—a winged sparrow—a line of beauty—a gleam of light—a morning's dew-drop, or an evening's zephyr unnoticed or disregarded by Him? No! He despiseth nothing that He has. made. How much less will He regard with indifference, or look with a frown upon the weakest, obscurest, faintest putting forth of the faith of His own Spirit in the soul! If the lowliest product of nature—fading in its beauty, and evanescent in its duration—is arrayed with loveliness and invested with interest worthy of His notice, how much more the tenderest bud, the lowliest flower of divine grace in the renewed heart!

Not only is faith precious in itself, but the trial of faith is precious. The Holy Ghost thus asserts this truth: "The trial of your faith being much more precious than gold that perisheth, though it be tried with fire." The process as here described is severe—it is the trial of fire. Yet that is the element by which the refiner tests and separates his precious metal. God condescends, as it were, to borrow from man an illustration of His wonder-workings in regard to our faith. He places it in the furnace heated by fire. Thus we find how frequently and pointedly the figure is employed in the Bible. We read of a "fiery furnace" (Dan. iii. 6); of the "fiery darts of the wicked" (Eph. vi. 16); of the "fiery trial" (1 Pet. iv. 12); of "the baptism of fire" (Matt. iii. 11); and in the words already quoted—"the trial of your faith, though it be tried with fire." And yet, severe and painful, and, to all appearance, destructive as this process is to which the faith of God's elect is subjected, it is described as one of the precious things of God in the experience of the saints. Why so? Let us see.

The trial of faith is precious because it attests its reality. Apart from its trial, what an uncertainty attaches to faith! Untried faith is uncertain faith, just as unsmelted ore is suspicious ore. A believing man knows not upon what he is really leaning until God brings his dependence to the proof. Has he wealth? Has he strength? Has he friends? Has he influence? Has he interest? Has he gifts? How far he may be secretly and unsuspectingly leaning upon one or more of these and not upon God, he cannot know until God tries him. But when all these creature-dependencies, these human supports, tremble and fall from beneath him—when the flood-tide of sorrow has swept them away, or the wintry blast of adversity has scattered them, then comes the grand test of his true support,—he stands or falls, raises his head in hope or droops it in despair, just as is the reality and strength of his faith in God. Trace in some of its illustrious examples the sustaining power of real faith in the hour of its severe trial. "I had fainted," says the Psalmist, "unless I had believed to see the goodness of the Lord in the land of the living." In an earlier stage of his tried experience we read, concerning this man of God, that, "David was greatly distressed; for the people spake of stoning him,…but David encouraged himself in the Lord his God." In the prophecy of Habakkuk, there occurs a remarkable and beautiful instance of a like result of a severe trial of faith: "Although the fig-tree shall not blossom, neither shall fruit be in the vines; the labour of the olive shall fail, and the fields shall yield no meat; the flock shall be cut off from the fold, and there shall be no herd in the stalls: yet will I rejoice in the Lord, I will joy in the God of my salvation." Trace the power of real faith when brought to the trial of that most certain and solemn of all tests—a dying hour: "My flesh and my heart faileth: but God is the strength of my heart and my portion for ever." It would seem impossible to surpass these instances of the supporting, sustaining power of real faith in the hour of extreme trial. And yet there is one—the most illustrious—that distances them all, extraordinary and precious though they are. When suspended upon the cross, amidst its agony and gloom, in the exercise of a faith that doubted not, staggered not, Jesus clung to a frowning, hiding, deserting Father, exclaiming—"My God, my God, why hast thou forsaken me?" Behold the Man—the God-man—the Author, the Giver, the Sustainer, and the Finisher of your faith, treading the path of faith's trial, and leaving you an example that you should follow His steps. Thank God, then, believer in Jesus, for every fresh evidence of the reality of that faith, which is "like precious faith" with the faith of the Son of God. The test may be severe, the trial may be fiery, yet if it confirms you in the blessed assurance, "I know in whom I have believed," you cannot afford to lose it, scorching and painful as the furnace may have been; that trial may be as severe as Abraham's, when commanded to slay his son—as David's, when the people talked of stoning him—as Job's, when hurled from the pinnacle of health, affluence, and adulation to the lowest depth of sickness, poverty, and contempt—as Daniel's, when cast into the lion's den—as the three children, when thrown into the fiery furnace—or as Paul's, when the messenger of Satan buffetted him—nevertheless, it is the ancient path to glory, and severe though the trial, blessed, eternally blessed, will be the result.

The trial of faith is precious, because it purifies faith. In its own nature faith, as it comes from God, is pure and without alloy. Essentially there is no admixture whatever with the faith the Holy Ghost inspires—it is as pure, sinless, and untainted as was our humanity when it first came from the hands of God. But, as the mountain stream which starts from its hidden source pure and sparkling, partakes of the earthiness and tint of the soil through which it courses its way into the vale beneath, so the faith which proceeds from God holy and unmixed, mingles with the hidden corruption and unbelief of the heart in which it dwells, and thus becomes alloyed and impaired. Hence the necessity and the preciousness of its trial. The fire separates—the furnace purifies—the crucible refines; and so, in the happy experience of the believer, the trial of faith becomes "much more precious than gold, though it be tried as by fire." Oh to have the dross of carnality, and the alloy of unbelief, which so dims the lustre and paralyses the vigour of faith destroyed! Nothing, after the fiery trial, may be left, of all that looked so divine, so holy, and so spiritual, but one grain of the pure gold of faith—yet that one grain of faith, obscure, infinitesimal as it may seem, outweighs in its real value millions of worlds, and it shall never, never perish.

But we may illustrate the preciousness of faith by its actings and fruits. Faith is a wonderful plant in the garden of the soul—it yields all manner of precious fruits, and, like the tree of life in the midst of the streets of the New Jerusalem, it bears fruit all the year. Dear reader, there is no holiness in the soul but faith is its root. Springing from, resting in, and looking to Jesus, from whom its fruit is found, faith produces love, joy, peace, patience, holiness, humility, and every grace that adorns the character, and beautifies the walk of a believer in Jesus. Faith is precious, too, in its wonder-workings. It hath a powerful faculty of sight and of extraction. It can see both sides of the guiding pillar—the cloudy and the bright. It can extract a smile from God's frown, love from God's displeasure, mercy from God's judgment, encouragement from God's refusal, hope from God's delays; can find a door of hope in the valley of Achor, and can sing as sweetly in the dreary night season as in the bright and sunny day. Wonderful triumph of faith that can say, "The Lord gave, and the Lord hath taken away, blessed be the name of the Lord!" Thus faith, laying one dispensation over against another—placing in the scales apparent opposites and contradictions in God's government—can see light in darkness, can produce harmony from discord, and can gather encouragement from defeat; and, dipping its pencil in the darkest colours of sad and gloomy providences, can trace upon the canvas of the Christian's life some of its most brilliant and cheerful pictures.

From this general view of the fruits of faith, let us specify two or three in particular.

What is peace but a blessed fruit of faith? The peace which God gives, which the Holy Ghost creates, which the Atonement of Christ secures, and which in its nature and blessedness "passeth all understanding," is only received from precious faith dealing with a precious Christ. Were you, my reader, banished like John to some lone isle, bearing with you but a fragment of the Bible—that fragment the single but full and sublime declaration, "Being justified by faith, we have peace with God through our Lord Jesus Christ"—it were enough to calm, cheer, and assure your mind, amidst all the dreadful consequences of sin, with the hope of a full acceptance with God through Christ. Oh, how real and tranquillising the peace which simple faith brings into the soul the moment Jesus is seen as the "Prince of peace," as "making peace," as "our peace," and as bequeathing "peace," His last legacy of love to His saints! All peace is contained in that one word—Reconciliation. Reconciled to God through the peace-making, peace-speaking "blood of the everlasting covenant," there is no longer any ground of condemnation, nor fear of hell. "If God be for us, who can be against us?" God pacified towards us, no matter who accuses or condemns; the believing sinner, at peace with God through Christ, can afford to be at war with the world, the flesh, and the devil. Beloved, bring all your sin and guilt to the atoning blood of Jesus, and the "God of peace" will give you peace; and "when He giveth quietness, who then can make trouble?"

And what is true joy—a twin grace with peace—but a precious fruit of faith? The apostle reminds us of this—"Now the God of hope fill you with all joy and peace in believing." In the same proportion to the directness and simplicity with which your faith deals with Christ, looks to Christ, lives upon the fulness of Christ, rests in the complete salvation, the finished work of Christ, draws all its evidences and hopes from Christ, will be your "joy in God through our Lord Jesus Christ." Nothing can enkindle this holy joy in the heart but a believing view of what the Lord Jesus is, and what He has done. It is only a sense of full pardon, of free justification, of gracious adoption, of the hope of glory, that can awaken real joy in the soul of a believing sinner. What joy can there be in the heart of a convicted felon, or of a condemned criminal, or of a convict paying the sad penalty of his crime in lonely exile, toil, and degradation? None whatever. But convey to him a free pardon, unbar his prison, break his manacles, and bid him go free; restore him to his country, his family, his home, and, bruised and broken though that heart be with a consciousness of guilt and a sense of shame, you yet have awoken in its sad chambers the sweetest chimes, and joy, entrancing joy, thrills and dilates his bosom. Such is the picture of a soul cleansed from the guilt of sin, and freed from the condemnation of the law by a believing acceptance of the Lord Jesus Christ. That moment Christ is received into the lowly, penitent, and believing heart—the instant that Christ is seen paying the great debt, suffering the penalty, enduring the condemnation—a joy springs up in the soul such as never thrilled an angel's heart, and all this joy is "joy in believing" "In this rejoice not," says the Saviour, "that the spirits are subject unto you; but rather rejoice, because your names are written in heaven." Oh, how much more joyful would the saints of God be did they deal less with themselves, and more with Jesus! They look at their sins, pore over their unfitness, pine at their leanness, and succumb to their failures and infirmities, their poverty and emptiness, and so all sweet, sacred joy droops and dies within their souls. But, "the joy of the Lord is your strength." "The meek shall increase their joy in the Lord." And seeing that the Lord has "clothed them with the garments of salvation.

and has covered them with the robe of righteousness,"it is the priv-ilege of their soul "greatly to rejoice in the Lord, and to be joyful in their God" (Isa. lxi.10). But, beloved, remember that Christ's joy can only re-main in you, and your joy be full, as in childlike faith you look directly, and only, and constantly to Christ. "We joy in God, through our Lord Jesus Christ, by whom we have now received the atonement." Oh for a higher tone of holy joy amongst the Lord's redeemed! Who in this vast universe have such reason to make the valley resound and the mountain echo with the glad notes of praise, as you who are freed from servitude, who are delivered from hell, and who are on your way to heaven, to spend your eternity — "for ever with the Lord?" Beloved reader, if you are saved — if, in the exercise of the lowliest faith, you can cherish the hope of acceptance, as a poor sinner, with God through Christ — you may rejoice in tribulation, and glory in infirmity, and count the sufferings of this pres-ent time not worthy to be compared with the glory that will be revealed in you. "Rejoice in the Lord, and again I say, Rejoice."

This precious faith is equally the parent of all holiness, and in this view is not less precious to the child of God. There is no true holiness apart from faith in the Lord Jesus — it is the root of all real sanctification. "Puri-fying their hearts by faith" (Acts xv. 9). "Faith, that purifieth the heart and worketh by love" (Gal v. 6). How much is there in the outward religion of many that has all the appearance of holiness, but which is yet unholy in the sight of a holy God! The religious worship, practices, and duties of some, clothed with an air of sanctity so profound, and which awaken the awe, win the admiration, and elicit the applause of so many, pass for noth-ing with that infinitely holy Being concerning whom it is written by the Holy Ghost, "Without faith it is impossible to please God." Faith is a re-vealing, emptying, impoverishing grace — it gives its real possessor to see the depravity of his own nature, the vileness of his own heart, the worth-lessness of his own righteousness, and the innumerable flaws, spots, and failures of all holy spiritual doings. It opens the eye, too, to Christ, and by its gentle and persuasive influence leads the soul, thus emptied and impoverished, to Him, as having all fulness of righteousness, all riches of grace, all soothings of love treasured up for the "poor in spirit," and for those who "hunger and thirst, after righteousness." Faith resting in Christ, beholding Him who is invisible, will mould and influence the be-liever's entire walk. It begets holy principle, and holy principles inspire holy practice, and a holy practice will be "filled with the fruits of righ-teousness, which are by Jesus Christ, unto the glory and praise of God" (Phil i. 11). This precious faith will influence a man to walk prayerfully, circumspectly, and vigilantly. His daily prayer will be, "Let integrity and uprightness preserve me." In his worldly calling he will seek to glorify God. The false balance, the scanty measure, the exaggeration of the seller, the depreciation of the buyer, the rash speculation, the prodigal expen-diture, the grasping covetousness, love for the world, its pleasures, at-tire, and show, an uncharitable, unforgiving, censorious, malicious spirit, with all the corruptions and sinful infirmities of our fallen nature, — true faith, looking to Christ and dealing with eternal realities, will constrain the believer to war against, crucify, and conquer. "This is the victory that overcometh the world, even our faith." Oh for more of this heart-purifying, soul-elevating, Christ-assimilating, God-glorifying, heaven-attracting faith! When your worldly business opposes God's glory, your interests Christ's honour, your temper the Spirit's witness, your conduct the high and heavenly calling you profess, remember that true faith will not cause a moment's hesitation as to your duty. Oh that at that moment, the most critical it may be of your life, when the balance quivers between self-interest and the Divine honour, your faith may take one close view of the cross, one piercing glance into eternity, and so bring you off more than a conqueror, covered with the deathless acclaim and reward of a Christ-exalting triumph!

Precious, indeed, is that faith that leans upon God in adversity, that goes to Jesus in trial, and that repairs to the Spirit in sorrow. Precious faith, that finds a promise for every condition, a helper in every emergency, a soother for every sorrow,—that can hope against hope, taste a sweet disguised in every bitter, and see a bright light veiled by each dark cloud. This is the true gold that procures all blessings and enriches its possessor with all good. He that has faith in God has every desire of his heart fulfilled. He can dive into the treasures of God's word and say, "All these are mine, for they are my father's epistles of love." He can turn to the Redeemer's fulness and exclaim, "It pleased the Father that all this fulness of grace, and truth, and love, should dwell in Jesus for me." He can repair to the throne of grace and say, "Here I am permitted to draw near to God, burdened with sin, laden with want, oppressed with trial, assailed by temptation, crushed with sorrow, casting, by an act of faith, all my care upon Him." Is not that precious faith that enriches my poverty, that dignifies my meanness, that guides my perplexities, that cheers my loneliness, that calms my grief, that defeats my foes, that paints a bow upon every cloud, and that brings all heaven into my soul? Yet such is the fruit of that faith of which God is the giver, the Spirit the author, Christ the object, and a poor, empty, unworthy soul the happy possessor!

But rich and inviting as this subject is, we must conduct the present chapter to a close. In doing so, suffer me to exhort you not to despair when God sees fit to deal with you as He did with the father of the faithful—assure you of a promise, and then put death into all the means leading to its fulfilment. Be it so—that promise, lifeless though it may seem, yet stands good against all that militates against its accomplishment. One affirmative of God may be weighed against ten million negatives of man,—one Divine promise against a universe of human improbabilities and impossibilities,—a grain of faith against a pyramid of unbelief. "Let God be true, and every man a liar." With second causes faith has nothing to do. It sees God only, deals with God only, believing that "with God all things are possible."

Beware of making a Christ of your faith, precious as it is. If you are staying away from the Saviour because your faith is weak, you are substituting your faith for Christ—the channel for the Fountain of comfort, peace, and salvation. If I have a mission to the sovereign of these realms—some petition to prefer—and I linger upon the steps that conduct me to the royal presence, or in the corridor that leads me into the royal chamber, what marvel if I have no audience, and, consequently, no response to my request? That lofty flight of steps, that magnificent corridor, are but introductions to my approach to the sovereign, not the sovereign herself. Such is faith! Divine and precious as it is, faith is but the path that leads us to the King. And although it is often with hesitation and weakness we tread this royal pathway, yet each new step upon which we place our foot brings us nearer to Jesus. We must, however, beware of lingering upon the steps, or of loitering in the ante-rooms, substituting our going to Christ for our having actually come to Christ. Onward we must press, discouraged not by our slow, nor elated by our rapid progress—counting nothing of our faith but as a mean to an end—that end our full reception of the Lord Jesus—until we find ourselves in the royal presence, "beholding the King in His beauty." It follows, then, that faith does not save you, it being but the instrument of salvation; that your weak faith is no reason why you should stay away from Christ, and that your strong faith is no plea recommending you to Christ. It is Christ, and Christ only, from first to last, that saves; and your faith is precious and valuable only as it brings you to Him to be saved through His imputed righteousness alone. The truth we are endeavouring to explain is so vital and important; we would venture to simplify and enforce it by another illustration. The ship riding in the roads heaves not her anchor in order to aid the little boat which has just put out from the shore, and contending with wind, and tide, and wave, struggles to approach, her. But casting forth a line, she bids the frail vessel grasp it and draw itself to the ship. Thus, it is not the ship that approaches the boat, it is the boat that approaches the ship. Trembling soul, setting out for Christ, quitting the shore of a sinful, delusive world, and loosening yourself from the strong grasp you have long had of your own righteousness, let me remind you that Christ is in heaven, and that He cometh not down again from above to meet the soul battling with sin, and guilt, and unbelief in its struggles to come near to Him. What, then, doth He? He giveth an exceeding great and precious promise—"Him that cometh unto me I will in no wise cast out;" and bidding the sinner take hold of that promise by faith, He invites it to approach Him and receive all the blessings of salvation, and all the treasures of grace of which He is the Author, the Head, and the Giver. Faith does not bring Christ to the soul (the blessed Redeemer is self-moved—moved by His own graciousness and love), but faith brings the soul to Christ. Faith fastens itself upon Jesus, "exalted a Prince and a Saviour to give repentance unto Israel, and remission of sins," and so it draws the soul to Christ. "Say not in thine heart, Who shall ascend into heaven? (that is, to bring Christ down from above;) or, Who shall descend into the deep? (that is, to bring up Christ again from the dead). But what saith it? The word is nigh thee, even in thy mouth, and in thy heart: that is, the word of faith, which we preach; that if thou shalt confess with thy mouth the Lord Jesus, and shalt believe in thine heart that God hath raised him from the dead, thou shalt be saved." Here is the divine cord that draws the sinner to Jesus, and will, if taken hold of in simple earnestness, assuredly bring the weakest, most trembling, and unworthy soul to the Saviour. "If thou wilt believe in thine heart,…thou shalt be saved."

Then, let no sin-distressed soul, bending over this page, despair of being saved. Numberless, aggravated, great as your sins may be—death and condemnation staring you full in the face—confronted as if by the grim, gloomy instrument of your execution—behold, here is a full and free pardon asking but the acceptance of your faith. "Only believe." When the trembling jailor of Philippi rushed into the cell of Paul with the memorable inquiry, "What shall I do to be saved?" did the apostle send him to religious ordinances, or to duties, or to pious doings—to baptism, to the Lord's supper, to prayer, and fasting, and charities? Oh no! These were proper in their place, but sadly out of place here, and therefore most improper. But what is the work the apostle puts the anxious penitent upon?—the work of believing. "Believe in the Lord Jesus Christ, and thou shalt be saved." This is the work,—"And this is the work of God, that ye believe in Him whom He hath sent." And when a poor woman came and poured an alabaster box of precious ointment upon His head, what did Jesus say to her? What was the act which He commended? He mentions not her tears, though she wept; He speaks not of her fondness, though she kissed His feet; He commends not her liberality, though her anointing was very costly and precious. He does not say, Your repentance has saved you, your love has saved you, your liberality has saved you; but He says, "Woman, thy faith hath saved thee; go in peace." He passes by all her other qualities, and places the crown of acceptance upon the head of her faith. Dear reader! Jesus is just the same at this moment that He was then—as ready to receive, accept, and save you—as ready to crown your feeble, trembling faith with such a diadem of glory as angels never wore. "Go in peace, thy faith hath saved thee." Oh that with the believing, weeping father in the Gospel, you may exclaim, "Lord, I believe; help thou mine unbelief."

Is it with you a season of great strait, difficulty, and want? Now is the time to set faith to work. Your faith may long have been inactive and dormant. The sword has so long reposed in its scabbard that you can with difficulty withdraw it, now that it is a time of need; and your arm has become so enfeebled from disuse that you can scarcely wield the sword even when drawn. But God has sent this pressure in order to restore and quicken your confidence in Himself. Oh, have faith in God that He will appear in your behalf, and glorify Himself in you. His name is Almighty—God all-sufficient. Listen to the language of one who thus, from a chapter in his own deep experience, unfolds the blessedness of that simple, believing confidence in God to which we would urge you in this hour of need:—"I have seemed to see a need of everything God gives me, and want nothing that He denies me; there is no dispensation though afflictive, but either in it or after it I could not have done without it. Whether it be taken from me or not given to me sooner or later God quiets me in Himself without it. I cast all my concerns on the Lord, and live securely on the care and wisdom of my heavenly Father. My ways are in a sense hedged up with thorns, and grow darker and darker every day; but yet I distrust not my good God in the least, and live more quietly in the absence of all, by faith, than I should do, I am persuaded, if I possessed them all I think the Lord deals kindly with me to make me believe for my mercies before I have them. The less reason hath to work on, the more freely faith casts itself on the faithfulness of God. I find that while faith is steady nothing can disquiet me, and when faith totters nothing can establish me. If I tumble out amongst means and creatures, I am presently lost, and can come to no end; but if I stay myself on God, and leave Him to work in His own way and time, I am at rest, and can sit down and sleep on a promise when a thousand rise up against me; therefore my way is not to cast beforehand, but to work with God by the day. 'Sufficient unto the day is the evil thereof.' I find so much to do with my calling and my heart that I have no time to puzzle myself with peradventures and futurities. Faith lies at anchor in the midst of the waves, and believes the accomplishment of the promises through all these overturning confusions and seeming impossibilities. Upon this God do I live, who is our God for ever, and will be our guide unto death. Methinks I lie becalmed in His bosom; as Luther, in such a case, I am not much concerned, let Christ see to it. I know prophecies are still dark, and the books are sealed, and men have all been deceived, and every cistern fails. Yet God abideth faithful, and faithful is He that hath promised, who also will do it. Many things now I might say, but enough; O brother! keep close to God, and then a little of the creature will go a great way. Maintain secret communion with God, and you need fear nothing. Lay up all your goods in God, so as to be able to overbalance the sweetness and bitterness of all creatures. Spend no time anxiously in forehand contrivances for this world; they will never succeed; God will turn His dispensations another way. Self-contrivances are the effects of unbelief. I can speak by experience, would men spend those hours they run out in plots and contrivances in communion with God, and leave all to Him by believing, they would have more peace and comfort."

Such, then, is the preciousness of faith—it is so precious that none but God can bestow it, and when bestowed it is so precious that it brings into the soul, as the queen-grace, untold blessings in its royal retinue. It has been remarked by an eminent minister of Christ, now in glory, that were God to limit him to one prayer it would be the apostle's—"Lord, increase our faith." And this is no exaggerated sentiment, because the increase of faith brings with it an increase of love, joy, peace, obedience, and every grace of the Holy Ghost. But while not content with any limit to your growth in this grace of faith, yet remember for your encouragement who think you have no precious faith, that it may exist in the soul, and for the most part does, in the smallest degree. Who will affirm that he has yet attained unto faith, small even as the grain of mustard seed? Then we ask such a boaster that he say to this mountain, Be ye cast into the sea; to this sycamore tree, Be thou plucked up: for our blessed Lord has told us that "if we have faith as a grain of mustard seed, nothing shall be impossible unto us." Thank God, then, for the least degree of faith, though it be less than the grain of mustard seed, for the smallest measure will conduct you fully into heaven. And yet forget not that there is no difficulty that faith in God, however small, cannot surmount, no mountain it cannot level, no tree it cannot uproot, simply because it deals with the power of God. Calling to its aid omnipotence, allying itself with the Almighty, it can thrash the mountains small, and make the hills as chaff, it can leap over a wall and run through a troop, and though often lame and halting, it yet can take the prey.

We conclude the present chapter with a brief glance at the crowning act of precious faith—the glory it brings to Jehovah;—and this is the crown of its preciousness. If the faith of a child of God terminated in himself—

even though it were to put him in the full possession of heaven—it would come short of its highest, holiest, noblest end. It is worthy of God that He has made all things to centre in Himself. "The Lord hath made all things for himself" (Prov. xvi. 4). "I have created him for my glory" (Isa. xliii. 7). In no being in the universe has God put forth so much of His glory, and by none will He finally appear so illustrious as a believer in the Lord Jesus Christ. God has done more for that saved soul, and will more magnify His great name in him, than for all the unfallen intelligences of heaven. He will appear more glorious, His perfections will shine forth with more full, harmonious, and complete lustre in one sinner saved, than in the final and eternal destruction of the myriads who people the regions of the lost. In the case of the lost, justice and holiness appear in awful severity; but in them that are saved, justice and holiness—yet more awfully illustrated in the soul-sorrow and dying agonies of Jesus—are seen blended with love, mercy, and grace; so that men and angels see more of the divine glory in the salvation, than in the condemnation of man. It is the glory, then, of faith, and the perfection of its preciousness, that it gives glory to God. "The reason why faith is said to give glory to God is, because faith answers God's faithfulness. Great faith is said to give glory to God: one of the special commendations of Abraham's faith is, 'He was strong in faith, giving glory to God' (Rom. iv. 20). God magnifies His name of faithfulness above all His name; the believer magnifies his faithfulness by his believing; therefore he gives glory to God. There are three honourable services that some men get put into their hands, and which are denied to angels. There is preaching of Christ, suffering for Christ, and believing in Christ. Let us consider wherein there is an honouring of God by believing; for it is a point very rarely believed. Who is there of believers that think that by bare believing they give God more glory than any other way they can do?

"Faith gives glory to God, because it brings nothing to Him but poverty, want, and emptiness. All graces bring something to God, but faith brings nothing. Love brings a flaming, burning heart to God; repentance brings a bleeding, broken heart to God; obedience brings a working hand to God; patience brings, as it were, a broad back to God, let Him lay on what He will; poor faith brings just nothing, but the poor man's bare hand and empty dish. The poorer man comes to God the more glory to God. It is remarkable that, in those cases wherein we bring something to God, we are very apt to carry away something of the glory that belongs to Him: faith brings nothing at all to God; it brings no more than broken bones and sores to the great Physician (Rom. iii 27).

"Faith glorifies God, for it seeks all in Him, and from Him: as it brings nothing to Him, so it expects everything from Him, whatever its wants be. The language of faith is, 'All my wants be upon Thee, O Lord;' there is no other way of bearing them; it expects all from Him, and from the single warrant of His word. (John iii. 33.)

"Faith always glorifies God, for it ventures its all upon His word. The believer is still in this frame, in the exercise of faith: 'Now, here I have God's faithful promise; and if it should fail me, I should certainly sink for ever. My soul, body, reputation, privileges of the gospel, all my concerns whatsoever, are all laid upon the faithfulness of God; they are all put in that bottom of the ship; if I miscarry, I am gone for ever.' Who is there of believers that believes this, that a bare adventuring of thy eternal salvation upon the Son of God, by virtue of the promise of God, brings more glory to God than all things else can do? (1 Cor. i. 30, 31.)"[1]

If this be true—and most true it is—then, beloved, besiege the throne of grace for more of this Christ-crowning, Spirit-honouring, God-glorifying grace of faith. Oh, it is the mightiest grace of the Holy Ghost in the soul, and because it is so, it brings the richest revenue of praise to the Triune Jehovah! Behold, how like a queen she enters the soul, her train composed of the costliest material, her train-bearers the sister- graces of the Spirit. "The king's daughter is all glorious within; her raiment is of wrought gold." Seek, O seek it, then; earnestly, diligently, importunately seek it. Every new deposit of this precious coin augments your real wealth; and every new victory this grace of faith achieves adds another precious stone to the diadem of glory with which your Saviour is crowned. Whatever may be your present circumstances, "have faith in God." Stand still, and see His wonder-working on your behalf. He will smite that rock—He will part that sea—He will level that mountain—He will exalt that valley—He will roll from off the tomb of thy buried mercy the stone thou canst not move. Only have faith in Him! "Commit thy way unto the Lord, trust also in him, and he shall bring it to pass." Thus, your soul, in the exercise of this "precious faith" that looks from self, ceases from man, and trusts alone in God, shall repose in Him, acquiescent, tranquil, and safe as an infant on its mother's breast. Then will the Psalmist's enviable experience be yours—"Surely I have behaved and quieted myself, as a child that is weaned of his mother: my soul is even as a weaned child."

> "Leave God order all thy ways,
> And hope in Him, whate'er betide;
> Thou'lt find Him in the evil days,
> Thy all-sufficient strength and guide;
> Who trusts in God's unchanging love,
> Builds on the rock that nought can move.
>
> "What can these anxious cares avail,
> These never-ceasing moans and sighs?
> What can it help us to bewail
> Each painful moment as it flies?
> Our cross and trials do but press
> The heavier for our bitterness.
>
> "Only thy restless heart keep still,
> And wait in cheerful hope; content
> To take whate'er His gracious will,
> His all-discerning love hath sent.
> Doubt not our inmost wants are known
> To Him who chose us for His own.
>
> "He knows when joyful hours are best,

---

1   Traill.

He sends them as He sees it meet;
When thou hast borne the fiery test,
And art made free from all deceit,
He comes to thee all unaware,
And makes thee own His loving care.

"Sing, pray, and swerve not from His ways,
But do thine own part faithfully,
Trust His rich promises of grace,
So shall they be fulfill'd in thee;
God never yet forsook at need
The soul that trusted Him indeed."[2]

---

2   G. Newmarch, 1653.

Chapter III.

THE PRECIOUSNESS OF TRIAL.

"The trial of your faith, being much more precious than of gold that perisheth."—1 Peter i. 7.

It is the preciousness of trial in general, including the preciousness of the trial of faith in particular, to which the apostle thus refers. We propose, therefore, to amplify the truth, and to illustrate in the present chapter the preciousness of all those trials of which, more or less, the saints of God are partakers. This view may present the subject of trial in a point of light more soothing and sanctifying than the reader has been wont to contemplate it. You have thought of trial, have anticipated trial, have met trial, have shrunk from trial as the patient recoils from the surgeon's lance, forgetting that that very trial was the needed process by which God was about to work out some great good in your personal experience; and that, so far from being dreaded, it should be welcomed as amongst the most precious things of God, the richest blessings of the everlasting covenant. The points we propose to illustrate are—trial—the preciousness of trial—and the blessings that spring from trial.

The term is expressive. It refers to a process by which the character or strength of a thing is tested. The engineer tries the base of his arch, the architect tries the foundation of his building, the refiner tries the nature of his ore. The word trial thus acquires a significant import in relation to that disciplinary process by which God proves His people. Trial, then, becomes a necessary element in the schooling and training of the children of God for duty and service upon earth, and for enjoyment and glory in heaven. Exempt the Church of God from trial, and she is excluded from a process the results of which are incalculable in her experience.

It will tend to open this subject more forcibly, if we consider who the Lord tries in the sense in which the term is now employed. There is one passage in God's book which contains—as many brief sentences of inspired truth do—volume in a word, and it will supply the answer to the question, Who does the Lord try? "The Lord trieth the righteous." The furnace in which God places His people—in other words, the process of trial by which He proves them—is not the same by which the ungodly world is tried. "The fire in Zion, and His furnace in Jerusalem," are only for His own elect. He has the crucible for gold, and the crucible for earth—the fire of love, and the fire of wrath; and in nothing will He more distinguish His own people from the ungodly,—the gold from the "reprobate silver,"—than in the mode by which both are thus dealt with. He tries the righteous because they are righteous; He chastens His sons, because they are sons; He reproves, rebukes, afflicts them, because He loves them, having "chosen them in the furnace of affliction." What touching words of Christ are these—who can read them without emotion?—"As many as I love I rebuke and chasten." Again, "Whom the Lord loveth he chasteneth, and scourgeth every son whom he receiveth." Thus, it is His own people, His righteous, His holy ones, on whom His afflictive hand is often the most sorely and heavily laid. "The Lord trieth the righteous."

But what does the Lord try? It is not our fallen nature that He tries, the existence of whose depravity is clear and unmistakeable. There wanteth no proof that we are sinful and corrupt, and that "in our flesh there dwelleth no good thing." But the Lord tries His own wondrous work of grace in the soul. He tries everything that is divine, and good, and holy in the regenerate. He tries their principles, He tries their motives, He tries their graces, He tries their knowledge, He tries their experience, He tries His own work. Take, for example, a few of the spiritual graces which He more especially brings to the test of trial. He tries the believer's love. "Lovest thou me more than this?" is often the probing question of Jesus to His disciples. He will test the reality, the sincerity, the strength of our love to Him—whether it can confide in Him when He smites, cling to Him when He retires, obey Him when He commands—whether it will entwine around Him the closer that the storms seek to tear it from its hold. "Canst thou resign this blessing? wilt thou undertake this service? art thou able to drink this cup, or bear this cross for me?" is the significant language of many a trial with which the Lord trieth the righteous. Happy if thy love sustains the test of its sincerity, and thy heart replies, "Yea, Lord; Thy love inspiring my love, Thy grace helping my infirmity, Thy strength perfected in my weakness, I can—I will—I do."

The Lord tries also the patience of His people. There is, perhaps, no grace of the Spirit, or adornment of the Christian character more overlooked than this, and yet there is not one more precious, God-honouring, and beautifying. To find this divine and rare pearl, we must often pass from the surface of society, and seek it—where, indeed, the piety and taste of few lead them—amid scenes of suffering, of grief, of adversity. In some secluded apartment, on some couch of languor, or bed of sickness, shaded by penury and loneliness, this divine grace may exist—no eye beholding its sparkling amid the surrounding gloom, but His whose "eyes are over the righteous, and whose ear is open to their cry." There may be seen the patient, quiet spirit of a humble believer in Jesus, enduring without a murmuring word, bearing without a rebellious feeling, suffering without a hard thought of Him who has smitten—with a calm, submissive, dignified surrender to the Divine disposal—the will of God. And yet, who, in whatever path he walks, finds not, in some circumstances of his daily history, the "need of patience?" The trying circumstances of life—the chafings of the hourly cross—the constant contact with dissimilar tastes, uncongenial minds, unsympathising hearts—the delays in answer to prayer—the ceaseless pain—the restless head—the nervous temperament, to which the buzzing of a fly is agony—above all, the hidings of God, the tarrying of Jesus, the suspension of the Spirit's consolation—all, all demand the exercise of that patience with which the believer possesses his soul. This is the grace the Lord tries! Ah! how little know we of the impatience of our spirit—the petulance and unsubmissiveness which will brook no delay, which frets against the Lord, and rebels against His dealings—until the Lord tries us. But He tries our patience only to increase it. Humbled under the conviction how rebellious and repining is our spirit, we are led to cry mightily to God to vouchsafe to us this grace, meekly to endure, silently to suffer, and cheerfully to do His will. "The Lord direct your hearts into the patience of Christ." "Ye have need of patience, that, after ye have done the will of God, ye may receive the promise." We are exhorted to "let patience have her perfect work, that ye may be perfect and entire, wanting nothing." "Here is the patience of the saints."

I have spoken of the trial of faith. Without recalling the train of thought already pursued, it may be well briefly to remark, that faith being the queen-grace of the graces—all others constituting her regal attendants—the Lord especially tries this grace of the believer, and by so doing He indirectly tries and so strengthens all the cognate graces of the soul. Thus, we read, "The trial of your faith worketh patience." And what are the ends to be accomplished in the trial of faith? The Lord tries our faith to test its genuineness, to promote its purity, to invigorate its power—thus to bring us into a more intimate acquaintance with Himself. Never should we try God as we do did He not try us as He does. We should, alas! be content to travel many a stage without Him. No child-like sense of dependence—no holy communings—no seeking His will—no trying of His love, faithfulness and wisdom. How seldom would the Lord see our uplifted face, or our outstretched hands, or hear the plaint accents of our voice, did He permit this grace to lie sluggish and stagnant in the soul. But it is "living water" which Christ has deposited within the regenerate, and trial is needed to keep it pure, sparkling, and ascending. Be ye sure of this, then, beloved, that the Lord thus exercises your faith only to make you a richer possessor of this most enriching of the graces. It is a kind process of Jesus by which He seeks your greatest good. The more your faith is tried, the more it deals with God, and travels to Christ; and it is impossible for you to spend one minute with God, or to catch one glimpse of Christ, and not be sensibly and immeasurably the gainer. The more your faith leads you to the throne of grace, the more precious will prayer become. The more your faith deals with the atonement of Christ, the more will the glory of His work unfold to your mind. The more your faith takes hold of the Divine promises, the more will it be confirmed in the truth of God's word. Thus faith—so supernatural and wondrous a grace is it—transmutes everything it touches into most precious gold, and so confereth upon its tried but happy possessor "greater riches than the treasures of Egypt."

But who can travel the circle of all the trials to which the saints of God are subject? How great their variety! how peculiar often their character! Each child of God seems to move in a groove peculiar to himself,—to revolve round the great centre in an orbit of his own. The Lord deals with us as individuals that we may have individual dealings with Him. Therefore, among the catalogue of the Christians trials, those of an individual nature may take the precedence of all others. It is a great mercy when we can retire from the crowd and deal with God individually—when we can take the precious promises to ourselves individually—when we can repair to Jesus with individual sins, infirmities, and sorrows, feeling that His eye bends its glance upon us, His ear bows down to us, His hand is outstretched to us, His whole heart absorbed in us, as though not another claimant, suitor, or sufferer unveiled a sorrow or preferred a request—as if, in a word, we were the solitary object of His love. Oh, deal with Christ personally, even as He deals personally with you. His invitation is, "Come unto me," —and He would have you come, —and you cannot honour Him more—recognising His personality, and His personal relation to yourself, and disclosing your personal circumstances, making confession of personal sin, presenting personal wants, and unveiling personal infirmities, backslidings, and sorrows.

But, in addition to personal, there are often relative trials, which many are called to experience. It is impossible for feeling hearts not to make the circumstances of those to whom they are bound by close and tender ties of love and friendship in a measure their own. The religion of Jesus is the religion of sympathy. It teaches us to "weep with those that weep, and to rejoice with those that rejoice" —to "bear one another's burdens, and so fulfil the law of Christ." And what a touching exemplification of this our religion did its great Author present when bending over the grave of Lazarus; as the evangelist tells us—"Jesus wept." He had griefs of His own—oh, how bitter!—but He buried them deeply and silently within His breast, and seemed to feel and to weep only for the griefs of others. "In all their afflictions he was afflicted." And thus, too, it often is with the Christ-like believer. Concealing his personal sorrows, and bearing in lonely and uncomplaining silence his own burden, he is often found, from his unselfishness and sensibility, to be more deeply afflicted and oppressed by the sorrows and burdens of others. "Who is weak, and I am not weak? who is offended, and I burn not?"

But there are spiritual trials peculiar to the children of God. The world, as it cannot sympathise with the joy of the believer, so it cannot participate with his spiritual sorrow. The Lord tries the righteous as righteous. What knows the world of trials springing from the indwelling of sin, from the temptations of Satan, from spiritual darkness, from the conflict of unbelief, from the infirmities of prayer, from leanness of soul, coldness of love, hardness of heart, perpetual tendency to spiritual relapse? Nothing whatever! But such are the soul exercises of many a saint of God, and these constitute his sorest trials.

But it is not so much on the fact of the Christian's trials that we would dwell, as upon a particular aspect of those trials which—especially in the actual process of trial—we are prone to overlook—their preciousness. The apostle clearly intimates this—"The trial of your faith being much more 'precious than of gold." It is to the preciousness of the trial of faith, not so much to the preciousness of faith itself, to which he refers. Let us briefly pursue this idea, and see in what respects the child of God may contemplate his trials as among the precious things of God.

Trial is precious, because that which it tries is so. The work which God brings to the test of affliction is worthy of all the pains He takes to prove its reality, to promote its purity, and to advance its growth. Nothing is so precious, so costly, so indestructible as the work of the Holy Ghost in the soul. If, beloved, you have a broken heart for sin, if you possess faith less even than a grain of mustard seed, if there glows in your heart a solitary spark of Divine love, or there beats in your soul a throb of spiritual life, — if, in a word, there is the outline of the restored moral image of God; faint and imperfect though it is, no figure can illustrate its beauty, nor words describe its worth. It distances all idea in its intrinsic preciousness. Now this is the work the Lord tries. These are the Divine principles, holy emotions, heavenly feelings He brings to the test. He tries it because it is worth the trial, and so the trial itself becomes a precious thing because it has to do with a precious work.

Trial also derives a value from its being the discipline of a loving Father. The moment faith can see the extraction of any drop of the curse from the cup of sorrow, and trace in its ingredients nothing but the elements of love, wisdom, goodness, faithfulness, righteousness, it realises the costliness of the discipline. The very rod is loved because it is the rod of Him who is "Love" The chastening is sweet because it is parental. And the true believer exclaims, "My Father designs by this to teach me some salutary lesson, to inculcate some divine truth, to rebuke me for some folly, to correct me for some sin, to recall my truant heart, to restore my wandering soul, to endear Himself, and by detaching my affections and sympathies from earth's attractions, to allure and bind them closer to heaven. Precious trial that is the dictate of a wise and holy discipline, that leaveth traces of a Father's hand, that is loving in its origin, loving in its nature, loving in its results!"

Trial is precious because it increases the preciousness of Christ. It is in adversity that human friendship is tested. When the wintry blast sweeps by, when fortune vanishes, and health fails, and position lowers, and popularity wanes, and influence lessens, then the summer birds of earthly friendship expand their wings and seek a warmer clime! The same test that proves the hollowness of the world's affection and constancy confirms the believer in the reality, power, and preciousness of the friendship of Jesus. To know fully what Christ is we must know something of adversity. We must be tried, tempted, and oppressed — we must taste the bitterness of sorrow, feel the pressure of want, tread the path of solitude, and often I be brought to the end of our own strength and of human sympathy and counsel. Jesus shines the brightest to faith's eye when all things are dark and dreary. And when others have retired from our presence, their patience wearied, their sympathy exhausted, their counsel baffled, perchance their affection chilled and their friendship changed, then Christ approaches and takes the vacant place; sits at our side, speaks peace to our troubled heart, soothes our sorrows, guides our judgment, and bids us "Fear not." Beloved reader, when has Christ appeared the nearest and most precious to your soul? Has it not been in seasons when you have the most stood in need of His guiding counsel and of His soothing love? In the region of your heart's sinfulness you have learned the value, completeness, and preciousness of His atoning work, of His finished salvation. But the tender, loving, sympathetic part of His nature, you have been brought into the experience of only in the school of sanctified trial. Oh, how precious has that trial made Him! Into what sacred intimacy and close fellowship and conscious nearness has it brought you. When He has approached with an expression so benignant, with a look so winning, with words so soothing, with an influence so tranquillising, and told you that He was acquainted with your sorrow, entered into your loss, felt all the keen, delicate touches of your grief; and then spoke words of comfort to your spirit, bound up your broken heart, gently drew you into a sweet, holy, cheerful submission to His will and full justification of His dealings, oh, has He not enthroned Himself upon your soul at that moment more supremely and firmly than ever? You once thought you knew Him, and you did in some degree, but now, in the depth of your hallowed sorrow, a sorrow into which the Man of sorrows and the Brother born for adversity has enshrined His whole self, you exclaim, "I have heard of thee by the hearing of the ear; but now mine eye seeth thee." We ask, Is not trial a precious discipline, a precious correction, a precious school, that leads you more fully into the heartfelt experience of the preciousness of the Saviour? Shrink not from, nor rebel against, that which makes you more intimately acquainted with your best Friend, your dearest Brother, the tender, sympathising, Beloved of your soul. You will know more of Jesus in one sanctified trial than in wading through a library of volumes or in listening to a lifetime of sermons.

It is impossible either to contemplate the costly results of trial, and not find an evidence of its preciousness. Trial is a fruitful process; and, though often painful as the incisions of the amputating knife, the results, like those incisions, are salutary and healthful. Sanctified trial opens an outlet for the escape of much soul-distemper. Deep-rooted, hidden, and long pent-up evil, the existence of which has been as a fretting sore, inflaming, irritating, and impairing the whole spiritual constitution of the soul, has by this process been thrown off, and thus a more wholesome state and healthful action has supervened. Oh, what selfishness, what carnality, what rebellion, what worldliness, what secret declension, has God's lancet brought to light, revealing it but to inspire self-abhorrence, sin-loathing, and sin-forsaking—and all this the costly fruit of a deeply sanctified affliction!

Trial, too, stirs us up to lay hold upon God in prayer. Nothing, probably, in all the Lord's means of grace and dispensations of providence so leads us to prayer, incites us to call upon the Lord, as the pressure of affliction. And so high a privilege is access to God, so sweet a spot is the throne of grace, so great and holy the blessings that spring from a waiting of soul upon the Lord, that must be a wholesome discipline that leads to such results. Oh, count it a precious trial, a golden affliction, that brings your heart into a closer communion with Christ! Your Elder Brother's voice may, like Joseph's, sound harshly and alarmingly upon your ear, filling you with fear and foreboding; yet it is the voice of your Brother, the "voice of the Beloved," and it speaks but to rouse you to a more full, confiding opening of your heart in prayer. Oh, precious trial! Oh, heaven-sent affliction! that breaks down the barriers, removes the restraints, thaws the conjealings that intercept and interrupt my fellowship with God, and with His dear Son Christ Jesus. Our heavenly Father loves to hear the voice of His children; and when that voice is still, when there is a suspension of heart-communion, and the tones are silent which were wont to fall as music upon His ear, He sends a trial, and then we rise and give ourselves to prayer. Perhaps, it is a perplexity, and we go to Him for counsel; or it is a want, and we go to Him for supply; or it is a grief, and we go to Him for soothing; or it is a burden, and we look to Him for upholding; it is an infirmity, and we repair to Him for grace; it is a temptation, and we fly to Him for succour; it is a sin, and we repair to Him for pardon; but, be its form what it may, it has a voice—"Rise, and call upon thy God!" and to God it brings us.

How much, too, does deeply sanctified trial correct our false judgments. We conceive dark thoughts of God's character, wrong views of His dealings, crude interpretations of His word—our judgments often miscarry in their opinions of persons, of actions, and events; but when under Gods hand how much of this is corrected. The passing tempest has swept the clouds away, cleared our intellectual, and purified our moral atmosphere, and a brighter, serener sky has smiled upon us from above, and our path has become easier and pleasanter. We see God's character and our own in a different light—His so glorious, our own so vile. We interpret His dealings differently and more favourably, and begin to learn that there is no individual who has not, perhaps, more in his character to admire and love than to censure and condemn; and that there is no event in Divine Providence that has not a lesson of truth and a message of love.

We are deeply indebted to trial—and it thus fully sustains its character as among the precious things of God—as authenticating the fact of our divine sonship. Erase sanctified trial from the catalogue of the Lord's dealings with you, and you would cancel one of the strongest evidences of your adoption. What earthly father corrects not the waywardness, self-will, and disobedience of his child? and shall not our heavenly Father, in the exercise of a wisdom and love yet greater, employ a holy and wholesome discipline towards His children? Every stroke of His rod is a proof of His love, and every correction of His hand an evidence of our sonship. How tender and touching the admonition, "My son, despise not thou the chastening of the Lord, nor faint when thou art rebuked of him. For whom the Lord loveth he chasteneth, and scourgeth every son whom he receiveth." Thus, then, our hallowed afflictions and trials are among the choice, precious things of God, because they are signs and seals of our gracious adoption into His family. Be not cast down, O tried believer! as though some strange and untoward thing had happened to you. Misinterpret not the dealings of God, as though your present sorrows, difficulties, and trials, were marks of His displeasure, and evidences against your true and divine relationship. Many of the Lord's people who appear exempt from those trials by which others are sorely afflicted are prone to argue from thence against their being the true children of God. Most true is it that the religion of Jesus is the religion of the cross, and that there never was a true Christian without a cross. And yet the painful misgiving, arising from exemption from the crosses which others bear, may itself be the cross the Lord appoints you. The heart-searching and prayer, the earnestness and anxiety, which this conviction produces, may be just the self-discipline which those peculiar trials—from the absence of which you augur ill against yourself—are designed to effect. God can as richly teach, and as deeply sanctify us by the absence as by the presence of a trial. But ah! are there no crosses other than reverse of circumstances, loss of health, chilled affection, changed friendship, heart-crushing bereavement? Yes, beloved reader; this body of our humiliation, the power of indwelling sin, the assaults of Satan, the seductions of the world, the wounding of the saints, spiritual becloudings and despondencies, is enough, in the absence of all external trial, to discipline the heart, to humble the soul, and keep the believer near to the cross of Jesus. Thus there is no believer without a trial, and no Christian is without the cross.

"A lady of rank and great piety complained that, whereas in Scripture the cross is everywhere spoken of as useful and necessary for the children of God, yet she, for her part, must acknowledge that hitherto the Lord had never deemed her Worthy of one, and that this often raised within her melancholy thoughts and doubts whether she was one of His children or not. Gotthold said to her—I confess that complaints like yours are not common, inasmuch as few Christians have any ground to lament a lack of the cross, while others, whose share of it is exceedingly small, nevertheless imagine that it is quite as large as they are able to bear; and in particular, those who are yet unaccustomed to it, are prone, to fancy that their cross is too great and heavy for them. As for your case, however, it seems to me that you are actually bearing a cross without being conscious of it. You are vexed with gloomy thoughts because you have no cross. These gloomy thoughts, however, appear to me to be themselves a considerable cross, and also a very salutary one, for they not only evince, but nourish and augment your desire to resemble the Lord Jesus, and to take up your cross and follow Him. Besides, the words of our Saviour, 'Whosoever doth not bear his cross, and come after me, cannot be my disciple,' relate not merely to the common hardships of human life, but are also and especially to be understood of the crucifixion of the old man, of his sinful lusts and desires, of self-denial and the subjugation of the will. For the rest, we cannot and ought not to make crosses for ourselves, for this would end in hypocrisy. The Lord holds the cup of affliction in His own hand, and pours out of it when and as much as He will. That He has spared you hitherto, acknowledge with humble gratitude; He is the Searcher of hearts, and perhaps knew that, with the cross, your heart would not have felt towards Him as it has done without it. Recollect, however, that the drama of your life has not yet been played to the end, and that, for ought you know, your gracious God may still have some little cross in reserve for you, to be imposed in due time. The fiercest tempests often come in the evening of the finest summer days, and it is after the pure wine has been run off that the lees are wont to follow. It ought to be another ground of gratitude to God, that He has given you time to prepare for all emergencies, and provide yourself with the armour necessary for your defence."[3]

It is not the least hallowed result of sanctified trial, thus increasing its preciousness, the deeper acquaintance into which it brings us with God's word. In trial we fly to the Scriptures as the unfailing source of guidance and comfort. Whatever may be the nature of our sorrow, or the singularity of our path, we are sure of finding in God's word light, sympathy, and soothing corresponding therewith. God sends us into this school of affliction to learn. Thus He dealt with David—"It is good for me that I have been afflicted, that I might learn thy statutes." God's word at all

---

3   "Gotthold's Emblems."

times should be our study and delight. "Let the word of Christ dwell in you richly in all wisdom." But there is, through outward distractions and inward conflicts, a tendency to neglect the word, to lose our relish for its sweetness, or to turn from its faithful rebukes. And as a parent or a teacher sometimes employs the rod to stimulate his pupil to learn, so our Heavenly Father, our Divine Teacher, often sends His rod of correction to drive us to the study of the truth; then we testify, "It is good far me that I have been afflicted (corrected, chastened, rebuked), that I might learn thy statutes." And oh, with what increased clearness and beauty does the Bible often unfold to us in the time of precious trial! We understand the Scriptures now as we never did before. We may have consulted critics and expositors, and by our own ingenuity and skill have endeavoured to penetrate the sacred mysteries of the word, and yet but to little perception of the truth. But the rod of correction has proved our best expositor under the guidance of the Spirit of truth! "Then opened He their understanding, that they might understand the Scriptures." Dark, mysterious, and trying providences—trials which we thought so untoward—have been our best commentaries on the deep things of the word. What a honied sweetness, in our personal experience, has the bitterness of trial imparted to it! We did not know that there was so much sweetness in the word until we found so much bitterness in the world; nor so much fulness in the Scriptures until we found so much emptiness in the creature. We see the Bible now to be full of Jesus—Christ its revelation, its glory and sweetness, its Alpha and Omega, its beginning and end. Satiated with creature comforts, and surfeited with self-satisfaction, we had loathed the manna of the word, and it had no more relish to our spiritual than the most insipid element to our natural taste. But sweet, sanctified, precious trial has led us to the Book of the tried—God's own word—and we have "rejoiced at it as one that findeth great spoil." With the Psalmist we have testified, "How sweet are thy words to my taste! yea, sweeter than honey to my mouth." "This is my comfort in my affliction: for thy word hath quickened me." Oh welcome, then, cheerfully and submissively the precious trial that renders more precious in your experience the preciousness of God's word.

The time of trial often sets us upon a closer examination of our Christian progress and hope. In the season of worldly sunshine and prosperity, gliding along upon the smooth and calm current, how much do we take for granted as to our true spiritual state. We deem all right within because all is smiling without. The world smiles, friends approve, ministers commend, the heart flatters, and the candle of the Lord shineth round about us—alas! alas! with what slight evidences of conversion, with what dubious marks of grace, with what a slender hope of heaven, are we then satisfied! How shallow our self-acquaintance, how imperfect our knowledge of Christ But the trial comes, bearing the disguise of a foe, yet in reality a friend. And now the first blast of adversity scatters the fig-leaf covering, and destroys the beautiful tresselled wall which our own hands had constructed for our beauty and defence. What we thought was substance proves but a shadow, what we imagined was a reality proves but an appearance. The faith we thought so strong, the love we thought so fervent, the grace we thought so real, the growth we thought so unmistakeable, all, all vanish before the dealings, the probings, the siftings of the Searcher of hearts in the day of trial. Trial has brought us to our right place—the feet of Jesus. There, in the spirit of self-examination, of self-loathing, of self-renunciation, we have been led to ask, "Will this evidence serve me when I come to die? will this love give me boldness in the day of judgment? will this faith present me faultless before the throne of God and the Lamb?" Thus relinquishing our vain fancies, our foolish dreams, our dubious evidences, we have been enabled to take a renewed hold of Christ, to fly afresh to the fountain of His blood, and to enfold ourselves more closely within the robe of His righteousness. Thus emptied, humbled at His feet, we praise and adore Him for the discipline that consumed the dross, scattered the chaff, swept from beneath us the sand, and that strengthened our evidences, brightened our hope, unfolded the Spirit, and enthroned the Redeemer, more vividly and supremely within our soul. O precious trial! dark though thou art, that yet bearest beneath thy sombre wing blessings of grace so sacred and costly as these!

As a moral discipline it would seem impossible to overrate the preciousness of trial. No believer has been placed in a true position for the formation, development, and completeness of his Christian character who has not passed in some degree through this discipline. Not more essential is it that the vessel of the artificer should be exposed to the heat of the furnace, in order to impart transparency to the material, consolidation to its form, and brilliance and permanence to the colours his pencil has traced upon it, than it is for a "vessel of mercy whom God has afore prepared unto glory," to be tried though it be as by fire. From this moral discipline there is in the family of God no exception. It is a remark of the seraphic Leighton—true as it is beautiful—that, "God had but one Son without sin, and never one without suffering." How touching and conclusive the argument and appeal of the apostle—himself purified in this crucible and instructed in this school—"Ye have forgotten the exhortation, which speaketh unto you as unto children, My son, despise not thou the chastening of the Lord, nor faint when thou art rebuked of him: for whom the Lord loveth he chasteneth, and scourgeth every son whom he receiveth. If ye endure chastening, God dealeth with you as with sons: for what son is he whom the father chasteneth not? But if ye be without chastisement, whereof all are partakers, then are ye bastards, and not sons. Furthermore, we have had fathers of our fresh which corrected us, and we gave them reverence: shall we not much rather be in subjection unto the Father of spirits, and live? For they verily for a few days chastened us after their own pleasure; but he for our profit, that we might be partakers of his holiness. Now, no chastening for the present seemeth to be joyous, but grievous: nevertheless afterward it yieldeth the peaceable fruit of righteousness unto them which are exercised thereby." Thus is it clear that chastisement or trial is an evidence and seal of adoption; and that without it we should lack that spiritual discipline, apart from which there is no proper symmetry and completeness of Christian character. Who has not marked the wide and striking difference in the character and deportment of a child trained beneath the wholesome discipline of a parent, and a child who has grown up without that discipline, left to its own self? To what is that difference to be traced but the forming influence of discipline in the one, and its entire absence in the other? There is a development and strength of character, a maturity of mind and mellowed refinement of feeling and address in the child thus schooled, which you in vain look for in the child neglected. "A wise son heareth the instruction of his father." In the Hebrew this passage may be literally rendered, "A wise son is the chastisement of his father." On this text, thus rendered, in all probability the Jews founded their proverb, "If you see a wise child, be sure that his father has chastised him." Now, how gracious and tender is our heavenly Father to condescend thus to deal with us! In everything would He sustain the relation He stands to us as a Father. Not only in loving us, thinking of us, providing for us, guiding and keeping us, but also chastising us. He has undertaken a father's office, and He will fully and faithfully discharge it, even though it may compel the frequent and painful, though loving and righteous, use of the rod. Oh to be assured that this stroke is a fresh seal of adoption! Who would not cheerfully exclaim, "The cup which my Father hath given me, shall I not drink it?"

And yet we think there is a yet higher end accomplished by precious trial, even than this authentication of our adoption. We refer to the Divine holiness to which it assimilates us. "He for our profit, that we might be partakers of his holiness." Next to his justification, sanctification must be the grand aim of the believer; and whatever is promotive of this must be precious. God would make us happy, but He can only make us happy by making us holy. Happiness and holiness are cognate truths: they are relative terms; they are twin sisters. He must be happy who is holy. Sin is the parent of all misery; holiness the root of all happiness. Now the holiness which God would bring us into sympathy with, and make us partakers of, is His own holiness. There is much that passes in the religious world for holiness which is spurious in its nature, and which is disowned by God. There is no real holiness but that which moulds us into the Divine image—that which makes us God-like. We cannot possess God's essential holiness, but we may partake of His imparted holiness. In the same sense in which we are said to be "partakers of the Divine nature" (2 Pet. i. 4), we are "partakers of the Divine holiness." What a portrait is a child of God purified, sanctified, and disciplined by trial! God is the divine original; he is the human copy. Upon that heart softened, upon that spirit subdued, upon that will laid low, the holy Lord God has imprinted, inlaid, His own likeness. And as the polished mirror reflects the likeness of the man who looks into it, and as the glassy lake images the sun that beams down upon it, so does the disciplined child of God,—the grossness of the fleshly eliminated from the spiritual—the dross of the natural separated from the divine—his purified soul reflects, and sparkles, and shines with the holiness of God. Oh, to be like God, who would not welcome the trial, exclaiming with the psalmist, "I know, O Lord, that thy judgments are right, and that thou in faithfulness hath afflicted me." How tenderly, soothingly, lovingly does your Father address you, His tried child—"My son, despise not thou the chastening of the Lord" Is there rigour in the discipline?—there is love in the rod. Is there bitterness in the cup?—there is sweetness upon its brim. Is there acuteness in the suffering? there is soothing in the relation—"My son!" Never can He forget in the severest discipline, in the most painful correction, that He is our Father, and we His children. "Is Ephraim my dear son? is he a pleasant child? for since I spoke against him, I do earnestly remember him still: therefore my bowels are troubled for him; I will surely have mercy upon him, saith the Lord." Never does God employ a rebuke without a cordial, or the pruning knife without the balm. How frequently the mercy precedes, and thus prepares for, the judgment. It was so in the case of our first parents. Ere God pronounces the awful sentence, He breathes the gracious promise. Mercy digs the channel of judgment—prepares and paves its way. Thus, God's corrections, rebukes, and chastisements come tempered, softened, and subdued; and like the smitings and reproofs of the righteous, are a "kindness," and "an excellent oil, which shall not break the head." Thus it is that the tried believer can look into the face of his Father and say, "Righteous art thou, O Lord, when I plead with thee; yet let me talk with thee of thy judgments" (Jer. xii. 1). How sweetly and tenderly did Jesus blend the warning with the consolation, "In the world ye shall have tribulation, but in me ye shall have peace!" Our Lord wisely and graciously presents the world to us as a scene of sorrow, trial, and tribulation, but the counterpart shall be that in its midst we shall experience His presence, love, and grace as our peace. Thus the remark of a quaint writer holds good, "Affliction's rods are made of many keen twigs, but they are all cut from the tree of life. It is a great mercy to have a bitter put into that draught which Satan has sweetened as a vehicle for his poison." Never is the believer so near to Christ's heart, and the Spirit's comforts, and Heaven's joys, as when the flood of dark and broken waters is surging beneath and around him, lifting him upon their crested billows. The higher the ark which bore the Church of old rose upon the flood, the nearer it mounted toward heaven. As earth receded, heaven approached; and the vessel, floating away upon the bosom of the swelling deep, mounted higher and higher. Is it not so with the believing soul when floods of great waters come into it? As these waters swell and rise, sinful follies, worldly vanities, carnal pursuits, pride, self, and ignorance, disappear, and the soul gets nearer to heaven. Precious trial that buries earth's vanity and corruption, and unveils heaven's joy and glory to the soul! Thus out of the eater comes food. The trial that looked so threatening has brought such mercy. The cloud that seemed charged with electricity empties a fruitful shower. Oh, trying seasons are our most spiritual, most prayerful, most Christ-endearing, Christ-conforming seasons, and so trial becomes precious. "Stars shine the brightest in the darkest night; torches are the better for the heating; grapes do not come to the proof till they come to the press; spices smell sweetest when pounded; young trees root the fastest for shaking; vines are better for bleeding; gold looks the brightest for scouring; glow-worms glisten best in the dark; juniper smells the sweetest in the fire; the palm tree proves the better for pressing; cammomile, the more you tread it the more you spread it. Such is the condition of all God's children; they are then most triumphant when most trampled, most glorious when most afflicted; often most in the favour of God when least in man's; as their conflicts, so their conquests; as their tribulations, so their joys; they live best in the furnace of persecution, so that heavy afflictions are the best benefactors to heavenly blessings, and when afflictions hang heaviest corruptions hang loosest, and grace that is hid in nature, as sweet water in rose leaves, is then most fragrant when the fire of affliction is put under to distil it out."[4] Favoured child of God, whose Fathers discipline in providence and grace wafts such blessings into the soul! Precious trial that makes Jesus more precious, the throne of grace more precious, the discipline of the covenant more precious, holiness more precious, the saints of God more precious, the word of God more precious, and the prospect of going home to glory more precious! "Happy the believer who, the more afflictions assail him, cleaves the more closely to the Lord. Like the traveller overtaken in a storm, who, when the rain beats upon him, or the snow drifts upon his person, or the mountain wind drives furiously against him, lays firmer hold of his cloak and wraps it closely around him, he, amidst the storm of troubles, keeps faster hold of the 'Man who is an hiding-place from the wind and a covert from the tempest.'"

A time of trial is a time of sensibility. God often sends it for this very end. There is nothing in the gospel of Christ that forbids emotion, everything to awaken it; there is nothing in the religion of Jesus to crush sensibility, everything to create it. Christianity is a religion of feeling—deep, hallowed, sanctified feeling. It is the only religion that thoroughly appeals to our emotional nature, that touches the deep, hidden springs of our humanity, and tells us we may—weep. With Christ's tears at Bethany, and with his drops of blood in Gethsemane before us, surely we may express the deepest sympathy with the adversity of others, and may indulge in deep, chastened grief with our own. Weep on, then, beloved mourner! We would not seal up those tears. "Jesus wept," and you too may weep. "No chastening for the present is joyous, but grievous;" therefore, it is no sin to give expression to emotion, to indulge in sensibility, to "water our couch with tears, and to make our bed to swim." Without a measure of grief our affliction would leave no trace of good. When God speaks, we should hear; when He smites, we should feel. Only let your grief be moderate, chastened, and submissive, embodying its sentiment, and expressing its intensity in the language and spirit of the "Man of Sorrows," "Not my will, O my Father, but thine be done."

What shall we then say to these things? Shall we not count among the precious things of God, not the least precious, the trial whose discipline removes from us so much evil, and confers upon us so much good? How little should we know experimentally of the Lord Jesus—what depths there were in His love, what soothing in His sympathy, what condescension in His grace, what gentleness and delicacy in His conduct, what exquisite beauty in His tears, what safety beneath His sheltering wing, and what repose upon His loving heart, but for this very adversity. Your ark is tossed amidst the broken waters, but you have Christ on board your vessel, and it shall not founder. He may seem, as of old, "when asleep upon a pillow," ignorant of, and indifferent to, the storm that rages wildly around you; yet the eye of His Godhead never slumbers, and He will, and at the best moment, arise in majesty and power, hush the tempest and still the waves, and there shall be peace. And will you not then count that a precious adversity that awakens in your breast the adoring exclamation, "What manner of man is this, that even the winds and the sea obey him?" Yes; Christ treads the limpid pathway of your sorrow. He comes to you

---

4   Spencer.

walking upon the sea of your trouble. He approaches to quell your fears, to calm your mind, to give you peace. And but for this alienation of property, this sore bereavement, this terrible calamity, this wasting disease, this languor, suffering, and decay, these restless days and wakeful nights, oh, how many a precious visit from the Beloved of your soul would you have lost! Be still then; trial will bring a precious Jesus to you; and the presence, the love, the sympathy, and the grace of Jesus will lighten, soothe, and sweeten your trial. We shall soon be at home, where "God shall wipe away all tears from their eyes; and there shall be no more death, neither sorrow, nor crying, neither shall there be any more pain." The last truth of God will be seen, the last lesson of holiness will be learned, the last taint of sin will be effaced, and there will be no more need of sorrow's discipline, nor the hallowing influence of precious trial; the last ember of the furnace will be extinguished, the last wave of trouble will die upon the shore, and we shall be for ever with Jesus. Until then, "commit your way unto the Lord," leave your concerns in His hands, "trust in Him," and come up from the wilderness clinging to His almighty arm, and leaning upon His loving breast, to uphold you in weakness, to soothe you in grief, and to bring you home to Himself, where the days of your mourning shall be ended, and "God shall wipe away all tears from their eyes."

> "When sore afflictions crush the soul,
> And riven is each earthly tie,
> The heart must cling to God alone:
> He wipes the tear from every eye.
>
> "Through wakeful nights, when rack'd with pain,
> On bed of languishing you lie,
> Remember still your God is near
> To wipe the tear from every eye.
>
> "A few short years, and all is o'er;
> Your Borrows, pains, will soon pass by;
> Then lean in faith on God's dear Son,
> He'll wipe the tear from every eye.
>
> "Oh, never be your soul cast down,
> Nor let your heart desponding sigh,
> Assured that God, whose name is Love,
> Will wipe the tear from every eye!"[5]

---

5   Mrs Mackinlay.

Chapter IV.

THE PRECIOUSNESS OF GOD'S THOUGHTS.

"How precious are thy thoughts unto me, O God! how great is the sum of them!"—Psalm cxxxix. 17.

It is marvellous that God should think of us as He does. That, infinitely great and holy—all worlds, all beings, all events occupying His mind—He should yet have individual thoughts of us, those thoughts not mere passing glances of the mind, but involving the pre-determination and pre-arrangement of each event, circumstance, and step of our personal history, trivial though it be as a hair falling from the head—is a truth too mighty to grasp were it not too precious to refuse, and too divine to disbelieve. You have, doubtless, beloved, often appeared in your own view so obscure, and insignificant a being—a mere cypher in the great sum of human existence, a single drop in the vast ocean of human life—as to be almost at an infinite remove from God's notice. You could not, indeed, relieve yourself from the conviction of individual responsibility, nor stifle the reflection that for each transaction of the present life the future holds you accountable; yet that, isolated and solitary, perchance, poor and mean, as you may be, God, the great, the holy Lord God should think of you, notice you, regard you, set His heart upon you—that His thoughts, more precious than the ocean's gems, and more numerous than the sands which belt it, should cluster around you, clinging to you with a grasp so fervent and intense as to lift you to the distinction and privilege of a being in whom, the Divine regard were solely and supremely absorbed—is a truth distancing all conception, and well-nigh overwhelming you with its mightiness. And yet so it is! Each child of God dwells in His heart, and engages His mind as though he were the sole occupant of this boundless universe—a tiny insect swimming in the ocean of infinity. Such is the truth to which the psalmist gives utterance in a burst of devout, impassioned feeling, "How precious are thy thoughts unto me, O God! how great is the sum of them!" "Unto me!" Here is faith attracting to, and concentrating upon, its individual self all the precious thoughts Jehovah has of His people. Oh, there is not a thought of His wisdom, nor a thought of His love, nor a thought of His power, nor a thought of His grace which does not entwine itself with the being, and blend itself with the salvation of each child of His adoption. The subject now engaging our meditation is—the preciousness of God's thoughts—and may the theme lay low all high, towering, sinful thoughts of ourselves, and inspire and raise our holy, grateful, adoring thoughts of

43

Him—His glory, beauty, and love—until, with a depth of adoration, and an intensity of affection, worthy the theme, our hearts respond, "How precious are thy thoughts unto me, O God! how great is the sum of them!" Let us first contemplate a few characteristics of God's precious thoughts of His saints.

God's thoughts of His people are—infinite. Believers deal too little with the infinitude of God. Hence the tendency to "limit the Holy One of Israel." Thus, too, it is, that our confidence in God is so hesitating, our views of His power so dwarfish, our love so defective, and our requests and expectations so contracted. "I am a great King, saith the Lord God." All His thoughts are vast, infinite, worthy of His greatness. His electing thought of us was a great thought; His thought of redeeming us was a great thought; His thought of making us divine by the regeneration of the Holy Ghost is a great thought; His thought of bringing us to glory to enjoy Him fully and for ever is a great thought. All these thoughts of God are as great as they are precious, as precious as they are great. O child of God! think not lightly of the thoughts God has of thee—they are so vast, nothing can exceed, so precious, nothing can equal them. The thoughts of an Infinite Mind encircle and enfold thee more closely and fondly than the ivy clasps the elm, or the mother her new-born infant. Whether they appear clad in darkness, or robed in light, they are equally the great and precious thoughts of thy covenant God and Father. "How precious art thy thoughts unto me, O God! how great is the sum of them!"

God's thoughts of His people are—hidden. The thoughts of the Invisible One, they must necessarily be so. It is His glory to conceal until it becomes His wisdom and love to reveal them. Treasured up in the Divine Mind, they repose in profound mystery until each circumstance in our daily life unfolds and makes them known, then we learn how real and how precious God's thoughts of us are. There is not a moment, beloved of God, that the Lord is not thinking of you; nor is there a moment that He is not, in some form or other, embodying those thoughts in His gracious and providential dealings with you. His wisdom withholds, and His love veils them, until the event transpires that gives them utterance and form. Therefore, when God is silent, let us be still; when He speaks, let us hearken. Hidden to us though His precious thoughts are, they are all known to Him. "I know the thoughts I think towards you, saith the Lord; thoughts of peace and not of evil, to give you an expected end." Attempt not, therefore, to fathom the Divine Mind, or to penetrate the thoughts that are hidden there. Know thou, that they are thoughts of everlasting love, thoughts of assured peace, and let this bring your heart into silent, patient waiting, until all these thoughts shall stand unveiled in His wise, loving, and holy dispensations, here, and in heaven's own light hereafter. Enough is revealed by Christ to satisfy you that God's thoughts of you are thoughts of reconciliation—that there exists not in the Divine Mind a solitary thought adverse to your well-being. Jesus, our Friend, reposes in His people the same confidence His Father has reposed in Him. "All things that I have heard of my Father I have made known unto you." Jesus is the expression and embodiment of our Father's mind. Jesus is God thinking, God loving, God working, God redeeming. "He that hath seen me hath seen the Father." Be not, then, troubled in mind at the dark and mysterious in your path. God is dealing well with you. By His light you shall walk through darkness. Confiding in the wise and loving, though concealed, thoughts of your heavenly Father, your trustful heart can respond, as those thoughts gradually unfold, "How precious are thy thoughts unto me, O God!"

Unchangeableness is another characteristic of God's thoughts of His people. This is self-evident, since they are the thoughts of the Unchangeable One. Change implies imperfection. God is a perfect Being, consequently He cannot change. "I the Lord change not." With Him is "no variableness, neither the shadow of a turning." He may vary His providences, multiply His dispensations, and shift the ever-moving scene of human life, but—

"His eternal thoughts move on,
His undisturbed affairs."

How precious is this truth to the child of God! Human thoughts change; mind itself fails, and with it fades from memory countenances that were familiar, and names that were fond, and scenes that were sacred. Human thoughts that cluster and cling so warmly and closely around us to-day, ere many weeks are past, attracted by new objects of interest, or absorbed by new engagements of time, have fled and gone, and we are alone and forgotten. But there is One whose thoughts of us never change, whose mind never ceases for a moment to think of us. "O Israel, thou shalt not be forgotten of me," is His own loving declaration. Directing us to a mother—the last earthly home of human tenderness, sympathy, and love—He tells us, "She may forget, yet will not I." Beloved, whatever fluctuation you find in human thought, or change in human affection, God's thoughts of love, and care, and faithfulness, are changeless. Have they ever darted into your heart like solar beams, causing that heart to sing for joy? Then, though in darkness, loneliness, and sorrow you are led to exclaim, "Hath the Lord forgotten to be gracious?" God still bears you in His thoughts and on His heart. Relatives may forget, friends may forget, the saints may forget, but thy God never can. He thinks of you at this moment as lovingly, as carefully, as from all eternity. Once in the thoughts of thy covenant God, thou art in those thoughts for ever. Be not cast down, then, if God appears to forget you. "My way is hid from the Lord," says the desponding Church. "No," says God; "I have engraved thee upon the palms of my hands; thy walls are continually before me." Amidst all your mental wanderings, your fickle, faint thoughts, of Him, He still remembers you. In the multitude of your anxious and perplexed thoughts within you, awakened by a sense of your ungrateful oblivion of God, or by His trying and mysterious dealings, let this comfort delight your soul, that He never forgets you. But let us particularise some of God's thoughts of His saints.

He thinks of their persons. Each believer has a personal interest in the Divine Mind. The acceptance of our person before that of our sacrifice is God's order. It is man's folly, deep and fatal, to reverse this. "I will accept you and your sweet savour," says the Lord God—first, the persons, and then the offerings of His people. Now, the Lord's people are an accepted people—"accepted in the Beloved." You may, in some moments of spiritual despondency, appear to your own view so vile and uncomely as to be beyond the pale of God's loving and complacent regard. You can only think of, and view yourself with, the deepest self-abhorrence. And yet at that moment of spiritual prostration, your person, standing in Christ, clad in His imputed righteousness, and comely through the comeliness He has put upon you, is an object of His ineffable delight; and all His parental, gracious, and tender thoughts are entwined around you with a grasp from which nothing shall ever separate you.

He thinks of His own work in your soul—that divine kingdom of righteousness, joy, and peace in the Holy Spirit which has its home in every regenerate man. Its development and growth, its progress amidst indwelling sin, the fluctuation of spiritual feeling, the varied phases it assumes, the summer's drought, the winter's frost through which it passes—occupies the incessant thoughts of God. He has His eye upon that hidden kingdom of grace in the soul more intently, more fixedly, more benignantly than He views the most powerful and gorgeous kingdom upon earth. "The kingdom of God is within you," says the Saviour; and all other kingdoms shall fall and disappear, when this kingdom of grace in the saints shall emerge from its veiled obscurity and feebleness, and expand and brighten into an eternal kingdom of glory. Yes, beloved, God thinks of all the spiritual exercises through which you pass—your fears and hopes, your doubtings and your trustings, your high and your low frames, your infirmities of prayer, of faith, and love—yea, there is not a throb of your heart, not a feeling of your soul, not a thought of your mind growing out of the work of Divine grace within—all that elevates or depresses, that grieves or cheers, that shades or brightens—that does not engage the thoughts of thy God.

The thoughts of God, too, are occupied with the returns His people make. Nothing you do escapes His notice. What! is there anything done by you for God to which He is indifferent? Ah, no! He thinks of all your sincere desires to love Him, your lowly endeavours to serve Him, your earnest efforts to obey Him, your feeble, imperfect attempts to honour and glorify Him. He thinks of all the poor returns you make of loving toil, of patient endurance, of filial obedience. Have you a passing remembrance of Him as you thread your way through the crowd?—God thinks of it. Is there a gush of love welling up from your heart in secret communion?—God thinks of it. Bear you with stealthy step to an obscure abode the cup of cold water to moisten the fevered lips of some poor suffering saint?—God thinks of it. Have you relinquished some fond idol, or mortified some darling sin, or resisted some potent temptation, or discharged some act of self-denial for the honour of His name?—God thinks of it. Every habit you lay down, or cross you take up, or burden you bear, or yoke to which you bow for Jesus, shall be treasured up in the thoughts of thy God through eternity.

We have now, in the progress of our remarks, arrived at a delightful part of the subject—the preciousness of God's thoughts. And where is there a heart touched by divine grace that does not respond from its innermost shrine to the exclamation of David—"How precious are thy thoughts unto me, O God! how great is the sum of them!" They are in truth precious, than which nothing is really so. To feel that God has one loving thought of us, to know that He thinks of us—that He remembers us with a constancy which no forgetfulness on our part of Him can efface, to be quite sure that in His thoughts of love, His thoughts of peace, His thoughts of complacent delight, His true, constant, faithful thoughts we have a personal share—oh, there is a preciousness in this truth, a repose, a confidence, a sanctity, which distances all conception! "How precious are thy thoughts unto me, O God!" Let us go into a few particulars.

God's thoughts are precious in themselves—they are essentially precious. They must be so, since they are a Father's thoughts. How precious are His thoughts of eternal love towards us! What! is there no preciousness in this truth to your soul, beloved? I trust the honey from the comb is not half so sweet. "I have loved thee with an everlasting love, therefore with lovingkindness have I drawn thee." Is there no sweetness in this truth, in comparison of which all carnal sweetness is as gall? You have tasted the gracious stream, and found it sweet; but have you followed that stream to the fountain whence it flowed—the everlasting love of your covenant God—and tasted yet more sweetness there? Be ye assured of this, not one drop of honey distils into your cup, but it comes from the heart of God. It exudes from that "Tree of Life" which He planted in this sinful, sorrow-stricken world, scathed, wounded, by His own hand of justice. "Stricken, smitten of God, and afflicted, it pleased the Lord to bruise him; he hath put him to grief," that through this costly, touching, winning channel—the wounds of our Immanuel—might flow into our souls His everlasting thoughts of love. Then you exclaim, "Did God love me from all eternity? did He think of me then? was He preparing all my future happiness and eternal blessedness, treasuring up for me all grace here, and all glory hereafter?—O God! how precious are Thy thoughts of love to me!" Yes, they are precious, because they are God's thoughts, and not man's—divine, and not human—thoughts of Divine love, and not of anger—of peace, and not of wrath.

As redeeming thoughts they are precious. It was a thought, which could only find its conception in the Divine Mind, that of saving sinners by the sacrifice of God's beloved Son. No finite mind would ever have thought of saving man; once lost, he would to that mind seem lost irrecoverably. To secure the integrity of His moral government intact, the glory of His Divine nature unsullied—to harmonise justice with mercy, holiness with love, truth with grace, and thus to reconcile all the jarring interests of heaven in the salvation of sinners, by the blood of the Cross, was a thought worthy of God. Go to the cross of Calvary, and learn how costly and precious are God's redeeming thoughts of you. His thought of rearing that cross in the centre of a revolted part of His empire—of impaling upon it His only begotten and well-beloved Son, a sacrifice for the salvation of its rebellious subjects—His thought of laying all our sins and all our curse upon Jesus, extinguishing the fires of our hell by the life-blood of Immanuel—of opening the kingdom of heaven to us through the pierced, broken heart of Christ the Anointed One—oh, it were infinitely worthy of Him who is "wonderful in counsel, and excellent in working!" O God, when I read thy heart in the cross, in the wounds, in the tears, in the anguish, in the blood of thy Son, Jesus Christ, how precious are thy thoughts unto me!—thoughts that planned and accomplished my redemption, by an expedient so vast, and at a cost so precious.

Trace these thoughts of God as they compassed our path through all the days of our unregeneracy—how precious are they! We too much overlook this—the patience and forbearance of God during the period of our unconverted days. Surely the 'long-suffering of God' through all these stages and acts of enmity and rebellion was 'salvation.' How often, when gliding upon the treacherous rapid that bore us onward to the gulph, or when standing upon the brink of the yawning precipice, eternal wrath flaming beneath our feet, God thought of us in mercy and redeemed our life from instant and everlasting destruction! And along all the winding path of waywardness and sin, of worldliness and folly, still His thoughts of electing love and sovereign grace pursued us, nor lost their sight, nor relaxed their hold of us, until the appointed and happy hour that brought us into the bond of the covenant.

How precious His thoughts in conversion. What must the love and tenderness of those thoughts have been at the moment that saw us prostrate at His feet, all our self-righteousness, rebellion, and hostility, all our false dependencies and refuges falling in wreck and ruin from around us; and our soul in that blessed posture which He Himself has portrayed, as none but He could, in language the most tender and touching: "To this man will I look, even to him that is poor and of a contrite spirit, and that trembleth at my word!" Oh, what must have been His gracious, condescending, loving thoughts when He traced our first tear, saw our first sorrow, and heard our first appeal to His mercy! When afar off, he beheld us approaching in penitence and contrition, marked the downcast look, the hesitating step, the trembling heart, and heard the secret resolve, "I will arise and go to my Father, and will say unto Him, I have sinned." And when He looked and beheld the glance, the touch, the venture of faith on Jesus—saw the trembling soul embrace His blessed Son, receive His unspeakable gift, and trust in His great salvation—how precious must have been His thoughts of us at that moment?

How precious are His restoring thoughts. These may, at times, appear greater than His thoughts in conversion. Why? Because these restoring thoughts are after all our sinful wanderings, repeated backslidings in the face of love the most tender, of goodness the most unwearying, of faithfulness the most unwavering, of dealings the most kind. That still His thoughts of pardon and of restoration should follow us, seeking us, bringing us back, and restoring to our souls the joys of His salvation, oh, how precious in themselves are God's thoughts! "I have gone astray like a lost sheep; seek thy servant; for I do not forget thy commandments."

God's providential thoughts of His people are precious. God is thinking of our wants, of our circumstances, of our emergencies, every moment. His providential thoughts of us are anticipative; they prevent us with their goodness. That same God who fed Elijah beneath the sycamore tree,—who prepared a dinner for the disciples, weary with their night of fruitless toil, as they landed upon the shore,—who feeds the ravens when they cry, and makes those ravens feed His children,—who, when the meal and the oil are well-nigh exhausted, sends succour,—is our God of providence, all whose thoughts are acquainted with, anticipate, and supply our daily need and emergency. Blessed is it to trace a Fathers thoughts of us in our providential mercies: to feel that this good has come, this mercy has been bestowed, this table spread, this want supplied, this pressure met, this evil averted, by God's careful providential thought of us. Oh, how precious are these thoughts to him who lives upon a Father's bounty, who can trace a Father's hand, feel a Father's heart, and hear a Father's voice responsive to the petition, "Give us this day our daily bread."

But Gods thoughts are net only precious in themselves, they are so also in the personal experience of the believer. David's language expresses this, "How precious are Thy thoughts unto me, O God!" This is not an abstract truth—no revealed truth is so to the child of God. If through the truth he is sanctified—"Sanctify them through Thy truth"—then every truth of God forms an essential ingredient in God's grand recipe for all believers. Christ pledged the promised, and now given, Spirit, that "when He is come He shall guide you into all truth." Oh, did we more distinctly recognise this office of the Holy Ghost, and honour Him more by availing ourselves of His teaching—ceasing to "hear the instruction that causeth to err;" especially ceasing from our own fancied wisdom and attainments— we should not be the children in knowledge and the dwarfs in holiness that we are, but men in both. Into the personal experience, then, of this truth the Holy Spirit is prepared to guide us—the preciousness of God's thoughts. Oh, yes, they are precious at all times, in all places, and under all circumstances. Wreathed in dark clouds or glowing in sunlight, whatever the form they assume or the tint they wear, they are still the thoughts of a covenant God, and as such are inexpressibly precious to the believing soul. Who will affirm that thoughts of love—a creature's love though it be—are not precious? The fond remembrance borne to us from some remote spot, assuring us that time has not effaced nor distance annihilated that sacred affection, that early love that first enstamped its image upon the heart, is more precious to us than rubies. These thoughts of love thus wafted to us are more fragrant than the violet breath of spring. But oh, how do the thoughts of divine love distance this! That human heart must die, and in that very moment those thoughts of love perish. But God can fill and satisfy our souls with Himself in the entire absence of all creature good. How precious and soothing to our sad and lonely, perhaps aching and anguished hearts, is the reflection that God thinks of us in love! And when we deem no one bears us in fond remembrance—when our path is dreary, our faith is low, our comforts few—when resources are failing, and creatures are withdrawing, and Satan is tempting—when a train of untoward circumstances are weaving their net-work around our feet, forming a labyrinth to human ken of inexplicable and inextricable difficulties—and when, from the many and deep waters in which we sink, our appeal is heard, "My heart is overwhelmed; lead me to the rock that is higher than I"—oh, how precious to us then are the covenant, faithful, loving thoughts of our God!

There is another peculiar stage of Christian experience in which the soul experiences the preciousness of God's thoughts. We refer to the season of mental disquietude and depression, it may be of despondency and despair. You cannot at that moment command your mental powers, control your thoughts, or fix and concentrate them upon any consecutive train of serious and devout reflection. Oh, is it not then soothing and precious to be reminded that your heavenly Father has thoughts of you, that your High Priest in heaven has thoughts of you, that the Holy Spirit on earth has thoughts of you, that each Divine Person of the glorious Godhead has you in remembrance, breathing the words with which He once comforted His Church in the wilderness, "I know the thoughts that I think towards you, saith the Lord, thoughts of peace and not of evil, to give you an expected end." Oh, let no child of God—around whose mind thick clouds are hovering, walking in darkness and having no light, tempted to doubt God, to cast away his confidence and abandon his hope in Christ—yield himself to the desponding reflection that he has no place in God's thoughts of peace. Christian sufferer! child of the light walking in darkness! thy Father's thoughts of you never were more tender, compassionate, and faithful than at this season of mental gloom, of spiritual despondency. You may not behold Him through the cloud that shades Him from your eye; but He, from whom no darkness hideth, sees you, and knows the way that you take. Though you may have relaxed your hand of faith on Him, He has not withdrawn His hand of love from you, but is leading you by a right way to bring you to your heavenly and eternal home. "I am poor and needy, yet the Lord thinketh upon me."

Let this subject test the bearing of our minds towards God. What are our thoughts of Him? It is a mark of the ungodly, that "God is not in all their thoughts." It is a distinctive feature of the children of God, that they "think upon His name." Oh, is there an occupation of the mind to be compared with this? Thinking of God! meditating upon Christ! There is no other subject of meditation that can calm your perturbed thoughts, fix your wandering thoughts, purify your sinful thoughts, harmonise your perplexed thoughts, quench your panting thoughts, soothe and comfort your sad and mournful thoughts, as thinking upon God! Here is repose— here is peace—here is hope. Oh, that He did engage more of our thoughts! What an infinite, boundless, ennobling theme! "My meditations of Him shall be sweet." Thoughts of His love will comfort you in sorrow, thoughts of His power will calm you in danger, thoughts of His holiness will check you in temptation, thoughts of His wisdom will encourage you in doubt, thoughts of His all-seeing, all-pervading, all-enshrouding presence will sweeten the solitude, smooth the roughness, and illumine the gloom of your path homeward across the desert.

And remember how precious to His heart are your thoughts of Him. "They that feared the Lord spake often one to another: and the Lord hearkened, and heard it, and a book of remembrance was written before him for them that feared the Lord, and that thought upon his name." (Mal. iii. 16.) Imperfect, transient, sinful as your thoughts of God are, yet there is not a humble, grateful, adoring thought of Him in your heart that is not more precious to Him than countless worlds. Those worlds, innumerable and glorious, will ere long be swept from their spheres; but not one lowly, loving, holy thought of God, that once found a moment's home in your heart, shall ever be erased from His took of remembrance. These holy thoughts of God in Christ, that struggled amidst indwelling corruption—that, like grains of gold amidst beds of earth, sparkled in their veiled and lowly beauty, seen only by Him from whom nothing holy, as nothing sinful, is hidden—these thoughts of His love and faithfulness which, in seasons of depression, and circumstances of trial, and scenes of sorrow, darted, sun-like, athwart your gloomy desponding mind—"My Father loves me now, cares for me now, is thinking of me now—how precious are Thy thoughts unto me, O God!"—all, all comes up as a memorial before Him, more beauteous than morning light, more fragrant than the breath of spring, more costly, precious, and endurable than ocean's richest gems? No tongue can describe how precious and glorifying to Christ is a penitential, believing, loving, adoring, grateful remembrance of His name, welling up from the renewed heart of a poor sinner. He seems to say, "Hast thou, my disciple, one thought of Me? I have, for that one thought, ten thousand thoughts of thee. And when I seem to be deaf to thy voice, and silent to thy petition, and thou art led to exclaim, 'The Lord hath forsaken me, and my Lord hath forgotten me,' listen to my words—'Can a woman forget her sucking child, that she should not have compassion on the son of her womb? Yea, she may forget, yet will not I forget thee.'"

Seek the daily purification of your thoughts of God in the atoning blood of Jesus. All your truant, unbelieving, murmuring, rebellious thoughts, oh, take them to the Fountain which alone can blot them out, leaving no tracings upon God's tablet but your penitential thoughts of His holiness, your grateful thoughts of His love, your adoring thoughts of His glory, your peaceful thoughts of His grace! One holy, loving, adoring thought of His name He will never, never forget.

And suffer no humbling conviction of personal unworthiness, or blinding influence of deep sorrow, to veil from your mind the precious truth that God still thinks of you. You may be forgotten by some, and may deem yourself too insignificant and obscure to be remembered by others; but He upon whom all worlds hang, and all beings depend, has thoughts of kindness and of love towards you. Listen to His gracious declaration addressed to you, "Thou shalt not be forgotten of me, O Israel!" Oh, won-drous grace, matchless love, that entwines you, His beloved child, in His thoughts of peace, and care, and sympathy, with an intensity, individu-ality, and minuteness, which seem to exclude from His mind every other being in the universe, so completely does God absorb His people within Himself. Bereaved and desolate widow! God, thy God, thinks of thee, and of thy little ones. Lone and friendless orphan! God thinks of you, for "in Him the fatherless find mercy." Mourning one! God thinks of thee, for He has declared, "I, even I, am He that comforteth you." Wanderer, penitent and heart stricken! God thinks of thee, for He says, "I have surely heard Ephraim bemoaning himself. Is Ephraim my dear son? is he a pleasant child? for since I spake against him, I do earnestly remember him still: therefore my bowels are troubled for him; I will surely have mercy upon him, saith the Lord." Tried, tempted, afflicted one! God thinks of thee. "I know their sorrows," saith the Lord. "Come, my people, enter thou into thy chambers, and shut thy doors about thee: hide thyself as it were for a little moment, until the indignation be overpast." Sick one! amidst thy languor, pain, and solitude, thy God thinks of thee, for "He knoweth our frame, He remembereth that we are dust;" and He has promised "gen-tly to lead them that are burdened." Stay, then, your mind upon Jeho-vah-Jesus. "Thou wilt keep him in perfect peace, whose mind (margin, whose thoughts) is stayed on thee: because he trusteth in thee." Let nothing inexplicable in God's dealings with you unhinge your mind from this confidence in the wisdom, love, and righteousness of His procedure. Remember His declaration, "My thoughts are not your thoughts, neither are your ways my ways, saith the Lord. For as the heavens are higher than the earth, so are my ways higher than your ways, and my thoughts than your thoughts." (Isa. lv. 8, 9.) Thus, confide in those covenant, unchanging, loving thoughts of God, and believe that, high as the billows mount, these divine thoughts of your Father's love tower infinitely above all your unworthiness, sins, sorrows, and fears. Although at times so absorbed in a sense of your sinfulness and littleness you may appear to yourself but like an animalcule swimming in the ocean, or a mote floating in the sunbeam, yet the God who gave to that insect its being, and sustains its life, thinks of, and cares for, and loves you. Go, then, and exclaim, "How precious are thy thoughts unto me, O God! how great is the sum of them!" "Casting all your care upon him; for he careth for you."

> "Mighty God! on whom the care
> Of the whole creation lie;
> And whose ample bosom bears
> The load so patiently:
> 'Midst the worlds that lean on Thee,
> Thou hast loving thoughts of me.
>
> "Ever quickly Thou dost hear
> Thy children's feeble cry;
> And dost keep them everywhere
> Beneath Thy watchful eye:
> 'Midst the worlds that lean on Thee,
> Thou hast faithful thoughts of me.
>
> "Anxious care and heavy woes
> Oft agitate my breast;
> And no balm that hither grows
> Can give my spirit rest:
> But 'midst worlds that lean on Thee,
> Thou hast gentle thoughts of me."

Chapter V.

THE PRECIOUSNESS OF THE DIVINE PROMISES.

"Whereby are given unto us exceeding great and precious promises."—1 Peter i. 4.

The promises of God are the jewellery of the Bible. Every page of this sacred volume is rich and sparkling with these divine assurances of Jehovah's love, faithfulness, and power towards His people. We can scarcely cite, as illustrating His beneficence and forethought, a more appropriate and costly evidence of God's wisdom and goodness than this peculiar provision which He has made for the exigencies of His Church. It meets the believer at every step of his journey, confronts every circumstance of his life, and chimes with each phase of his mental and spiritual experience. Upon no spot in the wilderness can he plant his foot, strange and untrodden though that path may be, but a gem from this casket meets his eye, the sight of which inspires his heart with confidence, his spirit with comfort, his soul with hope.

Now, God, in giving us these divine assurances, proceeds with His Church upon the same principle which holds together the social fabric of human society, viz., promise and trust It is promise, in some form or other, and trust in that promise, which binds man to man; and it is the confidence we repose in his word which gives credence to his statements, his discoveries, and his testimonies; and which lures and sustains us in our individual path of acquisition and research. The promise of gold allures the avaricious, the promise of glory fires the ambitious, the promise of pleasure stimulates the worldly, the promise of intellectual reward sustains and animates the student. And although these promises may prove as visionary and fitful as a dream, yet, for the moment, they impart confidence and inspire hope. Thus man's credulity in man is the great ligament of human society, and the promise of reward the pole-star of his life. Now, our heavenly Father deals with His children precisely upon the same principle—of promise and trust. He speaks, and challenges our belief; He promises, and asks our confidence; He utters His word, and bids us rely implicitly on His love, faithfulness, and power to make it good.

Among the precious things of God, then, how inconceivably precious and indispensable are His promises! Imagine what would have been the condition of His children apart from the divine promises of which the blessed volume is so full. What must have been the desolateness, the sadness, and the sinking had we not the divine assurances of God's Word on which to rely; and in the realisation of which we are guided in our march heavenward, are upheld in weakness, cheered in depression, and conducted step by step to final blessedness. Oh, were it possible to erase from the sacred volume all those precious promises which cluster in its pages, like golden fruit bending from the Tree of Life, what a wintry gloom would enshroud the whole of your future, both the life that now is, and the life which is to come. Rob a man of God of the "precious promises," and you extinguish the sun of his moral firmament, and roll back the darkness and confusion of chaos. Rob him of the promises, and you cut off every spring of comfort and consolation that cheers and gladdens his heart in this vale of suffering and tears.

Another observation we make refers to the fact, that these are not the promises of man, but of God. They are the promises of Jehovah, the promises of an Infinite Being; the promises of a God who cannot lie—consequently He will fulfil them; and of a God of Omnipotence,—and consequently He possesses the power to make them good. We bid you keep this truth vividly before you, that the promises on which God has caused you to hope are the promises of Jehovah—consequently there is the certain pledge of their timely and complete fulfilment.

They are, moreover, comprehensive in their character, and are adapted to all the varied circumstances of individual history—so comprehensive and so adapted, that we cannot conceive of any condition in which you, as a child of God, may be placed, any circumstance by which you may be surrounded, any sorrow by which you may be depressed, any perils that may confront, any darkness that may overshadow you, or any wants of which you may be the subject, in which you may not find some promise of His blessed Word that meets your case. Away with the promises (as it regards my personal experience) if I thought there was a sorrow feeding at the core of my heart which God's word of promise could not console, an intricacy in my path through which it could not guide me, a bitter in the cup God causeth me to drink for which it had no sweetness. Beloved, we want you to keep this view of the precious promises of God's Word constantly before you. They are comprehensive, and adapted to all the circumstances of your personal history, and so prove themselves to be the precious promises of Jehovah.

Yet one more observation. These promises of God are covenant promises; that is, they are the promises of the new covenant of grace. We deal too much with the old covenant, and too little with the new. Our faith is too much of a Jewish faith, and too little of a Christian. A more glorious covenant is the covenant of grace; and its promises are "better promises"—promises of more precious blessings than ever appertained to the old covenant. They are all signed and sealed with the heart's blood of the Mediator of the covenant, and, consequently, they are the precious promises of our Covenant God. That covenant must be broken, the oath of that covenant must be violated, the God of that covenant must change, and the "blood of the everlasting covenant" must cease to be efficacious if one solitary promise on which your poor, trembling, and anxious soul hangs its all, should fail. They cannot fail, because they are the promises of the new covenant of grace. Well may they be called "exceeding great promises." They are the promises of a great God, and of a great covenant. They are "great," in themselves, because they promise us great blessings. They are "exceeding great," because they are the promises of Jehovah. They rest upon four foundations, or pillars; and so long as these pillars stand, so long must stand the precious promises of God's word. God's holiness is one pillar upon which they stand, which will not suffer Him to deceive; God's goodness is another which will not suffer Him to forget; God's truth is another, which will not suffer Him to change; God's power is the fourth, which enables Him to accomplish all that He has promised. With these few general observations, we now proceed to a more particular illustration of their preciousness and efficacy. "Exceeding great and precious" is the character given to them by the Holy Ghost, and the Holy Ghost never uses words without profound significance and meaning.

They are "precious promises," because of the source from whence they originate. What are these promises? They are the unfolding of the heart of God; they are the revelation of the mind of God; they are the exponents of the will of God; they are, in a word, God Himself. If a faithful and true friend, a man of probity, integrity, and honesty, who would rather pluck out his right eye, or sever his right hand than violate his word, makes us a promise, it is but another exhibition of his own self. In that promise we read his veracity, his kindness, his love. We receive the promise, believe the promise, act upon the promise, because we know the man, and feel sure that the promise is a reflection of his character. We want no other endorsement than the probity, integrity, and friendship of the promiser. Look at the promises of God. They are exceedingly precious, because of the source whence they originate. They are the throbbings of the infinite and deathless love of God. I cannot, with a weeping eye, light upon a precious promise, but the moment I see it I behold my Father's love exhibited and unveiled I read God's heart in the promise. I seem to hear the gentle, tender accents of His voice; therefore, as the revelation of my Father's love, the promises of God become exceeding precious. Oh, how often has your heart been touched with the kind promise of a parent! You have read in that assurance the love whence it originated. Beloved, read the love of your heavenly Father in the precious promises. They are but the echoes of His heart sounding from each page of the sacred volume.

They are precious, too, from the channel through which they flow. All the promises of God come to us through a channel—the same channel through which every blessing flows—but which, we fear, is too much overlooked, and in our sad forgetfulness of which we have such low thoughts of Jesus, and such dim views of God's love. Beloved, there is but one channel through which God bestows any blessing upon us. You ask what it is. I give it you in God's own precious words:—"There is one Mediator between God and man, the man Christ Jesus." All your blessings flow to you through Jesus. Your providential mercies, the higher blessings of grace—your sins pardoned, your name written in the Lamb's Book of Life, the glories of heaven unfolding to your faith—all flow to you through the one Mediator. Jesus is the medium through which the precious promises of the word come to us. We ask you, then, if the promises are not precious? if they do not derive inconceivable value and sweetness from the channel through which they flow? Oh, it is kind of God to send you a blessing or a rebuke through one who loves you! Dearly beloved, look at the precious promises. They all come to you through the merits, mediation, finished work, atoning sacrifice, the incessant and ever-prevalent intercession of the Lord Jesus Christ. Consequently, they become exceedingly precious. Nay, more than this. Every promise meets and centres in Christ. "All the promises of God are yea and amen in Christ Jesus." Not a solitary promise that buoys you above the surging billows, or that paints its bright bow on the dark cloud that overshadows you, or that distils its drop of sweetness into your nauseous draught, but that promise is in Christ, through Christ, from Christ and will be made good to you in virtue of your union with Christ. Here the case of many of God's saints is met who say, "I dare not claim the promise; I am so sinful, so unworthy, so unbelieving, I have so often looked at the promise and rejected the comfort that it gives, that I dare not now appropriate it." Dearly beloved, the ground on which you stand with regard to the promise of God, is the finished work of Jesus Christ; and these promises come to you in virtue of what Christ has done; consequently, there is not a sin-burdened, sorrow-stricken soul but may stretch forth his hand and receive these precious jewels as they flow out from the open casket of God's word.

They are precious in themselves. Take the promise addressed to a soul under a conviction of sin, spiritually and earnestly inquiring his way of pardon, acceptance, and salvation. The Holy Ghost has given you a deep sense of your sinfulness. You see your heart to be vile, your nature depraved; smitten with godly grief for sin, and bowed in the dust of self-abasement, you are almost on the brink of despair. But Christ's promise meets your case—"Come unto me, all ye that are weary and heavy laden, and I will give thee rest." "Look unto me and be ye saved all the ends of the earth." "Him that cometh unto me I will in no wise cast out." The moment your eye of faith, though misted with tears, can descry these promises, hope springs up in your heart. Oh, precious promise, that bids me come weary and heavy laden with sin to rest in the Lord Jesus Christ, and receive Him as all my salvation and all my desire! Will you not say that is an "exceeding great and precious promise," that bids the sin-weary find rest in Jesus? Or, are you oppressed by some of those varied mental and spiritual exercises that do so much cast down the child of God? How precious is the promise—"Why art thou cast down, O my soul, and why art thou disquieted within me? Hope thou in God, for I shall yet praise Him, who is the health of my countenance and my God." Or, are you a child of the light walking in darkness, no starlight, no sunlight, not a solitary beam to cheer your way—all spiritual gloom around you? Listen to that precious promise—"Who is among you that feareth the Lord, that walketh in darkness and hath no light, let him trust in the name of the Lord and stay himself upon his God." What a precious promise is that? Or, are you suffering from a sense of the Divine withdrawment, the suspended manifestations of the Lord's love to your soul? What a precious promise is this—"For a small moment have I forsaken thee, but with great mercies will I gather thee. In a little wrath I hid my face from thee for a moment; but with everlasting kindness will I have mercy on thee, saith the Lord thy Redeemer?" Or, conscious of backsliding and departure from God, having gone astray like a lost sheep, your heart smitten with godly grief, beginning to doubt the reality of your former Christian experience? Hear the touching words of the Lord—"Return, thou backsliding Israel, saith the Lord, and I will not cause mine anger to fall upon you, for I am merciful, saith the Lord, and I will not keep anger for ever. Only acknowledge thine iniquity." Oh, what precious promises are these to the poor, heart-broken penitent! Is there nothing in these gracious assurances that meets your case? Or, are you in trouble, difficulties hemming you in on every side, all things seeming to make against you? Is there no preciousness in that promise—"Call upon me in the day of trouble, I will deliver thee, and thou shalt glorify me?" Oh, how many a tried and afflicted saint, buffeting with the storm, has been buoyed up and kept above the waves by this one solitary and precious promise of God, "Call upon me in the day of trouble!" Or, are you assailed by the fiery darts of the enemy? Listen to the promises addressed to the tempted, "The Lord knoweth how to deliver the godly out of temptations." "There hath no temptation taken you but such as is common to man; but God is faithful, who will not suffer you to be tempted above what ye are able; but will with the temptation also make a way to escape, that ye may be able to bear it." Are you in deep affliction, in sore adversity? Listen to the promise of thy God—"When thou passest through the waters I will be with thee, and through the floods, they shall not overflow thee." "All things work together for good to them that love God." "Casting all your care upon Him, for He careth for you." Are you troubled because answers to prayer are delayed; because the vision tarries and appeareth not? The promise is—"Wait on the Lord, be of good courage, and He shall strengthen your heart." Are you anticipating an evil, looking at it in the distance, and trembling at its approach? Hear the soothing word of thy Father—"Come, my people, enter thou into thy chambers, and shut the doors about thee, hide thyself, as it were, for a little moment, until the indignation be overpast." Could sweeter chimes breathe upon your troubled spirit words more appropriate or more soothing? Are you afraid of coming short of eternal glory—of perishing at last in sight of heaven? Listen to the promise—"He that hath begun a good work in you will perform it until the day of Jesus Christ." "Now unto Him that is able to keep you from falling." Thus kept, how can you perish? Are friends and kindred alienated, and do you feel desolate and lonely?—"When my father and my mother forsake me, then the Lord will take me up"—"I will never leave thee, nor forsake thee," is the precious promise of thy God. Do the infirmities and weaknesses of age accumulate around you? "Even to old age, I am He, and even to hoar hairs will I carry you. I have made and I will bear. Even I will carry and deliver you." This is the precious promise to God's dear aged saints. Let us learn from these words to be very tender, sympathising, and patient towards the aged. They are dear and precious to the heart of God, and it is an honour—oh, how great!—to place our arm beneath the aged one whom God carries in His loving heart. Are you afraid of temporal poverty, that the cruse of oil and the barrel of meal will fail you? Hear thy God—"Your bread and your water shall be sure." "Seek ye first the kingdom of God and His righteousness, and all things shall be added to you." Are you in bondage through the fear of death? Cling to the precious promise—"This God is our God for ever and ever. He will be our guide even unto death." Thus have we travelled through a few of the varied circumstances in which you may be placed, for each one of which God has provided a precious promise, on which He causeth your soul to hope.

Precious, too, are these promises in the experience of His people. You can testify to their inconceivable preciousness. What, my beloved, would you have done without them? Have they not stanched many a bleeding wound? and dried many a falling tear? Have they not calmed many a perturbed moment? Have they not guided your feet through many a labyrinth, shed light on many a lonely path, been as oil on the broken waters of many a dark billow, and like voices of music have broken sweetly on many a dreary night of weeping and of woe? You have fled to them in times of necessity, have entwined your arms of faith around them in weakness, and having tested their soothing and support, you can put your seal to the truth, that the promises of God are "exceeding great and precious."

Precious are they, too, in the fruit they bear. Who can describe the peace and joy of the soul when faith takes hold of the Divine promises? Who will not say they are "exceeding great and precious promises," as he beholds the precious fruits these promises bring forth in the happy experience of the saint of God? With this bare outline of the subject, let us, in conclusion, refer to one or two practical inferences.

We exhort you, beloved, to take hold of the Promiser in the promise. The mere promise is nothing to us if we cannot descry that which underlies the promise, —and that which we are to deal with in the promise is, the Promiser Himself. Abraham staggered not at the promise of God, "because he counted Him faithful who had promised." He would have staggered at the promise of man, because it was so marvellous; but when he saw the Divine Promiser in the promise, he knew that what was impossible with man was possible with God, and so he believed Him faithful that had promised. Rest in Jesus, ye wearied and burdened ones, —rest in God, ye tried and tempted ones, —rest in the Holy Ghost, ye sad and mournful ones; for all the precious promises of God, on which He has caused you to hope, are but the unfoldings of God Himself. Deal, then, with the Promiser in the promise, and you will find the promise to be like a rock of adamant beneath your feet.

We exhort you to store your heart richly with the precious promises of God. Take them on board your bark plentifully, for you have yet many a storm to weather, and you will need them to ballast your vessel in the tempestuous sea. Furnish your memories abundantly with them; let your heart deal closely with them; the time will come when the promise will be more precious to you than gold, yea, than much fine gold; and when affliction cometh, and the dark cloud gathers, oh then, how precious will you find the promises of your Covenant God to be with which you stored your mind and fed your faith!

Recollect, they are God's gifts, and are not your purchase. "Whereby are given unto you exceeding great and precious treasures." Come, then, to God empty-handed. Do not reason and hesitate because of your past unbelief; but as gifts of God's free favour, welcome and trust in them.

God may sometimes write the sentence of death upon a promise, and everything in His providence may seem opposed to its fulfilment, though for years you have clung to it. Be not, however, staggered at that. There is a life in that promise, beloved, that never can die. Take, as an illustration, the seed you have sown in the earth. You go and look at it, and find it, apparently dead and decayed—a mass of dust only; but there is a vital principle there that cannot be lost, and in process of time that seed will germinate and become a beauteous flower. So is it with the precious promise of God. Month after month, year after year has rolled by, and you see no fulfilment of the promise; but wait God's appointed way and His ordained time, and the promise shall rise again in all its life, loveliness, and fruit. God will cease to be rather than not fulfil the word on which He has caused your soul to hope.

Walk in the holiness of the promise. Oh, those are solemn words in 2 Cor. vii. 1—"Having therefore these promises, dearly beloved, let us cleanse ourselves from all filthiness of the flesh and spirit, perfecting holiness in the fear of God." The crowning glory and preciousness of these promises is, that they are sanctifying, promoting that holiness of life "without which no man shall see the Lord." Having therefore these rich clusters of precious promises bending down from the Tree of Life, whence we may pluck them at all times, in all seasons, and under all circumstances, let your life be a holy life, and let the sanctifying influence of the promises mould and govern your conduct.

In all your future path "be ye followers of them who through faith and patience inherit the promises," in all their fulness, blessedness, and preciousness. Follow them as they followed Christ; imitate them as they imitated God; press after them as they pressed forward and reached the goal and won the prize, for ere long you too shall be put into their full possession—the promise of grace terminating and expanding in the full enjoyment of the promise of glory. And when the time of your departure is at hand, your work finished, your battle fought, and your victory won, and when the soles of your feet smite the chill waters of death, then shall you find the path through those waters all paved and glowing with the exceeding great promises of your covenant God. Standing upon these precious stones, when heart and flesh are failing, and you are about to leave a wife in lonely widowhood, or children in friendless orphanage—eternity, a solemn, untried eternity, unveiling its realities to your view—with what firmness will faith plant its feet upon these Divine promises—so shall you pass peacefully, triumphantly over Jordan, and all the harpers will meet and welcome you on the other side. The Lord grant that these exceeding great promises may become increasingly precious to our hearts, and purifying to our lives, and all the praise and honour shall redound to Him who has declared, "Heaven and earth shall pass away, but my word shall not pass away." Lord, help us to receive Thy promise, and to trust in Thee the Promiser!

> "How oft have sin and Satan strove
> To rend my soul from Thee, my God!
> But everlasting is Thy love,
> And Jesus seals it with His blood.

"The oath and promise of the Lord
Join to confirm the wondrous grace;
Eternal power performs the word,
And fills all heaven with endless praise.

"Amidst temptations sharp and long,
My soul to this dear refuge flies;
Hope is my anchor, firm and strong,
While tempests blow and billows rise.

"The gospel bears my spirit up;
A faithful and unchanging God
Lays the foundation of my hope
In oaths and promises and blood."

Chapter VI.

THE PRECIOUSNESS OF CHRIST'S BLOOD.

"The precious blood of Christ."—1 Peter i. 19.

The Word of God is the only book that conveys to us a correct idea of the sanctity and meaning of blood. The instructions of God as to its nature and use in the Levitical economy present the spectacle to the mind invested with an impressiveness awful in its character, and profound in its meaning. In God's eye blood was a sacred thing. The solemnity with which He regarded, and the vigilance with which He shielded it, are remarkably striking. We marvel not at this. By the instrument of blood Jehovah was to unfold His Divine character, illustrate His moral government, and achieve His miracle of mercy in behalf of fallen man, in a way so wonderful and resplendent as the intelligent universe had never beheld. That one thing—blood, was to fill the world with His glory, heaven with His redeemed, and eternity with His praise! Hence the sacredness and value of blood in God's view. What an impressive spectacle would meet the eye of the devout Israelite as he entered the temple to worship. He would see blood upon the altar—blood upon the sides of the altar—blood in the bowls of the altar—blood flowing around the altar; and in that blood, so profusely shed and minutely applied, his penitent heart would confront the truth, "Without shedding of blood there is no remission;" and his believing eye would behold the "precious blood of Christ, as of a lamb without blemish and without spot," "slain from the foundation of the world."

Such is the vital truth which is now to engage our thoughts. Among all the precious things of God there is not one so precious, so inestimable, so influential, as the "precious blood of Christ." All salvation, all purity, all peace, all holiness, all hope, all heaven, is bound up in the atoning blood of Immanuel. There is no acceptance for the sinner, no cleansing for the guilty, no pardon for the penitent, no sanctification for the believer, but in the vicarious sacrifice of the Son of God. With nothing are honesty and tenderness of conscience, soul-prosperity, the power of prayer, purity of heart, holiness of life, unreserved obedience, peace, joy, and hope, so intimately related, so closely entwined, as the "precious blood of Christ." It becomes, then, of the greatest moment that we should have scriptural, spiritual, realising views of this great truth. The point at which we are liable to come short is, not so much our depreciatory views of the essential worth of atoning blood as of the necessity of the application of it to the conscience. How few there are of the Lord's people who are walking with the blood upon the conscience! "For this cause many are weak and sickly among you, and many sleep." We detect this deficiency and defect in the experimental religion of many, by the absence of a wakeful conscience, of deep spirituality of mind, of minute confession of sin, of closeness of walk, and a Christ-like temper and spirit. Nor this alone. To what may we trace the doubt and uncertainty as to their personal salvation, the want of assured peace, joy, and communion with God, which imparts a sickly hue to the Christianity of so many, which dims their light, impairs their vigour, and makes them so easy a prey to Satan's assaults and the world's seductions, but to the absence of close dealing with the atoning blood? The application of blood was a truth distinctly seen, even amidst the dim twilight shadows of the Levitical and prophetical dispensations. The blood of the sacrifice was of no avail until it was applied, brought into contact with the object. That object then—whether a person or a thing—became relatively holy. Touched by the sacrificial blood it was regarded as sanctified—as set apart for the holy Lord God; but until the blood was applied it was a common thing. How glorious the gospel of this! The believing soul must come in contact with the atoning blood of Christ; and in order to maintain holiness and closeness of walk with God—the essence of true religion—and to pass through life's duties, trials, and temptations, as a royal priest, realising our high calling of God, there must be the constant application of the blood of Christ. We will not anticipate subsequent parts of this chapter, but proceed to lay the basis of our subject by directing the reader's attention to the essential dignity and worth of the "precious blood of Christ."

It would seem impossible, by any illustration or argument, to over-estimate the intrinsic value of Christ's atoning blood. There are some things in religion of which we may entertain a too exalted and exaggerated conception. For example, we may have too high a view of the Church of Christ, exalting it above Christ Himself. We may hold too exaggerated and too exclusive views of Church ordinances, displacing and magnifying them, substituting their observance for vital religion, for a change of heart, for faith in Christ exclusively for justification. But no such danger lies in our study of the blood of Christ. Here our views cannot be too high, our contemplation too profound, our hearts too loving and adoring.

Consider for a moment, beloved, the ends that were accomplished by the shedding of Christ's blood. We often estimate the value of a mean by the end it secures. The Atonement of Christ was to meet the claims of God's moral government. By man's sin its holiness had been invaded, its authority contemned, its sanctions, laws, and commands outraged. Over all its glory a cloud had passed. God's eternal purpose was to save man. But He could save him only by an expedient that would remove that cloud and cause the glory it shaded to shine forth with deeper and more resplendent lustre. The expedient that would thus meet the claims of the Divine government must be Divine. The Atonement that would link justice with mercy, and holiness with love, in the salvation of the Church, must be infinite in its character, and priceless in its worth. Such, in a few words, were the two grand ends to be secured, and which were secured, by the offering up of the Lord Jesus Christ. Viewed only in this light, how precious does the blood of Christ appear! Blood that could harmonise the Divine attributes—uphold the righteousness of the Divine government, making it honourable and glorious in God to save sinful man—must be precious.

It is precious blood, because it is virtually the 'blood of God.' This is a strong but a scriptural expression. Paul, in his parting address to the Ephesian elders, employs it—"The Church of God, which He hath purchased with His own blood." This it is which stamps the atoning blood of the Saviour with such dignity and virtue—it is the blood of Jehovah-Jesus. It possesses all the worth and glory of the Godhead—all the divine virtue and efficacy of the Deity. From this it derived its power to satisfy, its virtue to atone, ifs efficacy to cleanse. And this is the reason why one dropof this precious blood, falling upon a sin-burdened conscience, in a moment dissolves the weighty load, and fills the soul with joy and peace in believing. And this is why there exists not a stain of human guilt which the atoning blood of Immanuel cannot utterly and for ever efface. Why, in a word, it is blood that "cleanseth from all sin."

But it follows that it is the blood of a pure and sinless humanity, and this by no means lessens our idea of its preciousness. A deep mystery, we admit, is the incarnation of God; but mystery confronts us everywhere, and in everything; therefore it would be unphilosophical, as unbelieving, to cavil at this fundamental doctrine of Christianity—the profoundest mystery in the universe—because it transcended, though it does not contradict, human reason. Our humanity is the incarnation of a spiritual nature; we are not one, but three parts—body, soul, and spirit—and yet we do not deny our own being. Let us go to Bethlehem, and see this great sight, not to reason, but believe, not to fathom, but adore. How great the folly of man in his endeavour to sound the depths of God's infinity! Here, then, exists an essential element of preciousness in Christ's blood—it flowed from arteries untouched, untainted by the virus of sin; from a humanity upon which not a breath of pollution had fallen. "He knew no sin." Begotten by the Holy Ghost, He was that "holy thing" born of a virgin. "Holy, harmless, undefiled, and separate from sinners," He came into the world, lived in it, died in it, and left it as pure and immaculate as the Deity He enshrined. His Godhead wore not the tainted fleece, was clad not in the leprous garment of our fallen, apostate, and sinful nature. A holy Saviour offered up a sinless Atonement for unholy, sinful man. Hence the preciousness of His blood. Look at it, beloved, in this light, and let your hearts glow with love, adoration, and praise, as you kneel before the cross, and feel the distilling upon your conscience of that blood, that pardons, covers, cancels all your guilt. From this view of the essential preciousness of Christ's blood, let us consider its preciousness to God.

We have referred to the law of the Levitical dispensation relating to blood. The minute directions which God gave concerning it marked the sacredness and significance of blood in His holy eyes. Can we for a moment suppose that the blood of the Atonement offered upon the cross of Calvary should not be of yet more infinite worth and preciousness to God? Beloved, we believe that of all the great truths upon which in this volume we are expatiating, we shall find in the hour of death this to be the most essential, supporting, and comforting—the preciousness and acceptableness to God of that Divine sacrifice for sin upon which, in that awful moment, we are relying—to know then that God is well pleased with that blood upon which, as a poor, guilty sinner about to appear in eternity, we rest; and that in its acceptance we are accepted, by its virtue wo are washed whiter than snow, and that through its merit we shall appear before God in righteousness—surely, with this truth witnessed to by the Holy Ghost in our souls, death will have no sting, and the grave no terror.

The atoning blood of Christ must be precious to the Father, because it is the blood of His own Son. There was an essential, close, and endearing relation between the Victim and the Offerer. Is the blood of a child precious to the heart of a parent? Thus precious was the blood of Jesus to God. Oh, methinks, if ever God loved His Son, He loved Him then! Gazing from His throne in glory upon the awful scene on earth, He saw the Son who dwelt in His bosom from eternity impaled upon the accursed tree, suffering the just for the unjust, vindicating the rectitude of His government, and pouring out His holy soul unto death, that He might bring us unto God.

But there was not only the yearning of parental affection in God, but in the sacrifice of His beloved Son He beheld the salvation of His Church fully and for ever secured. In that vital stream He saw the life, the spiritual and eternal life, of His people. His everlasting love had found a fit and appropriate channel through which it could flow to the vilest sinner. Divine Mercy, in her mission to our fallen planet, approached the Cross of Calvary, paused—gazed—and adored. Then dipping her wings in the crimson stream, pursued her flight through the world, proclaiming, in music such as angels had never heard, "Glory to God in the highest, and on earth peace and good will to men!"

And when God raised His Son from the grave, exalted Him to glory, set Him at His own right hand, and then sent down the Holy Spirit, the seal of His acceptance was affixed to His own deep sense of the preciousness of Christ's blood. "Herein is love, not that we loved God, but that He loved us, and sent His Son to be the propitiation for our sins." Trembling soul! approach this Atonement. God has accepted it—will not you? Surely you may with confidence and hope rely upon that sacrifice with which He has thus declared Himself well pleased. You cannot come to it too hopefully, nor rely upon it too implicitly, nor believe in it too simply, nor rejoice in it too fervently. It is precious to God, and, in virtue of its preciousness, your person is precious, your prayers are precious, your offerings of love are precious—fragrant to Him as the "smell of a field which the Lord hath blessed." Plead but the precious blood of Christ for renewed forgiveness, urge it as your argument in prayer, and draw from it your motive to self-surrender as a holy, living sacrifice to God, and you shall not fail of acceptance with the Holy One.

But there is another view of our subject which illustrates the endearing character of Christ's blood. It is not only precious to God, but it is also precious in the experience of the believer. God will make that precious to His people which is precious to Himself. He will endear to their hearts that which is dear to His own. It is precious to the saints, because it is the blood of their Great High Priest. There was no personal relation between the sacrifice and the priest under the Levitical dispensation. But here the Antitype transcends the type. We see in the blood of Christ the blood of one who stands to us in the varied and tender relations of a Priest, a Shepherd, a Friend, a Brother, a Kinsman, a Redeemer. Oh, to travel to the cross and behold in that illustrious Sufferer One who combined in Himself every endearing, tender, and precious relation! It was no stranger who hung there. It was no wayfaring man of grief who died there. It was our Elder Brother, our Goel, our Friend. How precious, then, to our penitent, believing, loving hearts must that blood be! With what reverence should we speak of it, with what faith should we trust in it, with what gratitude should we welcome it, and with what holiness of life should we shew forth its praise!

As all his salvation it must possess an indescribable preciousness to the believer. There is no salvation for the soul but in the atoning blood of Immanuel Whatever else presents itself as such is a delusion and a snare. Baptism is nothing here. Sacraments are nothing here. Priestly power is nothing here. Works of human merit are nothing here. The blood of Christ—God's own expedient—stands unrivalled and alone, the only hope of a lost sinner. The teaching and authority of God's Word are decisive and ultimate on this momentous and vital point. Christ's sacrifice is declared to be a "propitiation through faith in His blood" (Rom. iii. 25); "Being justified by His blood" (Rom. v. 9); "We have redemption through His blood" (Eph. i. 7); "That He might sanctify the people with His own blood" (Heb. xiii. 12); "Who hath washed us from our sins in His own blood" (Rev. i. 5); "These are they which came out of great tribulation, and have washed their robes, and made them white in the blood of the Lamb: therefore are they before the throne" (Rev. vii. 14). In these declarations it will be seen is inscribed the great essential truth—Salvation alone by the atoning blood op Christ. This is the 'Stone' which is set at nought by all who seek some other way to heaven—who build their hope upon the sand—a way the end of which is death. But "neither is there salvation in any other; for there is none other name under heaven given among men whereby we must be saved." Before the power and glory of this one precious name, every false religion shall vanish, and to it every knee shall bow. Around a dying bed the scaffolding of all ecclesiastical systems falls, leaving the man who has reposed his all upon it, to his ghostly hope. But to that departing soul, to whom the savour, power, and preciousness of the name of Jesus is as ointment shedding its fragrance round the room where disease, and death with united force are battling with life, oh how supporting, soothing, and hope-inspiring is the precious blood of Christ which is felt at that awful moment, when the transgressions of a life crowd upon memory, to "cleanse from all sin!"

The peace which flows from the application of the atoning blood of Christ increases greatly the believer's sense of its preciousness. Who can describe the repose of conscience, the mental serenity, the heart-ease which this blood seals upon the believing soul? It must be experienced to be understood. Beloved, as your eye traces this page, there may rage within your breast, unknown and unsuspected by others, the storm of sin's conviction. So sunlight and serene is, perhaps, the surface, not a shadow or a wavelet betrays the hidden and deep emotion. And yet you feel yourself a sinner—a lost sinner—the chief of sinners. You are filled with sin-loathing, selfabhorrence, sorrow, and grief. A deep conviction of your utter vileness, unworthiness, and hell-deserving is the cause. And what is the remedy? The precious blood of Christ! Brought beneath that blood, as like a crimson tide it flows from the cross, peace—perfect peace—the peace of God which passeth all understanding, will flow into your soul, and there shall be a great calm. And then will you joyously exclaim, "I am at peace with God through Christ. The tempest is hushed; the thunder-cloud has passed away; the Sun of Righteousness pours its golden beams into my soul, and heaven and earth seem to meet and kiss each other."

The present efficacy of the atoning blood must form an endearing element to the heart whose pantings and breathings are for purity. This will need no argument to those of my readers who are wont to keep a vigilant oversight of the spiritual state of their souls. You will feel, beloved, that you cannot close your day, in which, despite the greatest watchfulness and prayer, there will be found, in things done, or in things undone, much to produce contrition and humility, without a fresh application to the Fountain. The atoning blood of Jesus is of present efficacy. This, one of its essential elements, is much overlooked. Many of the Lord's people postpone an immediate confession of sin and application to the blood. The effect is to produce searedness of conscience, and a kind of moral ossification of the heart, most injurious to personal holiness. The conscience thus losing its tenderness, and the heart its sensibility, sin comes to be seen in a light less abhorrent, sanctification less sought, and Christ less endeared. Remembering, then, that it is an open and a flowing Fountain—that no sin, no backsliding, however great and aggravated, dare interdict or intercept your approach, repair immediately in faith to the blood, wash, and be clean. The atoning blood of Immanuel is the Divine Bath of the soul. Take an illustration. The physical man is kept healthy and vigorous only by perpetual ablution. And he is not acting in obedience to the laws of his being, as well as the commands of his Maker, who, deeming as unworthy his notice the claims of his physical structure to his regard, despises those precautionary measures, and refuses to employ those restorative and sanative means which God has imposed for the preservation and recovery of bodily health. We have no more right to trifle with the body than with the soul. If, as a professing Christian, suffering from wasting disease you refuse to avail yourself of the sanative aids God has kindly placed within your reach, the skill and the appliances His providence has provided, you are, undoubtedly, acting presumptuously, and not in faith. God has ordained the mean as the end, and no man can attempt to sunder them without violence to his own best interests, and dishonour to God. With this we must blend the thought, that all means of recovery are futile without His blessing; but that, looking to Him in prayer and confidence, we shall realise the truth of His word—"And the prayer of faith shall save the sick." Or, if that petition is withheld, it is but to confer a blessing yet more precious—it may be, the soul's translation to that world of blessedness, "the inhabitants of which shall no more say, I am sick." And now let us return to the truth thus illustrated.

Infinitely more needful is the constant cleansing of the soul. We repeat the assertion, that atoning blood is the Divine laver of the believer. The existence of a fretting leprosy within, and the hourly contact with a raging plague without necessitates perpetual soul-ablution. Let it not be supposed that we are advocating a habit calculated to impress the mind with light thoughts of sin, or to make Christ its minister. Far from this will be the effect of a constant and conscientious dealing with Christ's atonement—of frequent bathing in the blood. The blood of Christ is sanctifying, as well as purifying. It not only effaces the immediate stain of guilt, but it intensifies the heart's thirst for holiness. No believer can cultivate an intimate acquaintance with Christ, or bathe frequently in the fountain of His blood, and not experience a growing sanctification. It is the blood of a holy sacrifice, and it leaves the traces of holiness wherever it flows. And when he comes afresh and closely to the "blood of sprinkling," and again goes forth to the Christian conflict, it is to fight more successfully, to walk more circumspectly, and to yield himself more unreservedly unto God. How clearly and forcibly does the apostle put this truth—the sanctifying influence of the blood. "Now the God of peace, that brought again from the dead our Lord Jesus, that great Shepherd of the sheep, through the blood of the everlasting covenant, make you perfect in every good work to do His will." (Heb. xiii. 20, 21.) Let it not, then, be supposed, that in pleading for frequent application of the Saviour's sacrifice, a constant cleansing from sin, we advocate a lax, careless walk. We believe that the heart is only thoroughly examined, sin is only deeply known, principles, motives, and aims are only closely sifted, analysed, and seen, by the power of the atoning blood of Christ. The blood not only cleanses, but it searches; it not only purifies, but it probes. Its influence is powerful and penetrating, imparting a keen perception of sin where its existence and taint were not seen or suspected. In proportion to the filtration of a lake, or the polish of a mirror, is the power of reflecting the object imaged upon the surface. Keep thy heart, O believer, much beneath the cross, thy conscience in frequent and close contact with the blood, and the slightest touch of sin will make thee restless and unhappy until thou hast confessed, and God has forgiven. This is the secret—which, alas! few see, or care to know—of preserving the garments white amidst pollution, the mind serene amidst turmoil, the heart happy amidst sorrow, the life radiant and transparent as the sun, and the spirit temper, and carriage Christ-loving, and Christlike. Oh the wonders of the precious blood of Christ! Who can exalt it too highly, adore it too profoundly, love, magnify, and honour it too deeply and exclusively? Will it not constitute the theme of our study, the burden of our song, and the source of our bliss as ages roll on, and never cease to roll? Beloved, the surprise then will be, that here below we should have prized it so little, travelled to it so unfrequently, and glorified it so imperfectly, and have regarded it with an affection so fickle and so cold!

The last is not the least precious view, to the Saints of God, of the atoning blood of Christ, which this chapter presents—viz., its voice and power in heaven. It is a delightful, sanctifying truth—the pleading of the blood within the vail that now separates the saints of the Most High on earth from the glory of the upper and inner sanctuary. Our great High Priest hath passed within that vail, has entered into that sanctuary, bearing in His hands the blood He shed on Calvary. And with that blood—basing His intercession upon its divine and changeless efficacy—He pleadeth for the Church with an individual, momentary, and ceaseless intercession. Surely the present power of the blood in heaven will not admit of a moment's doubt in his mind who remembers its virtue ages antecedent to its oblation. God, in anticipation of this sacrifice, upon the promise of Christ to give Himself an offering, extended His full forgiveness to those who, amidst types, and shadows, and symbols, believed in the "Lamb slain from the foundation of the world." Upon Christ's bond to release His Church, long before the actual payment of the ransom, the "prey was taken from the mighty, and the lawful captive was delivered." God accepted the Saviour's suretyship, and extended pardon to Adam, and Abel, and all the Old Testament believers, upon trust and credit of a future sacrifice. Thus did the atoning blood of Jesus do what the law never could have done—"redeem from transgressions under the first testament;" and, by its antecedent and anticipative merit, procure the "remission of sins that are past." If, then—and this is our argument—the blood of Christ was so efficacious ages before it was shed, how much more efficacious is it at the present moment, now that it is actually shed! The testimony of the Holy Ghost touching this truth is clear and conclusive:—"Christ being come an High Priest of good things to come, by His own blood He entered in once into the holy place, having obtained eternal redemption for us." (Heb. ix. 11, 12.) "Christ is not entered into the holy places made with hands, which are the figures of the true; but into heaven itself, now to appear in the presence of God for us" (ver. 24). "The blood of Christ, which speaketh better things than the blood of Abel." Here, then, blood is one of the precious things of God—most precious! Christ is sitting at the right hand of God, enveloped in the incense-cloud of His merits, praying for you with a ceaseless and successful advocacy. Amidst your trials and toils, your temptations and sins, your wants and woes, your fears and tremblings, the voice of Immanuel's blood speaks for you in heaven, and that voice is echoed back to earth in the succourings, upholdings, and soothings, in the strength, grace, and love which its pleadings secure for you below.

And what a balm for the sin-distressed conscience is the precious blood of Christ! There grows not in the universe another tree whose balsam can heal the wounded conscience but this Tree of Life—a crucified Saviour. O beware, beloved reader, of a false healing! "They have healed the hurt of my people slightly," says God; that is, imperfectly, falsely. There is no balsam for a wounded conscience but that which exudes from the wounds of Christ. "With His stripes we are healed." Bring your wound to Christ's wounds, and it is in a moment healed. "Heal me, O Lord, and I shall be healed." David testifies, "I cried unto Thee, and Thou hast healed me." And is not this the especial office and gracious mission of Jesus? Listen to His precious words: "He hath sent me to heal the broken-hearted." Oh the luxury of a broken heart for sin, thus soothed, bound up, and healed by "the precious blood of Christ!" Who would not cry, "Lord, subdue, break, dissolve my heart for sin; let its grief be never so deep, pungent, and bitter, may it but be brought into contact with the virtue, the peace, and preciousness of Thy most precious blood?" Again, we beseech you, beware of a spurious healing! Remember, no tear can heal a wounded conscience—no confession can heal it—no sacrament can heal it—no minister can heal it—nothing in this wide universe can heal it but the precious atoning blood of Christ. That can heal it in one moment. It can efface, not only the faintest breath of guilt from the troubled conscience, but it can wash out the deepest, darkest, foulest blot of sin that ever existed upon the human soul. Think you there is no pardon for you? Deem you beyond the pale of salvation because you are so great, or so aged a sinner—"a sinner of a hundred years old," it may be? Look at Adam, the poisoner of his species, the murderer of his race. The precious blood of Christ availed for him, and in virtue of it he is now in glory, the greatest, the chiefest, the head of all sinners, hymning the high praises of the blood that brought him there. Will you, then, hesitate to believe? will you despond and despair while this monument of saving mercy, of sovereign grace, of Christ's atoning blood, stands as "a pattern to them which should hereafter believe on Him to everlasting life?"

Are you approaching the solemnities of a dying hour? Oh, turn you now from everything but the precious blood of Christ! Let go every object but the cross. Relax your hold of churches and creeds, duties and ordinances, ministers and saints, and let one object absorb every thought, and feeling, and desire—filling the entire scope of the brief and solemn space that now divides time from eternity—the precious blood of Christ! Cast yourself upon it in simple believing—look at it with the feeblest, dimmest eye of faith, and it will speak pardon, peace, and joy to your soul, unvailing to your departing spirit a hope radiant with immortality.

Beware of the false religions of the day. They are all designed and tend to vail the cross of Jesus. We want no other 'altar' than Christ. We need no other sacrifice but His. Christ is our only altar; Christ is our only sacrifice; Christ is our only door into heaven; Christ is all, and in all. Value ministers, churches, ordinances, means of grace, only as they are stepping-stones that lift you above themselves, and lead you upward and onward, closer and closer to Jesus. Around Him entwine the arms of your faith; clasp Him to your loving heart; and be ye sure of this, that such is His grace, such His compassion, such His tenderness, sympathy, and love, He will never tear from His bosom the poor, trembling, penitent soul that has fled within it for shelter. Approach this divine Altar, this one finished Sacrifice, ye poor in spirit—ye that smite upon the breast—ye that mourn for sin— ye that cry, "Unclean, unclean!"—ye that see your own righteousness to be but filthy rags—ye that disclaim and abjure every other salvation, and lay your mouth in the dust, acknowledging your iniquity, transgression, and sin; draw near to this atoning blood, and behold your welcome in the free grace of a sin-forgiving, sin-pardoning God. This precious blood will give you liberty—this precious blood will give you peace—this precious blood will sign and seal you as one upon whom the 'second death' shall have no power. Then, when Christ is coming, and the trumpet is sounding, and the dead are rising, and the great white throne is unvailing, and all are pressing round it for judgment, then will be fulfilled, as never before, the precious promise of God—"And when I see the blood, I will pass you by." Sprinkled with that blood, sheltered by that blood, washed from every stain in that blood, not a drop of divine wrath will light upon you; and you shall hear the Judge of all pronounce you pardoned—accepted— saved! Then will it be said of you—"These are they who came out of great tribulation, and have washed their robes, and made them white in the blood of the Lamb. Therefore are they before the throne." And from every heart and tongue of that goodly company of apostles, and prophets, and martyrs, and the spirits of just men made perfect, will the glorious anthem swell—"Unto Him that loved us, and washed us from our sins in His own blood, and hath made us kings and priests unto God; to Him be glory and dominion for ever and ever. Amen." Oh the bliss of that moment! May it be ours to join that number, and to unite in that song! Amen, and Amen.

> "We have an Altar and a Priest
> Within the riven vail—
> All typal sacrifice has ceased,
> Remove that 'altar rail!'
> With holy boldness venture nigh;
> The Golden Altar stands on high.
>
> "'Tis sprinkled with the costly blood
> On which the Father smiles,
> That blood which from the Offerer flow'd
> For all whom sin defiles.
> Look there, and meet your Father's eye,
> There learn the priestly mystery.
>
> "The brazen altar smokes no more
> On which the Victim lay,
> Where sin's unmeasured doom He bore,
> When thou hadst nought to pay;
> 'Go forth without the camp,' and see
> What God's High Priest hath done for thee.
>
> "Then look within 'the Inner Shrine,"
> Where now He pleading stands,
> Not God's High Priest alone, but thine—
> What say those wounded hands?
> The Father, when those scars He heal'd,
> Once, and for aye, thy pardon seal'd.
>
> "Though now in heaven, the Priestly King
> Long minister'd on earth;
> His life one 'whole burnt-offering,'
> Sweet-savour'd from his birth;
> The fragrance of that life divine
> Perfumes and fills 'the Inner Shrine.'
>
> "No 'rood screen' shields it from the eye
> Of those whose sight is true;
> That 'Inner Shrine' in yon pure sky
> Is open now for you.
> All conscience-cleansed and free from sin,
> The full-robed Priest says, 'Welcome in.'

"Behold those jewels on His breast,
Each as a signet graved!
Close to that bosom, warmly prest,
Lie those by Jesus saved;
And thou art saved, whoe'er thou art,
If Jesus has thy willing heart.

"The golden frontlet on his brow,
With 'Holiness' inscribed,
Tells that the law is honour'd now,
In vain with tinsel bribed:
The perfect work of One alone
Will God's all-searching justice own.

"Hark to the music of those bells!
How sweet their silver voice!
Of Peace, Good-will, and Grace it tells—
How canst thou but rejoice,
When God Himself delights to hear
Those silver tones salute His ear?

"A golden lamp sheds forth its ray;
The Spirit is your guide;
He shews the New, the Living Way—
The rent vail opens wide:
A seven-fold light that lamp imparts,
And courage gives to trembling hearts.

"And say, hast thou not oft regaled
Upon that living Bread,
Which, when all earthly comfort fail'd,
Your craving spirit fed?
That heavenly Manna, Shew-bread sweet,
Which none but white-robed priests may eat.

"The Laver stands. If earth-defiled,
Go, wash thy hands, thy feet,
And simply as a pardon'd child
Approach the Mercy-seat;
Within the vail your censer bring,
And bum sweet incense to the King.

"For know, that since God's Lamb was slain,
All typal rites have ceased;
Nor till Melchisedec shall reign,
May earth behold a priest, gave those who, wash'd in Jesus'
blood,
Are now made white-robed priests to God.

"They walk 'the outer court' a while,
But live within the vail;
Look out and weep, look in and smile,
And chant the melting tale
Of Him who bless'd the bread and wine—
'The Priest' within 'The Inner Shrine.'"[6]

6   By the Author of "Wild Thyme."

Chapter VII.

THE PRECIOUS ANOINTING.

"The precious ointment upon the head, that ran down upon the beard, even Aaron's beard: that went down to the skirts of his garments."— Psalm cxxxiii. 2.

It is to this striking emblem—the anointing oil—rather than to the truth it illustrates, the present chapter especially relates. The truth illustrated in this beautiful passage, we admit, is a great and holy one—brotherly love. "Behold, how good, how pleasant it is for brethren to dwell together in unity!" Would that we saw more of it in the professing Church of God! Then would the disciples of Christ be more marked and distinguished as such. "For by this shall all men know that ye are my disciples, if ye have love one to another." But it is the holy and precious anointing itself to which we especially direct the reader's attention. The subject is of essential importance. It is the personal possession of this anointing that constitutes our true Christianity. The religion of vast numbers is but the religion of sentiment, the religion of form, the religion of ritualism—a religion utterly destitute of one particle of this divine and precious anointing. It is therefore of the greatest importance that each reader of this work should institute the most rigid self-scrutiny to ascertain his real possession of the Holy Ghost, the Anointer and the anointing, without an interest in which we possess but "a name to live while we are dead;" "having a form of godliness, without the power thereof." To aid the devout reader in his inquiry into this subject, it will be our object to illustrate the precious nature of this divine anointing,—its application to Christ, the true spiritual Aaron and Head of the royal priesthood,—and its communication through Him to all who form a part of the one Anointed Priesthood. Oh that as we meditate upon this soul-reviving truth, the "oil of gladness" may diffuse its influence and fragrance through our souls, endearing Him to our hearts whose precious "name is as ointment poured forth" to those who know and love it.

The office of the priesthood under the Levitical dispensation was regarded as one of the highest designations of God in His Church. The priest stood, as it were, in God's place. He was Jehovah's vicegerent—the medium of communication from God to the people, and from the people to God. He was to receive the word from the mouth of God, and communicate it to the people; and, on their part, he was to make sacrifice, take of their offerings, and present them to the Lord. It will thus be seen that the priesthood was one of the highest and holiest offices in the Church of God.

73

It was in fact associated with royalty. Melchisedec was both a priest and a king—a royal priest. In this respect he was a remarkable type of our Lord Jesus Christ, who, by one of the prophets, is designated a "Priest upon His throne," and who stands to His Church in the twofold relation of King and Priest. Such is the dignity to which their union with Christ raises His people. They are, in virtue of that union, a "royal priesthood," "offering up spiritual sacrifices acceptable to God through Christ."

We have remarked, respecting the priesthood under the old economy, that, so important was the institution, the instructions God gave for the selection of the priests, and their designation to the office, were of the most minute and significant character. Our present subject limits us to a single and specific one—the anointing. The directions of God touching the composition of the unguent—the precious oil—by which Aaron and the priests were set apart to their holy office, are minute and instructive:—"Moreover the Lord spake unto Moses, saying, Take thou also unto thee principal spices, of pure myrrh five hundred shekels, and of sweet cinnamon half so much, even two hundred and fifty; and of sweet calamus two hundred and fifty shekels, and of cassia five hundred shekels, after the shekel of the sanctuary, and of oil olive an hin: and thou shalt make it an oil of holy ointment, an ointment compound after the art of the apothecary: it shall be an holy anointing oil. And thou shalt anoint Aaron and his sons, and consecrate them, that they may minister unto me in the priest's office." (Exod. xxx. 22-25, 30.) How deep and precious the spiritual significance of all this! The great truth it is designed to illustrate is the nature and preciousness of that holy anointing of which all the "royal priesthood" of Christ are partakers, and apart from which all religion, the most intellectual poetical, and strictly ritual, is vain and dead, spurious and worthless. One drop of this holy oil, this divine anointing, hath in it more of God more of Christ, more of the Holy Ghost, and more substance, sweetness, and preciousness, than all the religions of man, the most costly, splendid, and imposing, combined.

In one sentence we define the divine nature and the essential value of this precious anointing—it consists in the indwelling of the Holy Ghost in the soul. We marvel not, then, that in the typal unfolding of this truth, there should be such an accumulation of precious, fragrant, and costly things. And yet how far below the Antitype does it fall! What earthly things, the most rare and precious, can convey any adequate idea of the divine nature and the essential worth of the Holy Ghost? Who is He? There are those who would reduce Him to a mere attribute of God—an influence of the Most High—an emanation of the Deity—a divine principle! Alas! how many, even of the Lord's own people, have but the most dim and imperfect views of the personal dignity and official work of the Holy Ghost, who yet would recoil with abhorrence at the thought of holding a sentiment in the slightest degree derogatory to His glory. And amongst those who utterly and openly impugn the divine dignity of the Spirit, denying totally His personal oneness with the Godhead, to what subtle distinctions and hollow sophisms, in the enmity of the carnal mind to God's revealed truth, will they resort, rather than accept the plain and simple declarations of the Bible? But who is the Holy Ghost? Our mind is filled with sacred and solemn awe as we inscribe the words—The Holy Ghost is the third Person in the Godhead. When we open the revealed Word and read the words which compose the formulary of baptism, and the apostolic benediction, who can doubt this truth? Touching the former we read, "Go ye therefore and teach all nations (make disciples), baptizing them in the name of the Father, and of the Son, and of the Holy Ghost." (Matt. xxviii. 19.) Touching the latter it is written, "The grace of our Lord Jesus Christ, and the love of God, and the communion of the Holy Ghost, be with you all. Amen." (2 Cor. xiii. 14.) What shall we say to these distinct emphatic declarations? Doubt them? Cavil at them? Reduce them to figures of speech? Deny and reject them? God forbid! Beloved reader, is there no secret thought in your mind derogatory to the Divine Personality of the Holy Spirit?—no lurking suspicion of His claims to your love, worship, and obedience? Do you cherish towards Him like feelings of holy awe, filial reverence, and implicit faith with those with which you regard the Father and the Son? In a word, do you honour, and love, and pray to the Holy Ghost even as you love, honour, and pray to the first and second Persons of the ever-blessed Trinity? Oh, forget not that the debt of love, confidence, and obedience which you owe to the Spirit is the same! As you could not be redeemed and saved without the blood-shedding of the Son, so you could not be regenerated and sanctified but by the divine power of the Holy Ghost. Such, then, is the sacred anointing of the royal priesthood! The possession of the Holy Ghost, in all His divine perfections and official relations, by each believer in Jesus, is the precious anointing by which he is set apart as a priest of the Most High God. Can we conceive of any blessing more costly and precious? Of this blessing you are the recipient if you are a believer in the Lord Jesus. And the Word of God declares it:—"Ye have received the Spirit of adoption." "He hath given you the earnest of the Spirit." "The Spirit of God dwelleth in you." How easy were it to multiply these proofs!

Passing from the person of the Spirit, we advert for a moment to the work of the Spirit. How precious is that work!—so precious that all language, all imagery, fails adequately to express it. If, beloved, you are a temple, a sanctuary of the Holy Ghost, there is more of God, more of divine glory, dwelling within your soul, than in all the worlds that God has made, known and unknown. Oh, how imperfectly we estimate the value and high calling of a saint of God! But as we are to speak of this in a distinct chapter of the present work, we but refer to it now as illustrating the costliness of this anointing. The glory of a believer in Christ—like the glory of Him whose son he is—is a concealed glory. "The King's daughter is all glorious within." Where her dark corruption dwells, where the great conflict is passing, even there, amidst so much that is opposite in nature and hostile in spirit, the great glory of the child of God dwells, and all that hidden glory consisteth of the work of the Holy Ghost in the soul. A broken heart for sin, the spirit of self-abhorrence, the trembling faith in Christ, the thirst for sanctification, the breathings after God, are component parts of that divine and precious anointing which has sanctified you as a priest of the Most High God.

The influences of the Holy Ghost enter essentially into the precious anointing of the believer. What progress in the divine life can there be apart from these? This sacred anointing needs perpetual care and replenishing. The spirit of prayer in our souls—how restrained! The spirit of adoption—how it droops! The spirit of love—how it languishes! The spirit of faith—how it fluctuates! The spirit of Christ—how it wanes! But the Holy Spirit quickens, revives, and restores by fresh inspirations of His influence. A gale from Him bears on its wings life, fruitfulness, and fragrance. When the 'south wind' blows upon the soul, the spices thereof flow out, and Christ cometh into His garden, eats His pleasant fruit, and gathers His myrrh and His spice. And then, thus revived and refreshed by a renewed emanation of the Spirit's grace, the moral atmosphere in which the Christian walks is all permeated and perfumed with the fragrance of this precious anointing. Can you, then, estimate its worth? That heart-outpouring, that soul-breathing, that glimpse of Jesus, that hour of nearness to God, that moment's enjoyment of the Divine presence—oh! would you have bartered it for earth's choicest, costliest, fondest joys! Beloved, live not, as a priest of God, without the sensible inbeing of the Holy Ghost. Live in conscious union and communion with Him—seek to be filled with His influences. If prayer languishes—if grace decays—if affection chills— if there is any discovered relapse of your soul in the divine life, seek at once and earnestly the fresh communication of this divine anointing. "Let thy garments always be white, and thy head lack no ointment."

The indestructibleness of this anointing is the last element of its preciousness to which we allude. It is no small mercy to a child of God, that amidst the evanescence of spiritual feeling, the ebb and flow of Christian experience, nothing affects the imperishable nature of that divine anointing by which he was once and for ever consecrated to an unchangeable priesthood. All earth's perfumes evaporate and die; the blight is upon every flower, the curse is in every sweet; but here is that which can never be destroyed. Once the Holy Ghost quickens the soul with the breath life; once He enkindles a spark of love to God in the heart, once He breathes upon the believer this celestial perfume, he possesses a blessing which no age can impair, and which no circumstance can change. Hostile influences there may be which would seem to peril its existence—the indwelling taint of sin would threaten its purity and sweetness—yet nothing shall ever prevail to destroy the work of the Spirit in the heart of the regenerate. It is an anointing incorruptible—it has a fragrance imperishable. The power and perfume thereof shall go down with the believer into the grave, shall embalm and preserve the slumbering dust of God's elect, until, in the morning of the first resurrection, the trumpet of the archangel bids them rise to meet their Lord in the air. What behold I in that narrow house? What see I reposing in that clay-cold bed? A ruined temple of the Holy Ghost! Will it ever be restored again? Oh, yes! "We look for the Saviour, the Lord Jesus Christ, who shall change our vile body, that it may be fashioned like unto His glorious body, according to the working whereby He is able even to subdue all things unto Himself." (Phil. iii. 20, 21.) Thus precious is this holy oil, the divine anointing of the believer in Jesus. It imparts dignity to his person, for it constitutes him a priest-royal. It imparts fragrance to his sacrifices, for it makes them "an odour of a sweet smell, a sacrifice acceptable, well-pleasing to God." His prayers are precious, his praises are precious, his labours are precious, his every lowly act of love, obedience, and service is inconceivably precious to God, touched with this divine and holy oil. And as the perfume of the rose still lingers upon the broken and crumbled ruins of the shattered vase, so the divine perfume of the Holy Spirit's indwelling, regenerating, sanctifying grace shall cling to the believer, his works and labour and memory, long after death shall have ruined the material structure, and it shall have returned to the dust from whence it came. "The righteous shall be had in everlasting remembrance." "The memory of the just is blessed."

But while we thus maintain the essential indestructibility of this precious anointing, we would by no means fail to caution the believer against that which yet may seriously impair its vigour, obscure its beauty, and lessen its fragrance. Essentially it may not perish, influentially it may. Intrinsically it cannot be destroyed, efficiently it can. A noxious element may insinuate itself into this divine unguent, and blend with it a mixed and ungenial redolence. "Dead flies cause the ointment of the apothecary to send forth an ill savour: so doth a little folly him that is in reputation for wisdom and honour." (Eccles. x. 1.) An uneven walk, an unwatchful spirit, an unChrist-like deportment may blend with this previous anointing, and thus destroy its fragrance, and impair its power. The moral influence of the Church in the world is in proportion to her spiritual separation from the world. The light she emits throughout the earth will be graduated by her holy elevation above the earth. The chandelier which illumines an apartment is suspended from its centre. The Church of God is the world's moral chandelier. The Divine Sun from whom she receives her holy lustre, has condescendingly, but emphatically, pronounced her the "light of the world." It follows, then, that the spiritual influence which the Church is to exert in the world as a conservator of the truth, as a witness for Christ, and as an instrument to guide men to the Saviour, will be potent and successful, healthy and powerful, in proportion to her own moral elevation, holiness, and spirituality. What applies to the Church as a corporate body, equally applies to the individual Christian. Oh, what a blessing in the sphere in which he moves is a man of God, living under the rich anointing of the Holy Spirit! It is impossible he can be hid. "The ointment of his right hand bewrayeth itself." And the moral savour of that ointment—the holy, heavenly fragrance that floats around him—testifies to all who are brought within its influence, of God, of Christ, of eternity. See, then, that your religion is not half Christian, half Infidel—half Protestant, half Popish—half sincere, half compromising. Beware of the "dead fly in the ointment." Worldliness of living—covetousness of heart—an unforgiving temper—an earthly, grovelling mind—an uncharitable, censorious spirit—a want of integrity and uprightness of principle in your dealings with men—a secret rebellion of will against the government, the providence, the disposal of God, may just be that "dead fly." These may be the things, or others of a like character, which lessen your heavenliness of mind, impair your spiritual vigour, shade your divine light, vail your precious anointing, and render your moral influence as a labourer for Christ so little useful to man, and your walk as a believer in Jesus so little honouring to God.

A vital part of our subject remains to be considered—the confluence of this precious oil in the Lord Jesus Christ, the true spiritual Aaron of the "Royal Priesthood." We term this a vital truth, and justly so, because it is the source of all spiritual life to the believer. We are Christian in truth only as we are one with Christ. We are living branches in reality only as we have union with Jesus the Living Vine. We are an anointed priesthood only in virtue of our sacerdotal relation to Him, the Great High Priest of His Church. Here is—union; and this union is—life. Now, our blessed Lord Jesus was anointed with the Holy Ghost. His human nature was filled with the Spirit, and in this consisted His divine anointing, and in this anointing His consecration as the Royal Sacerdotal Head of a succession of royal priests. How clear and beautiful are the inspired testimonies to this truth! For example, in the Old Testament we read, "I have found David my servant; with my holy oil have I anointed him." (Ps. lxxxix. 20.) "Thou lovest righteousness, and hatest wickedness: therefore God, thy God, hath anointed thee with the oil of gladness above thy fellows." (Ps. xlv. 7). "Behold, O God, our shield, and look upon the face of thine anointed." Now, in what did this anointing of Christ consist but the fulness of the Holy Spirit? So we read, "God anointed Jesus of Nazareth with the Holy Ghost." (Acts x. 38.) So the indwelling fulness of the Spirit, "For God giveth not the Spirit by measure unto him." His humanity was indebted for the wisdom with which it spake, for the understanding by which it discerned, which made Him of "quick understanding in the fear of the Lord," for the power with which it wrought, and for the beauty which, amidst its humiliation and woe, made it so transcendently glorious, to the indwelling fulness of the Holy Ghost. Oh, what would our humanity be were it filled, as was the Son of God's, with the fulness of the Spirit! And if, in our Christian character, we would approximate to this model—in a word, if we would be. Christ-like—we must be more richly replenished with the Holy Ghost. "Hereby we know that He (Christ) abideth in us, by the Spirit which he hath given us." (1 John iii. 24.) We shall be assured of our union to Christ, of His home in our hearts, of our relation to the seed-royal, the true priesthood, by the inhabitation of the Spirit. O Divine and Holy Spirit! enter us, unworthy though we are; make Thy home in our hearts, vile though they be; breathe life and love, peace and joy, into our souls; quicken us, seal us, teach us, sanctify us, and make us divine, by making us Christ-like—happy, by making us holy,—and so fill and occupy us with Thyself that there may be no room for the reign of sin, the power of the world, and the love of self. Beloved, you cannot besiege the throne of grace for a more needed and a greater blessing than the fulness of the Holy Ghost. Think not that we employ an expression too strong when we speak of the fulness of the Spirit. It is recorded of Stephen that he was "full of faith, andof the Holy Ghost." And that this was not a peculiar or privileged case, the apostle exhorts all believers to be "filled with the Spirit." Seek, then, beloved, for your own soul this divine anointing. Be not satisfied with a measured bestowment of the precious blessing, but in earnest and importunate supplication open your mouth wide, that He may fill it! Oh the readiness of the Spirit to impart the boon! Oh the willingness of Christ, the Anointed, to satiate every longing soul, and to replenish every hungry soul from His own overflowing fulness! The straitness is in us, not in Jesus. Seek, then, with a seeking that will take no denial, the fulness of the Spirit!

The holy oil was poured upon the head of Aaron. This is most significant. The Lord Jesus—our Aaron—was anointed with the Spirit, as the Head of His Church. "He is the Head of the body, the Church." And the fulness of the Spirit that dwelt in Him was not for Himself alone, but to be communicated to all the members of His mystical Body. Trace the course of this holy oil thus poured upon the head of Aaron. It "went down to the skirts of his garment." How expressive and instructive the type! In virtue of our union with Christ, we become partakers of His precious anointing. So clearly and indissolubly are we one with Jesus, the Great High Priest, we share in all that He is, and partake of all that He possesses. He imparts to us His life, clothes us with His righteousness, washes us in His blood, replenishes us from His fulness, and will finally raise us to His glory, share with us His throne, and we shall reign with Him for ever.

This anointing that flows from Christ is received by us through faith. The life we live amidst daily conflict, trial, and toil, we live by the faith of the Son of God. This is the channel through which the sacred anointing flows down to us. What a mighty principle is this! When, at the close of the day, we throw our head upon our pillow, and in silent reflection review its brief history, we often marvel how we travelled through it. We look back upon the pressure, the temptation, the trial, the sorrow, and we are a wonder to ourselves. What was it that bore up and brought us triumphantly through? Oh, it was the power of faith conveying into our souls the fulness of Christ! It was the downflowing of this holy oil of grace and strength, of gladness and joy, from our enthroned and glorified Head that imparted wisdom in the perplexity, clearness in the judgment, strength in the temptation, fortitude in endurance, meekness in provocation, patience in suffering, and calmness, peace, and quietness amidst the keenness of sorrow and the surgings of grief. Faith leaning upon, and drawing from, Christ, is the secret of it all.

But not merely in virtue of union to Christ, or through the medium of faith, are we the recipients of this precious anointing. It flows from the loving heart of Christ, and is the free, spontaneous bestowment of His grace. There is not a being in the universe that Christ loves as He loves the saints. He is constantly ordering, and arranging, and disposing all events and circumstances for the promotion of their well-being. He would have His joy remain in us, and our joy to be full. And every feeling of holy gladness that thrills us, every spring of sacred joy that refreshes us, every gleam of divine sunshine that falls upon our path, is an emanation from the Divine anointing that distils from Christ upon our souls. Love is the source of it all, love is the conveyancer of it all, love is the end of it all. Light pours not more freely from the sun, nor water from the fountain, than does the "oil of gladness" flow from the heart of Jesus into the hearts of His saints. See how freely the precious anointing flows—"The Spirit of the Lord God is upon me; because the Lord hath anointed me to preach good tidings unto the meek; He hath sent me to bind up the broken-hearted, to proclaim liberty to the captive, and the opening of the prison to them that are bound; to appoint unto them that mourn in Zion, to give unto them beauty for ashes, the oil of joy for mourning, the garment of praise for the spirit of heaviness." O wonderful words! O precious announcements! Come, my soul, and listen! Jesus' anointing was not for Himself, but for others. It was for the "meek," it was for the "broken-hearted," it was for the "mourners in Zion," it was for the "captive," it was for "them that are bound," it was for those who are bowed down to the dust with the "spirit of heaviness." It was for poor, empty sinners—souls that hunger and thirst for righteousness—who feel their vileness, necessity, and nothingness; who come to Him as emptysinners to a full Saviour. Who lowers a full bucket into the well? Who carries a full pitcher to the spring? It is emptiness that travels to fulness. So must you come to, deal with, live upon, and receive from, Jesus. A full Christ and an empty sinner travel the same road, side by side, step by step, hand in hand, to glory. With no other will Christ walk. The proud, the self-sufficient, He knoweth afar off; and they know Him afar off. But the spiritual mourner, the broken-hearted, the poor in spirit, these are they upon whom Jesus delights to pour the oil of joy and gladness, which causes their hearts to glow, their faces to shine, their lips to praise. "Ointment and perfume rejoice the heart." One drop of this precious anointing will turn thy sorrow into joy, thy mourning into dancing, thy complaining into singing; make the name, the work, and sympathy of Jesus more fragrant and precious, and cause the lamp of love and holiness to burn more freely and more brightly than ever. Such are some of the precious privileges and blessings of a vital, inseparable union of a believing sinner with the Lord Jesus.

One instructive point yet remains to be considered. The precious ointment that was on the head of Aaron went down to the skirts of his garments: it reached to the extremity of his sacred person. The spiritual significance of this is peculiarly precious and encouraging to the "poor in spirit,"—to those whose self-acquaintance leads them to walk humbly with God. The humble, believing soul, that lies the nearest and the lowest at Christ's feet, receives the most abundantly of this overflowing and downflowing grace. There is no spot in the universe which concentrates upon itself so much blessedness—where meet and cluster, in focal power, so many holy, precious privileges, as the feet of Jesus. There we learn, there we receive, there we shelter. We are safe, because we are low—we are happy, because we are near. "He giveth grace to the lowly," and the lowliest, the most near, receive the most grace. Is this your place, O believer? Think not meanly of it. There is but one that surpasses it—it is the foot of the throne in glory! And no soul will find itself at the foot of the throne in heaven, that does not find itself at the feet of the Saviour on earth. The lowliness of the posture may possibly blind the eye to its peculiar blessedness: a bolder and more confident one may be considered preferable. But let us not be deceived; give me Mary's tears rather than Peter's boasting. Let me sit with her at the feet of Jesus, rather than stand with the self-confident apostle in the judgment-hall. In pleading for this lowly posture, we plead not for a state of mind that excludes holy joy, and an assured hope, as elements foreign to this condition. Far from it. The anointing of Christ—is it not the "oil of gladness?" and does He hot give "the oil of joy?" Most assuredly. Then, the believing soul that lies prostrate at His feet—close to the Fountain of all grace, sympathy, and love— partakes the most largely of the "joy of the Lord, which is the strength of their soul;" for "the meek shall increase their joy in the Lord." There, too, hope sheds her brightest beams. For if ever the "good hope through grace" which the gospel unvails, shines the most resplendent upon the soul, it is when, reclining at Jesus' feet, it clings in faith, glows in love, and melts in contrition.

Be exhorted, beloved reader, not to be content without the consciousness of this precious anointing. Rest not satisfied with but a "name to live." Do not surmise or trust that you are Christ's disciple, or child of God, but seek this inward, divine testimony. Plead with God the Holy Ghost to communicate to your soul freely and daily of this precious anointing. This holy oil will impart clearness to your mind, so that you shall have a "right judgment in all things;" it will impart sweetness to your temper, gentleness to your spirit, and will give you a lowly, loving, self-condemning heart. It will make more Christ-like your carriage towards others. Vacating the judgment-seat, and ceasing to be censorious, faultfinding, and condemning, you will be filled with charity and love: the grace of kindness will be in your heart, and the law of kindness on your lip. This precious anointing is so soul-transforming, so Christ-assimilating in its influence, that it is impossible to partake of it in any degree and not be like Jesus. When you see a religious professor proud in heart—lofty in spirit—covetous in his aims—condemning others, justifying himself—detracting, unsympathising, harsh,—you see one lacking this anointing. He is not sitting at the, feet of Jesus. It is only there that the believer sees so much to censure, to loathe, and to condemn in himself, that he has not an eye to discover, nor a tongue to revile; nor a hand to unvail the faults and imperfections of a brother. The holy oil empties and lays low. If in faithfulness it prompts to admonish and to rebuke, it will impart such tenderness, gentleness, and kindness of spirit, of tone, and of words, as shall be an "excellent oil" upon a Christian brother's head, winning him back to Christ by the irresistible law of love. And, oh, if your soul thirsts to know more of Jesus, seek more abundantly the influence of the Holy Ghost. Rest not until He reveals Christ to you. As a royal priest, anointed of God, you possess that indwelling Spirit, who is pledged to instruct, sanctify, and comfort you, until the Master comes and takes you home. "This anointing which ye have received of him abideth in you, and ye need not that any man teach you: but as the same anointing teacheth you of all things, and is truth, and is no lie, and even as it hath taught you, ye shall abide in him." Living beneath this anointing that floweth from the Head of His Church, down to the lowest, meanest, poorest, obscurest, feeblest member of His body, your heart will often sigh and long for his appearing, and will pray—"Come, Lord Jesus; come quickly."

Chapter VIII.

THE PRECIOUSNESS OF GOD'S CHILDREN.

"The precious sons of Zion, comparable to fine gold."—
Lamentations iv. 2.

In our endeavour to evade what from conviction we deem to be erroneous, there is often a tendency to verge to an opposite extreme of error. One of the most serious and popular errors amongst the many by which the truth of God is assailed is, the exaltation of the Church above its legitimate and assigned position in the Christian economy. With multitudes the Church is an idol, virtually a saviour. It is elevated to a pinnacle, enthroned as a sovereign, and invested with an authority and power which God never designed. Awful perversion of truth! In a word, the creed and the religion of numbers substitutes the Church for Christ, invades the legislative authority of God, and imposes upon the conscience of Christ's free disciples yokes which Christ's gospel nowhere enjoins. In avoiding this error we are, without due caution and study, liable to run into its opposite—the setting aside the value, the mission, and the glory of the Church of Christ altogether. Both these extremes are antichristian and fatal. Let us endeavour to find the truth that lies midway between them; and thus walking in the middle path, hold the truth in an equal balance, finding it instructive, sanctifying, and comforting. "Thus saith the Lord, Stand ye in the ways, and see, and ask for the old paths, where is the good way, and walk therein, and ye shall find rest for your souls." (Jer. vi. 16.)

It is the glory of God that He has in the world a Church—that it is composed of His elect, chosen from eternity, redeemed by Christ, and called by the Holy Spirit, a people gathered out of all lands, found in all Christian communions, and constituting, as a whole, an incorporate body, of which the Lord Jesus Christ is the Head. This body may be, as alas! it too much is, divided and sundered by differences of judgment on external and unvital points, but essentially and indivisibly it is one Church of God—one Family—one Bride of the Lamb—one spiritual house—and "all built upon the foundation of apostles and prophets, Jesus Christ himself the chief corner-stone," of whom, as such, we shall in a subsequent chapter of this work more particularly speak. Our present object is not so much to define the nature or expound the principles of Christ's one Church, as to assert its existence, unfold and illustrate its worth and preciousness. There is much sanctifying, comforting teaching involved in this truth—the preciousness of God's children. It is impossible to study it, and not rise from an admiration of the beauty, glory, and preciousness of the Church, to the transcendent beauty, glory, and preciousness of Him whose Church she is, in whose righteousness she is clothed, and in whose comeliness she is comely. "The precious sons of Zion, comparable to fine gold." Let us consider the title, and the preciousness of God's people, as suggested to our minds by this passage.

It is a high and honourable appellation "the sons of Zion." The world holds, the Church of God very cheap. No gold, nor fine gold is it in the eye and estimation of the ungodly. And yet the world owes its existence to the Church. The Church of Christ is, instrumentally and subordinately, the world's saviour. It is the conservator of the world, its salt, its light. Take out of the world all who are witnesses for God, for Christ, and for the Gospel—all who are living "godly, righteously, and soberly in this present evil world"—all who mourn for sin, who trample on their own righteousness, and trust alone in the righteousness of the Lord Jesus; in a word, all the good and holy and useful, and what remains but a mass of unmitigated evil—a world of unrelieved corruption—an empire wholly in rebellion against God, and in supreme subjection to Satan?

Thus, extract the salt, extinguish the light, sift the wheat, separate the gold, and eliminate the pure truth from the mass of error, and nothing is left but fuel for the final and fearful conflagration. This is the doom that awaits it when the last son of Zion shall have shaken its dust from his feet, and this earth shall no longer be the home and dwelling-place of the Church. Unclasp the vine that imparts beauty to, that climbs around, holds together and preserves the decayed and crumbling trunk, and it falls to dust and ruin. Thus will it be with this world when the Lord shall come and remove from it the Church which has so long been its moral preservation and its beauty. But the Church of God is His Zion, whom He loves, His dwelling-place. "Jehovah-Shammah"—The Lord is there—is its name. His Church is His only home upon earth. He dwells not in temples made with hands—the gorgeous cathedral, the Gothic abbey, the costly sanctuary, the material structure, planned, reared, and adorned by human device and art. A spiritual being, He can only dwell in the spiritual. "God is a Spirit," and His temple, His worship, and His offerings must be spiritual. Therefore has He declared that His fit, favourite, and only dwelling upon earth is the humble mind, the broken heart, the contrite spirit, the empty, lowly, penitent, and believing soul. Listen to His solemn averment of this great and holy truth:—"Thus saith the Lord, The heaven is my throne, and the earth is my footstool: where is the house that ye build unto me? and where is the place of my rest? For all those things hath mine hand made, and all those things have been, saith the Lord: but to this man will I look, even to him that is poor, and of a contrite spirit, and trembleth at my word." (Isa. lxvi. 1, 2.) This is the house we will build to the Lord, and this is the place of His rest! Does this page meet the glance of such a one? Blessed saint! There rears not its proud head a structure in the universe so distinguished as you. Your soul is the habitation of Him who is the "high and lofty One that inhabiteth eternity, whose name is Holy," who has said, "I dwell in the high and holy place, with him also that is of a contrite and humble spirit."

The Church of God, then, is His Zion. His people are denominated the "sons of Zion," in reference to the fact of the Church being the spiritual birth-place of His people. "As soon as Zion travailed, she brought forth her children." (Isa. lxvi. 8.) "And of Zion it shall be said, This and that man was born in her." (Ps. lxxxvii. 5.) The Church of God is the spiritual birth-place of His people. Every true child of God, every convert to Christ, is a son and a denizen of this city. He is born through the labours of the Church of Christ, he is nourished by the instructions of the Church of Christ, he is watched over and trained for heaven by the care and discipline of the Church of Christ, "who is the mother of us all." And "the Lord shall count, when he writeth up the people, that this man was born there." Oh precious privilege this, to be registered among God's people, to be "written amongst the living in Jerusalem," to be numbered with the children of God! Have you, my reader, any evidence that this is your honoured place? Does your name stand upon the sacred roll of those who are "called to be saints?" What if it should not appear when the Lord "writeth up the people!" Search, examine, and ascertain. Are you amongst the "mourners in Zion?" Do you "love her solemn feasts," and are you walking in her holy ways, your face fully set towards the Mount Zion of glory, of which John in the Apocalypse had a vision, "And I looked, and, lo, a Lamb stood on the mount Sion, and with Him an hundred forty and four thousand, having His Father's name written in their foreheads?" If this is your present condition, the Zion of God your spiritual home, and the God of Zion your covenant God, then may you clap your hands with joy. "Glorious things are spoken of thee, O city of God;" and in these "glorious things" that now are, and that are yet to be revealed, you shall share. Of the preciousness of the Lord's people—these sons of Zion—let us now speak.

The Holy Ghost compares them to "fine gold." "The precious sons of Zion, comparable to fine gold." We have yet much to learn, even the most deeply instructed, concerning the preciousness and privileges of God's people. Are we not in great danger of taking divine truth for granted? Instead of sifting its evidences, searching into its blessedness, and realising its power and sweetness in our souls, we give to it too much of a cold intellectual assent. We assume that the Lord's people are a privileged and precious people, but we little surmise how much blessedness, sweetness, and holiness is bound up in this truth—how much there is of God and of Christ in it. It is impossible, as we have remarked, to study the character and trace the history of God's Church, and not know more of the wisdom, power, and love of God. It is in the salvation of this Church that He has embarked all His glory, and has revealed Himself in a way that will fill all the celestial intelligences, saints and angels, with wonder, love, and praise through eternity. My reader, study the history of God's Church, for therein God is revealed in a volume second only in its grandeur, interest, and importance to the volume of His revealed Word. And now let us proceed to illustrate and open up the preciousness of the Lord's people—"The precious sons of Zion, comparable to fine gold."

We begin with the groundwork of the subject—the preciousness of God's people to God Himself. The proof He has given of this is His everlasting love towards them; His eternal choice of them to salvation; His anticipation of their fall in the first Adam, and His provision for their recovery in the second Adam. Who can read the following declarations, and not rise to a lofty conception of God's estimate of the worth and precious-ness of His people?—"Blessed be the God and Father of our Lord Jesus Christ, who hath blessed us with all spiritual blessings in heavenly places in Christ: according as he hath chosen us in Him before the foundation of the world, that we should be holy and without blame before Him in love: having predestinated us unto the adoption of children by Jesus Christ to Himself, according to the good pleasure of His will, to the praise of the glory of His grace, wherein He hath made us accepted in the Beloved." (Eph. i. 3-6.) Not His election of them only, which is the springhead of all the subsequent displays of His grace and favour, but His provision for their salvation, in the gift of His beloved Son, demonstrates God's estimate of their preciousness. Ponder the declaration of this truth—"In this was manifested the love of God toward us, because that God sent His only be-gotten Son into the world, that we might live through Him. Herein is love, not that we loved God, but that He loved us, and sent His Son to be the propitiation for our sins." (1 John iv. 9, 10.) Behold, beloved, how precious you are to God! That which God chooses, upon which He sets His eternal mind and heart, that which He secures to Himself at a sacrifice so great and costly, must be precious to Him. Upon no beings has He expended so much divine perfection, and in none has He made such illustrious dis-plays of His glory, as His saints. All His eternal decrees and purposes—all His everlasting grace and love—all His marvellous works in time, centre in this one body—His elect, redeemed Church, "to the intent that now, unto the principalities and powers in heavenly places, might be known by the church the manifold wisdom of God." His adoption of His people, in union with their election and salvation, forms another striking illustra-tion of their preciousness to God's heart, and of their beauty in His eye. "Having predestinated us unto the adoption of children by Jesus Christ to Himself." "As many as received Him, to them gave He power" (or priv-ilege) "to become the sons of God." (John i. 12.) "Behold, what manner of love the Father hath bestowed upon us, that we should be called the sons of God!" (1 John iii. 1.) "And because ye are sons, God hath sent forth the Spirit of His Son into your hearts, crying, Abba, Father.'› (Gal. iv. 13.) What more shall we say? Can anything add to the proof of God's estimate of the worth and preciousness of His people? He has loved them, chosen them, adopted them, saved them; and in each one and all of these suc-cessive demonstrations, He has declared to the universe how dear to His heart, and glorious to His eye, are "the precious sons of Zion, comparable to fine gold." In this Zion of His love and choice He dwells, displays the tokens of His especial favour, and shews forth His greatest glory. "For the Lord hath chosen Zion; he hath desired it for his habitation. This is my rest for ever: here will I dwell; for I have desired it. I will abundantly bless her provision: I will satisfy her poor with bread. I will also clothe her priests with salvation; and her saints shall shout aloud for joy." (Psalm cxxxii. 13-16.) And in the assurances He has given in His revealed Word of their ultimate and eternal glory—the final, full, and certain gathering together of all His children in their "Father's house" above—He has put the climax to the evidence of their worth and preciousness. "And they shall be mine, saith the Lord of hosts, in that day when I make up my jewels" (or, spe-cial treasure); "and I will spare them, as a man spareth his own son that serveth him." (Mal. iii. 17.) Well may God challenge His people, and say, "And now, O inhabitants of Jerusalem, and men of Judah, judge, I pray you, betwixt me and my vineyard. What could have been done more to my vineyard, that I have not done in it?" (Isaiah v. 3, 4.) When a God of infinite resources says He could have done no more, oh, what a stupendous, marvellous, overwhelming demonstration have we of the preciousness of His Church to His heart!

Thus far have we contemplated the Church of God in its collective form. But all that Zion is to God as a Church, it is to Him in its individual capacity,—"The precious sons of Zion." Each son of Zion is equally precious to Him as the whole. It cost Him as much love, as much power, as much grace, as much glory to save one sinner, as to save His whole elect Church. Who, then, can decide how dear you are to the Father? your person, your love, your obedience, your service, your offerings, regarded as His especial treasure, and as accepted in the Beloved? Angels are not so near or so dear to God as you. Their music is not so melodious as your poor, faltering praises. Their persons are not so glorious to Him as yours, clothed with the righteousness of His Son. Their tributes of adoration and glory are not so fragrant to Him as your sacrifices offered in faith and love, all-perfumed with the atoning merits of Jesus. He has pardoned your sins—has justified your persons—has provided, in Christ, for your necessities—is schooling and training you, by the hallowed discipline of the covenant, for the many-mansioned home He has provided, and Christ is preparing for you; and you shall dwell in His presence, and swim in His love, and bask in His glory through endless ages. Child of God! Son of Zion! is not this enough?

Equally precious are the "precious sons of Zion" to the Eternal Son of God. How shall we attempt to vindicate and unfold the love of Christ to His people—the great and costly proof of that affection which He has given? Who can fathom its depth, scale its height, or measure its length and breadth? That which is infinite is measureless; that which is eternal is boundless. And yet, though we may not compass its dimensions—for it is "a love that passeth knowledge"—we may "know the love of Christ." For the affection He bore us He voluntarily espoused our cause in eternity—bound Himself in an unalterable covenant to accomplish bur redemption, and, travailing in the greatness of His power and love, finished it. His love made Him willing to become incarnate, to assume our curse, to bear our sins, and to suffer and die in our stead. Rising from the dead, He completed our justification; and ascending up on high, He passed within the vail, "now to appear in the presence of God" as our Advocate and Intercessor. There is no other object upon earth that engages the thoughts or fills the heart of Jesus but His people. His presence, invisible and noiseless, yet real and powerful, perpetually surrounds them. Where the Kingdom is, there is the Sovereign; where the Body is, there is the Head; where the Church is, there is Christ. "Lo, I am with you alway, (literally, all days,) even unto the end of the world." For the accomplishment of the number of His elect, He preserves the world in existence—makes and unmakes empires—putteth down one, and raiseth up another—is guiding the deliberations of cabinets—is employing all human agencies—and is overruling every event and circumstance in the history of this vast universe.

But how precious to Him are the sons of Zion in their individual relation and history. Is there one who has ventured to appeal to His love—to trust in His grace—to accept His salvation, who is not more dear and precious than all the angels in heaven? Oh, how precious to Him the tear of godly sorrow—the touch of trembling faith—the look of lowly love—the offering of sincere gratitude—the yearning and longing of holy desire! So precious to Him are they, His ear is attentive to their faintest cry—His thoughts are never withdrawn from them for a moment—His hand is ever extended to succour, and they that touch them touch the apple of His eye. So precious, He sits at the fountain of grace to supply all their need—He bows His shoulder to their heaviest burden—He unvails His heart to their deepest sorrow; and in all places where they dwell, fulfils in their experience the beautiful prediction of the prophet, "He shall feed His flock like a shepherd; He shall gather the lambs with His arm, and carry them in His bosom, and shall gently lead those that are with young." O believer, live not without a deep, constant realisation of your preciousness to Christ, and of the depth, tenderness, and constancy of the love He bears towards you. All your present holiness, happiness, and succour, springs from your believing apprehension of this fact, that you are precious to the heart of Jesus. Let your faith grasp it, amidst the varied phases and changes of your Christian course, and it will be as a sweet flowing stream gliding and sparkling by your side all through the sandy desert, imparting swiftness to your feet in travel, strength to your hand in labour, nerve to your arm in battle,—soothing, reviving, and refreshment to your spirit when sad, faint, and drooping by the way. The Holy Spirit, testifying to your soul of the love the Saviour bears you, will remove all that constraint, shyness, and following Him at a distance, which too much characterises the bearing of so many of His disciples. Be assured of your personal interest in Christ, of your place in His affections, of your home and sanctuary in His heart, and no act of obedience, of love, or of service on your part, will be too costly. Your love to Him will be the inspiration and reflection of His love to you, proportioned in its degree and intensity to the vividness with which His is seen and realised. Nor for this alone would we love Him. Apart from all that He has done, and is doing now, Jesus challenges our admiration and affection. His personal worth, His official work, His glory, and His government, all demand our profoundest homage. This He receives from celestial beings, who, not having sinned, need no repentance, and not having fallen, need no Saviour; and this He will receive, in that day when to Him every knee shall bow, and every tongue shall confess; how much more is He worthy of it from those whom He has redeemed with His most precious blood! Reader, has your eye seen His beauty? has your heart bowed before His cross? have you fallen at his feet? and have you crowned Him Lord and Sovereign of your soul? Oh, what is Christ to you—despised, hated, and rejected?—or, adored, loved, and welcomed? Have you received Him, not as a helper, but as a Saviour—not as a model, but as a Redeemer? Is He all in all to you? If so, then doubt not your preciousness to Him. "I love them that love me." If His name is as ointment poured forth to your soul, it is an evidence that He has set you as a seal upon His heart and upon His arm, and will wear you as an ornament for ever.

Not less precious to the Holy Ghost are the children of God. It must be so, since He has renewed, sanctified, and made them His temple. The work of the Spirit is as essential to our salvation as the finished work of Jesus. There is in many a tendency to regard it as less important, and consequently, with proportionally less reverence and interest. Individuals who would shrink from holding a view of Christ's Atonement derogatory to the essential value and glory of that work, or calculated to neutralise its power, have yet been found to entertain views of the Godhead and work of the Holy Spirit, the effect of which has been to vail the glory of His divine person, and render nugatory His regenerating and sanctifying operation. And yet it is just as fatal an error to believe in the dogma of Baptismal Regeneration—the antagonistic error to the work of the Spirit—as to believe in the dogma of the Mass—the antagonistic error of Christ's sacrifice. So essential, then, is the work of the Spirit in the heart of the regenerate, so divine, holy, and efficacious is it, that all in whom it is wrought, however feeble and obscure it may be, are to Him "theprecious sons of Zion." So glorious and so precious to Him is the new creation of the soul, the universe has no beauty, no grandeur, no sublimity in His eye in comparison of it. Dwelling in the soul, He guards with a sleepless eye that new creation which His own Divine power and skill has wrought, and which no inward corruption or outward assault shall ever destroy. Precious to Him is every spiritual desire, every heaven-sent thought, every holy aspiration, every feeble, languid, yet sincere hunger and thirst of the quickened soul after righteousness. All your grateful remembrances of God, all your loving thoughts of Jesus, all your breathings after Him, all your pantings for deeper sanctification, your daily and sore conflicts with sinful desires, and wandering thoughts, and vain imaginations; your infirmities in prayer, your derelictions in duty, your failures in service, your falterings in obedience—all, all are cognisant to His unlumbering eye. And but for His inbeing, His ceaseless vigilance and divine power, this flood of evil, this whirlwind of passion, would upheave the foundations and carry away the edifice of your faith and hope. But the Holy Ghost is enshrined in every believer, and He guards this blood-ransomed, grace-won, and heaven-kept soul night and day, lest any being or anything hurt it. Oh that our hearts may bow in profounder adoration before this Divine Spirit, and ascend on the wing of more ardent, glowing, praiseful love to Him—listening to His voice more attentively, grieving His heart less frequently, and obeying His promptings more implicitly, who has wrought so great, so holy, so indestructible a work in our souls!

"The precious sons of Zion, comparable to fine gold." By this figure the Holy Ghost seeks to illustrate the relative preciousness of the Lord's people. Their clothing is costly, it is of "wrought gold," even the righteousness of God by faith in Christ Jesus. Their ornaments are costly, "comparable to fine gold," even the graces of the Spirit—"love, joy, peace, long-suffering, gentleness, goodness, faith, meekness, temperance"—awakening the admiration of those who have a spiritual discernment of their beauty: "Thy cheeks are comely with rows of jewels, thy neck with chains of gold." (Song Sol. i. 10.) This commendation of the Church, which is the commendation of all the Lord's people, is all the more precious, since it follows her own humiliating confession of unworthiness—"I am black." When the believer is low in his own eyes, he is exalted in Christ's. We are never more lovely in His view than when we appear the most uncomely in our own. These words of her Lord teach that though His people have many infirmities, yet there is exceeding great loveliness to be seen in them—they are "comparable to fine gold." There is, too, a plurality of ornament in the believer—not one jewel, but "jewels;" not one chain, but "chains of gold." The graces of the Spirit are not solitary and isolated, they are always conjoined and blended with others. The grace of imputed justification is a cognate grace of imparted sanctification, never separated in the believing soul. He who has one grace has all graces. How minutely does God describe the beauty with which He adorned the soul in conversion, and this is the distinguished condition of every true believer in the Lord Jesus—"I decked thee also with ornaments, and I put bracelets upon thy hands, and a chain on thy neck. And I put a jewel on thy forehead, and earrings in thine ears, and a beautiful crown upon thine head. Thus wast thou decked with gold and silver." (Ezek. xvi. 11-13.) Let us select one or two of these spiritual ornaments, as illustrating the preciousness of the believer to Christ.

How precious to Him is your love. Sincere love is precious, even as a human affection, find it in what heart you may. What must be His estimate of divine love in the human heart whose essence is 'love?' Oh, with what ineffable delight He gazes down upon a soul pulsating with a holy, divine affection towards Himself! Can you, beloved reader, say, "Lord, though I am the chief of sinners, the meanest of Thy saints, unworthy to loose the shoe-latchets of Thy disciples, a poor backslider, a slow traveller, a dull learner, a rebellious child, yet Thou knowest that I love Thee, that Thou art the sovereign of my affections, the beloved of my heart; that I am in covenant with Thee, Thy child, Thy servant, one of Thy precious sons of Zion, comparable to fine gold?"—then, beloved, your affection is inconceivably precious to the Lord.

How precious to Him is the obedience of His people. The loving, prompt obedience of a child—how grateful to a parent's heart! There is not an evidence of the sincerity of filial love more true or precious. The loving child is the obedient child; he obeys because he loves. Such is the test of love our adorable Lord—"the everlasting Father" of His people—has demanded. "If ye love me, keep my commandments." The Lord delights in the obedience of His people. He loves it above any other evidence of love. "To obey is better than sacrifice,"—the most rare and costly you can lay upon God's altar. One holy precept observed, one divine law obeyed, one lowly cross taken up, one cherished sin laid down for Christ's sake, has more of fragrance and acceptance in it to Jehovah than the most glowing, blinded zeal that ever bore a martyr to the stake. Beloved, in this spirit of filial love, search and study the commands of Christ, the laws and institutions of His kingdom, the precepts and examples of His gospel. Tamper not with convictions, do no violence to conscience, resist not the teaching and promptings of the Holy Spirit. If, on a careful research into God's Word, and a faithful examination of your own walk, you discover a command unobeyed, a precept unobserved, a self-denying cross from which, checked by the fear of man, you have shrunk, beware of a persistent course of disobedience! Oh, by all the love you profess to the Saviour, walk in obedience to His commands! They are not grievous, but pleasant; they are not arbitrary, but loving; they are not optional, but binding. Essential they may not be to salvation; essential they are to a holy and happy walk. We have already cited obedience to Christ as the test of love. Our Lord, on the same principle, has made conformity to His precepts an evidence of Christian discipleship. "Whoever doth not bear his cross, and come after me, cannot be my disciple." And, as if to win our reluctant hearts to obedience, in another place He emphatically says—"Take my yoke upon you, and learn of me; for I am meek and lowly in heart: and ye shall find rest unto your souls. For my yoke is easy, and my burden is light." Soon you will have done with the judgment of this poor world. With your head pressed upon a dying pillow, and with eternity slowly rising upon your view, human opinion will weigh but little with you then. Oh to meet the Saviour as a loving disciple, as an obedient child, bearing the "marks of the dying of the Lord Jesus," the scars and chafings of the rude and heavy, yet blessed cross, borne for Him! It will then be of little moment whether you ruled an empire, or swept a crossing; wore a mitre, or served the Saviour in the most obscure and lowly sphere of His Church. Found in Christ, standing "complete in all the will of God," you will hear the plaudit and receive the welcome of your Lord and Master—"Well done, good and faithful servant: thou hast been faithful over a few things, I will make thee ruler over many things: enter thou into the joy of thy Lord."

As belonging to the blessed number of the sons of God, remember that filial and cheerful acquiescence with His parental will is a distinctive feature. The precious sons of Zion are known by their submission to God. It is for this that they are chastened and disciplined, tried and purified; that, comparable to fine gold, they may emerge from the furnace a pure and holy reflection of the Divine image. This is the great secret of repose amidst restlessness, calmness amidst agitation, confidence amidst dark providences,—the will brought into complete subjection to the Divine will,—the heart beating in unison with Christ's heart. The moment you are led to see that all is right, that God has done it, and that it must be well done, you are happy. There is no happiness—not a moment's—in opposing God. Fretting against His dispensations, murmuring at His disposals, fighting against His dealings, resisting His providences, tossed amidst the waves of second causes, is just the uplifting of the flood-gates of all distress into the soul. But to lie down at His feet, as the wheat His hand has sifted,—to repose in His heart, as the child His rod has smitten,—to drink the cup His love has mingled, exclaiming, "Not my will, O my Father, but thine be done!"—this is happiness I indeed! Ye tried, afflicted sons of Zion, not less precious to the heart of Jesus are you because you are chastened. You have argued against yourselves, and have impleaded against God from the afflictive dispensations of His providence. You have deemed yourselves cast out of His heart, and out of His mind, and out of His sight,—"reprobate silver," and not "fine gold,"—because He has cast you into the "furnace that is in Zion." Listen to the language of one who thus reasoned, but soon discovered how false that reasoning was—"I said in my haste, I am cut off from before Thine eyes: nevertheless Thou heardest the voice of my supplications when I cried unto Thee." (Ps. xxxi.

22.) Be not hasty in the conclusion you draw from God's dealings with you. Wait patiently until He unvails the purpose, and clearly shews you the end of the Lord. "Be of good courage, and He shall strengthen your heart, all ye that hope in the Lord." Oh the blessedness, the quietness, the perfect peace of a cheerful acquiescence in the will of God! To have a blended will, a united heart, a submissive spirit with Him in His government of you, is to be like God. There is nothing more divinely assimilating and Christ-like. To be like Christ in Gethsemane is to be like Christ in the glory of His throne. To drink the cup in His spirit of profound submission, is to reign with Him for ever and ever. The Lord pardon where we have cherished the least rebellion against His dealings,—when we have refused to drink the cup,—when we have thought Him hard, and harsh, and arbitrary,—when we have, in our ignorance, supposed we could have devised, and planned, and arranged with more skill and wisdom, and with a happier result than He! May the intercession of Jesus on our behalf avert the correction which our murmuring, repining, and rebellion have evoked! May the sprinkled blood blend every thought, and feeling, and desire with Jesus!

> "I did Thee wrong, my God,
> I wrong'd Thy truth and love;
> I fretted at the rod,—
> Against Thy power I strove.
>
> "Come nearer, nearer still;
> Let not Thy light depart;
> Bend, break this stubborn will;
> Dissolve this iron heart!
>
> "Less wayward let me be,
> More pliable and mild;
> In glad simplicity
> More like a trustful child
>
> "Less, less of self each day,
> And more, my God, of Thee;
> Oh, keep me in the way,
> However rough it be.
>
> "Less of the flesh each day,
> Less of the world and sin;
> More of Thy Son, I pray,
> More of Thyself within.
>
> "Here moulded to Thy will,
> Lord, let Thy servant be;
> Higher, and higher still,
> More, and still more like Thee!"

It would be an imperfect close of this chapter were the spiritual reader not reminded of the animating truth, that among the "glorious things" that are "spoken of Zion, the city of our God," isthe future glory that awaits all her "precious sons." The latter-day glory of the Church, the new Jerusalem of the saints, the return of all the scattered children of Zion in triumph and joy to their final and eternal home in the new earth all radiant with righteousness, with a new heaven smiling from above, presents the most animating and sanctifying prospects that ever unvailed to mortal eye. The coming of the Lord Jesus in personal majesty and official glory to make up His jewels, to perfect the number of His elect, to gather together in one the scattered sons and daughters of Zion, and to present them in their essential and visible unity, "a glorious Church," to the Father, as His Bride, is the one all-revealed, all-consoling, all-inspiring, all-sanctifying hope of the saints. "Looking for that blessed hope, and the glorious appearing of the great God and our Saviour Jesus Christ" "Christ was once offered to bear the sins of many, and unto them that look for Him shall He appear the second time without a sin-offering unto salvation." With a hope before you so blessed and assured, what a motive to believers—what an incentive to devotedness—what a reason for watchfulness—what a bond of unity! What manner of persons ought we to be in all holy conversation and godliness! What separation from the world—what crucifixion of sin—what unreserved consecration to Christ—what wakeful vigilance—what patience in suffering—what meekness in persecution—what communion with the Invisible—what vivid realisation of eternal realities, should trace and track our every step towards the full consummation of our bliss! The Lord is at hand! Christ is coming! The Bridegroom is putting on His royal robes! The Bride is longing for His coming! All things indicate the nearness of His approach! The snow-clad mountains of this wintry, dreary world are already edged with the golden streaks of the up-rising Sun. Soon will that Sun appear in its full, its meridian splendour. "Let me go, for the day breaketh!" Sin—enchain me no longer! world—attract me no more! creatures—leave your shrine, and loosen your hold upon my affections! sorrow, suffering, trial—your hours are numbered! My Redeemer is coming! My Beloved is hastening! My Lord will soon appear, and receive me to Himself! "Let me go, for the day breaketh!" "In a little while He that shall come will come," for "the night is far spent, the day is at hand." Then will the magnificent vision of the Apocalypse be realised, "I John saw the holy city, new Jerusalem, coming down from God out of heaven, prepared as a bride adorned for her husband. And I heard a great voice out of heaven saying, Behold, the tabernacle of God is with men, and He will dwell with them, and they shall be His people, and God himself shall be with them, and be their God. And God shall wipe away all tears from their eyes; and there shall be no more death, neither sorrow, nor crying, neither shall there be any more pain: for the former things are passed away." Sons and daughters of Zion! on, then, and still on, praying, fighting, toiling, suffering, enduring, hoping, for "the morning cometh." Then, "the ransomed of the Lord shall return, and come to Zion with songs and everlasting joy upon their heads: they shall obtain joy and gladness; and sorrow and sighing shall flee away."

"Saviour! if of Zion's city
I through grace a member am,

Let the world deride or pity,
I will glory in Thy name.

"Fading is the worldling's pleasure,
All his boasted pomp and show!
Solid joys and lasting treasure,
None but Zion's children know."

Chapter IX.

THE PEECIOUSNESS OF GOD'S WORD.

"The word of the Lord was precious in those days."—1 Samuel iii. 1.

Amongst the precious things of God the saints of the Most High will ever regard as transcendency precious His revealed Word. But for this revelation we had known nothing of those precious things upon which this volume is designed to engage the reader's thoughts. The works of creation, varied and rich in their forms of beauty, while they testify to "His power and Godhead,"—thus leaving man inexcusable for his atheism,—nowhere supply an answer to the momentous question, "What must I do to be saved?" They bear a palpable and solemn witness to man's apostasy, but they testify nothing to his recovery. They tell of a fallen, but not of a restored humanity. They speak not of a Saviour—of a salvation—of hope—of heaven. I may wander in sad and pensive thought upon the sunny banks of its flowing rivers, I may tread its carpeted vales, or climb its cloud-capped mountains, revelling amidst its beauty, its grandeur, and sublimity, and yet find no repose for this restless mind, no peace for this troubled heart, no hope for this sinful and lost soul. Not a flower below, not a star above, tells me of—Jesus, a Saviour! I turn to the "glorious gospel of the blessed God," and my case as a ruined, self-destroyed, condemned sinner, is met by that single, but comprehensive and sublime announcement—"This is a faithful saying, and worthy of all acceptation, that Christ Jesus came into the world to save sinners." Beloved reader, the kingdom of nature, replete as it is with the wisdom, power, and benevolence of Jehovah,—every spire of grass, every lowly flower, every towering mountain, every glimmering star, rebuking the "fool's" denial of a God,—can never disclose how you may be pardoned, justified, and saved. No solution can it supply to the great moral problem of the universe—how God can be just, and yet the justifier of the ungodly. The "gospel of the grace of God," which these pages propose to unfold, meets to the utmost your case as a sinner, bringing life and immortality to light, and thus revealing to you a hope, resplendent and eternal, beyond the gloom and corruption of the grave.

In the prosecution of our subject, let it be premised that there are points which it is not our province to discuss. The reasonableness of a revelation from God,—the necessity of a revelation,—the fact that such a revelation is given to us in the Bible, are questions we must assume as established. It is rather to the worth and preciousness of God's Word, than to any line of ar-

94

gument in proof of its divinity, that we must bend our thoughts. And yet, let it not be supposed that we slight or undervalue evidence as substantiating the truth of the Bible. Everything that is solemn and precious to us as believers is bound up in the fact, that the Book upon which we ground our hope of the future is, what it declares itself to be, the Word of the Lord. The moment our faith in the divinity of the Holy Scriptures is shaken, everything else trembles with it. Life, in all its moral relations, wears another and a totally different aspect. Its foliage is withered, its flowers are blighted, its springs are embittered, and the entire landscape of the present and the future is enshrouded in gloom and despair. No marvel, then, that error should plant its strong and stem battery in front of this the most precious doctrine of our faith—the Divine inspiration of the Scriptures. How truly has the apostle described the unbelieving mind—"The god of this world hath blinded the minds of them which believe not, lest the light of the glorious gospel of Christ, who is the image of God, should shine unto them." We hold it, then, of infinite moment that our faith in the divinity of the Bible, in the plenary inspiration of the Scriptures, should grow stronger and stronger; and that whatever tends to instruct and confirm us in this doctrine of our faith,—be it a fact in history, a discovery in science, or a page in the volume of our personal history,—should be welcomed by us with eagerness, and be acknowledged, with devout thanksgiving and praise. The Lord keep you, my reader, from the low views of divine inspiration prevalent in this day! If this foundation be destroyed, or even apparently shaken, what else has your immortal soul to build upon but quicksand, every step, passing to eternity, over which sinks your soul deeper and deeper in doubt, darkness, and despair?

As the Word of the Lord, then, it is most precious. It could possess no real intrinsic worth apart from this fact. The Bible claims to be nothing less than the Word of God. "All scripture is given by inspiration from God," and "holy men of God spake as they were moved by the Holy Ghost." We part the lids of this sacred volume, and we listen to God's voice,—sometimes in terrific thunder, at others in entrancing music; now in sublime majesty, then gentle as an infant's whisper,—in mercy and in judgment God's Word speaketh. That infidelity should wish to disbelieve and stifle this divine voice speaking from the Bible, is no marvel, since, if the Bible be true, infidels have no hope. An illustration of this may be cited. The late William Wilberforce, when passing through a town in which a noted infidel was imprisoned for blasphemy, called to see him. He endeavoured to engage the unhappy sceptic in a conversation upon the Scriptures, but he declined, saying, that he had made up his mind, and did not wish his conclusions disturbed. Pointing to the Bible in the hands of his visitor, he remarked, in a manner which betrayed deep malignity of heart, blended with mental despair, "How, sir, do you suppose that I can like that Book, since, if it be true, I am undone for ever?" "No," replied the illustrious philanthropist and Christian, "this is not a necessary consequence, and need not be. This Book excludes none from hope who will seek salvation by our Lord Jesus Christ, who died for us, that whether we wake or sleep we may live together with Him." Thus infidelity rejects the Bible for fear it is true! We recur to the thought that God's Word is precious because it is truly and emphatically His Word,—the Word of Jehovah. And when the believer opens the Bible, it is with the profound and solemn conviction that he is about to listen to the voice of God!

But not only is the Word of God precious as a revelation of His being and perfections, but to the child of God it is peculiarly so as revealing the mind and will of God. What the thoughts and purposes of God were could be but dimly gathered from the external works and operations of nature. If these divine thoughts were ever made known to man, God himself must reveal them. "Canst thou by searching find out God? canst thou find out the Almighty unto perfection?" We cannot fully fathom even the finite mind; how much less the Infinite! If at all acquainted with the science of physiognomy, we may trace some faint glimmer in the human countenance of the mental emotions, but this is all the index we have of the hidden thoughts and feelings of the soul. Now, by a similar process, we may learn something of God. The face of nature—the natural countenance of God—is replete with his power, wisdom, and beauty. There is enough of His Godhead to confound and silence the deepest and loudest atheism of man. But nature can go no further. It leads me to the vestibule, but cannot conduct me into the glory within. It tells me there is a God, but it reveals not His nature and character as a Father and a sin-forgiving God. But where nature leaves me, revelation comes to my aid. Hence the high estimate in which God is represented as regarding His own Word. "Thou hast magnified Thy Word above all Thy name." That is, God has magnified His Word above every other manifestation of His name,—there being no such revelation and illustration of the Deity as is found in His revealed Word. Do the heavens and the earth declare the glory of God? Does providence testify to His divine government? How much more His revealed truth! Truly, "Thou hast magnified Thy Word above all Thy name."

As a revelation of His character, the Word of God is precious. What we gather of God's moral character from the kingdom of nature is more inferential than positive. From its creation, we infer the being of God; from its loveliness, we infer that God is beautiful; from its wonders, we infer that God is great; from the admirable unity and fitness of all its parts, we infer that God is wise; from the merciful blessings so richly and profusely scattered over its surface, we infer that God is good; and from the judgments which follow sin, and light upon the sinner, we infer that God is holy and just. But for the clear, positive, and complete revelation of God's character as a righteous, holy, wise, merciful, and sin-pardoning God, we must repair to His written Word. God has unfolded more of His moral character, perfections, and glory in the following words, spoken to Moses on Mount Sinai, amidst the awful emblems of His majesty, than in all the beauties, wonders, and sublimities of His created work:—"And the Lord descended in the cloud, and stood with him there, and proclaimed the name of the Lord. And the Lord passed by before him, and proclaimed, The Lord, the Lord God, merciful and gracious, long-suffering, and abundant in goodness and truth, keeping mercy for thousands, forgiving iniquity and transgression and sin, and that will by no means clear the guilty; visiting the iniquity of the fathers upon the children, and upon the children's children, unto the third and to the fourth generation." (Exod. xxxiv. 5-7.) What a glorious unfolding of God! What a foreshadowing of the yet richer unfolding of the gospel! If God was so glorious on

Mount Sinai, what must be His glory as revealed on Mount Calvary!

As a revelation of the love of God, His Word is inexpressibly precious. We want to know more than the mind of God. We are sinners, and we want to read His heart—His loving, gracious, sin-forgiving heart. We want to know, not only what His thoughts and purposes are, but what are His feelings towards us. Does He love us? Does His justice smile on us? Does His heart expand with mercy, and glow with affection towards us? The Bible alone supplies the answer to these momentous questions. There we read—as we read it tableted in no part of this vast and beautiful universe—"God is love." And when we approach the subject yet closer, penetrate more deeply into the heart of God, what a transcendent, marvellous unfolding of His love is presented in the gift of His beloved Son! Read the declaration, often read before, yet to be read again and again with deepening wonder, gratitude, and praise—"God so loved the world, that He gave His only begotten Son, that whosoever believeth in Him should not perish, but have everlasting life." "In this was manifested the love of God toward us, because that God sent His only begotten Son into the world, that we might live through Him. Herein is love, not that we loved God, but that He loved us, and sent His Son to be the propitiation for our sins." How precious ought that Word to be to our hearts which contains such declarations and reveals such truths as these! Well may the apostle exclaim, "Herein is love!" as if he had said, and he might have added, "and nowhere else but here!" Nowhere in the heavens above, or in the earth beneath, or in the waters under the earth,—no star, no flower, no creature, so reveals, expresses, and embodies the love of God as the gift of His dear Son to die for our sins. Oh, what love is this! "God so loved the world!"— so loved, that He gave Jesus! Jesus is the most precious exponent of God's love—Jesus descends from the bosom of His love—Jesus draws aside the vail of His love—Jesus is God's love expressed, God's love incarnate, God's love speaking, labouring, dying, redeeming. Beyond this it would seem impossible that love could go. Oh, let every affection of our heart, every faculty of our soul, every power of our mind, every action of our life, embody as its grateful response the words of the adoring apostle—"Thanks be unto God for His unspeakable gift!"

We are conducted to another view in the progress of our subject, illustrating the preciousness of God's Word. We refer to its gospel announcements. In this light, we cannot conceive of a more costly, precious blessing than the Word of God. The gospel is the most valuable treasure the believer possesses. Everything else is shadowy, chimerical, transitory, passing away. Nothing is real, nothing substantial, nothing satisfying and abiding, save the "glorious gospel of the blessed God." It is the glorious gospel, because it is replete with real glory,—it reveals a glorious God,—it makes known a glorious Saviour,—it proclaims a glorious salvation,—and it unvails the hope of a glorious immortality. And all other glory in comparison of the "glorious gospel of the blessed God" is as visionary and fleeting as a midnight dream. Nowhere does Jehovah appear so glorious as in the gospel of His grace. There He is revealed as a sin-forgiving God; there He is mirrored forth as a "just God and a Saviour;" there He is portrayed as a reconciled God in Christ; and there He is represented as standing in the relation, and exercising the love, of a—Father. O glorious gospel that presents such a view of God to the sinner's believing eye! "God was in Christ, reconciling the world unto Himself." What declaration can more clearly indicate the love of God to us, as the moving, originating cause of our salvation, than this? There is a marked, and we think, essential defect in the theology of many Christians touching this subject, which tends much to obscure the Divine glory, and to lessen in our view the greatness of God's love in man's salvation. We refer to the statements which represent God as angry, incensed, and vindictive, and as appeased, pacified, and reconciled by the death of Christ. Is not this an essential misapprehension of God's everlasting love to His people? Would it not appear from this representation of God that the Atonement of Christ was the originating cause of His love, rather than that His love was the originating cause of the Atonement? We think so. We look upon this notion of God as enshrouding the glory of redemption, by the palpably false view it presents of the Divine character. But the correct statement is the converse of this. God loved us— and as a result, Christ died for us. The Atonement of the Son of God was not the procuring cause, but the consequence, of the Father's love. Christ did not inspire God with love to man, but expressed it. He did not die to originate the Divine affection, but to expound and exhibit it. The love of God to His people was as eternal as the eternity of His being, as everlasting as His uncreated nature. "I have loved thee with an everlasting love." It panted, it yearned for an outlet. It sought and found it in Christ. The Atonement of Jesus, uniting and harmonising all the perfections of the Deity, supplied the channel through which the ocean of Divine love washed the shores of this earth, its soul-healing waves spreading like a sea of life over our sin-tainted, curse-blighted, sorrow-stricken humanity. When, therefore, the Scriptures speak of Divine reconciliation, as in the passage just quoted, we are to understand the full expiatory satisfaction given to God's moral government through the Atonement of Christ, by which His law is honoured, His justice is satisfied, His holiness is secured, His truth is maintained, and He appeared upon earth walking amongst men, "reconciling the world unto Himself."

But the experience of the believer supplies, perhaps, the most powerful and conclusive testimony to the preciousness of God's Word. We have not been advancing a vain thing, but a well-attested fact, in affirming the divinity and value of revelation. We are now about to cite the child of God—yea, the whole Church of Christ—as testifying to the preciousness of the Word of the Lord. How many a truth-experienced, gospel-believing, Christ-loving heart will respond to the words of David, "How sweet are Thy words unto my taste! yea, sweeter than honey to my mouth." What says Jeremiah? "Thy words were found, and I did eat them; and Thy word was unto me the joy and rejoicing of my heart." Corresponding with this is the experience of the universal Church, find it where we may, whatever may be the dissonance of opinion prevailing upon less essential and important questions of polity and worship.

It is precious to the believer, first, because it is divine, attested, experienced truth. Is it not so that, to you who believe in God's Word, every other word in comparison seems a fiction and a fable? And that, as you grow in grace, as your acquaintance with, and experience of, the Word of God deepens, as you near eternity, your hold upon everything else grows fainter and fainter, and your grasp upon it grows firmer and firmer? Now, God's Word is truth. He who is emphatically "the Truth," because He is essential truth, and the substance of revealed truth, has affirmed this in His sublime and memorable prayer—properly the Lord's Prayer—"Thy Word is truth." Pursue this thought for a moment There would seem to exist a necessity that it should be so, since it is the Word of the God of truth, partaking of the nature of that God whose truth it is. All that emanates from God must be a transcript, in some degree, of what He is. It is faintly so in the works of nature; yet more clearly so in the kingdom of providence; perfectly so in the empire of grace. The great truth, then, to which these three witnesses testify is this, "He is the Rock, His work is perfect: for all His ways are judgment: a God of truth and without iniquity, just and right is He." (Deut. xxxii. 4.) It follows then, as clearly as any conclusion can from its premise, that His Word is true—eternally, essentially, immortally true. True in the Saviour it reveals—in the salvation it declares—in the doctrines it expounds—in the precepts it enforces—in the promises it speaks—in the hopes it unvails—and in the threatenings it denounces. "Thy Word is truth." As divine truth, then, it is most precious to the believer who has staked his all of future and eternal happiness upon its veracity. Let your faith, beloved reader, have more close dealing with the truth of God's Word. Whatever gloomy and untoward providences may gather their shadows around your path, hold fast your confidence in the truth of God's Word. You shall find mutability in everything but this. God will vary His providences, but cannot alter His Word. "For ever, O Lord, Thy Word is settled in heaven." Heaven, with its resplendent glory and surpassing wonder—earth, with its countless myriads of beings, its beauty, and its history, shall be a thing of yesterday, not a vestige remaining to tell of its existence, its grandeur, and its greatness; but "the Word of the Lord shall endure for ever." All that God has whispered in mercy, or has thundered in judgment—the promise of love, the threatening of wrath—all the precious words upon which He has caused our souls to hope—the succourings pledged, the sure mercies covenanted, the assurances given, the consolations engaged, the oath sworn, shall all be fulfilled. Then, amidst the fluctuations and the vicissitudes of all sublunary things,—the home of childhood changed, the place of hallowed memories and sacred associations changed, the friends and companions of our choicest, sunniest years changed, adversity and death flinging their deep shadows upon life's landscape,—we will approach the closer and cling the firmer to the eternal, unchangeable truth of our God. Your faith, beloved, in God's word of promise may be severely tried by God's dealings with you inprovidence—the one may appear to oppose and contradict the other—but ever remember that God cannot deny Himself, nor alter the word that has gone out of His mouth. If the sentence of death seems pronounced upon the promise of God by His strange and mysterious procedure, forget not that there is yet life in the Word of the Lord; and that when the stone that sealed the tomb of all your mercy is rolled away, the Word upon which your soul has reposed, upon which your heart has lived, to which your faith has clung, and which has kept alive the spark of hope within your breast, shall come to life again, every sentence, word, and syllable fulfilled to the letter by Him of whom it is said, "It is impossible that God should lie." Oh, cling then to Christ's Word, as the mariner to the plank, as the mother to her infant, — yea, as a humble believer in that divine and gracious Saviour who has said, "Him that cometh unto me I will in no wise" — literally, "I will never, no, never, cast out."

As testifying of Jesus and His salvation, the Word of God must ever be transcendently precious to the believer. The Bible is, from its commencement to its close, a record of the Lord Jesus. Around Him — the divine and glorious Centre — all its wondrous types, prophecies, and facts gather. His Promise and Foreshadowing, — His holy Incarnation, Nativity, and Baptism, — His Obedience and Passion, — His Death, Burial, and Resurrection, — His Ascension to heaven, Second Coming to judge the world, and to set up His glorious kingdom, are the grand and touching, the sublime and tender, the priceless and precious truths interwoven with the whole texture of the Bible, to which the Two Witnesses of Revelation — the Old and the New Testaments — bear their harmonious and solemn testimony. Beloved, let this be the one and chief object in your study of the Bible — the knowledge of Jesus. The Bible is not a history, a book of science, a poem, — it is a record of Christ. Study it to know more of Him, — His nature, His love, His work. With the magnanimous Paul, "count all things but loss for the excellency of the knowledge of Christ Jesus your Lord." Then will God's Word become increasingly precious to your soul, and its truths unfold. You will trace the history of Jesus, — see the glory of Jesus, — admire the work of Jesus, — learn the love of Jesus, — and hear the voice of Jesus, in every page. The whole volume will be redolent of His name, and luminous with His beauty. Oh, what were the Bible to us apart from its revelation of a Saviour! Is there not great danger of studying it merely intellectually and scientifically, of revelling amongst its literary beauties and its grandeur, blind to its true value, and without any desire to know that precious Saviour who died for sinners, that Divine Redeemer who purchased the ransom of His Church with His own blood, that Friend who loves us, that Brother who sympathises with us, that enthroned High Priest who intercedes for us within the vail? May we not resort to it as mere controversialists, polemics, and partisans, searching it but for weapons of attack upon a Christian brother's system or creed, or quoting it but to give countenance and complexion to a favourite dogma? But do we study the "Word of Christ" spiritually and honestly, as those whose souls hunger and thirst for this the bread and water of life? Do we search it diligently and earnestly as for hid treasure — treasure beyond all price? Can we say with David, "O how love I thy law! it is my meditation all the day?" — "The entrance of thy Word giveth light; it giveth understanding unto the simple. I opened my mouth, and panted: for I longed for thy commandments," — "Thy Word is a lamp unto my feet, and a light unto my path." Do we read it with a child-like mind, receive it with a believing heart, bow to its teaching with reverence of soul, and receive its decisions in all questions of faith and practice as decisive and ultimate? In a word, do we search the Scriptures humbly, prayerfully, depending upon the guidance of the Spirit, to find Jesus in them? Of these Scriptures He is the Alpha and the Omega — the substance, the sweetness, the glory — the one, precious, absorbing theme. Listen to His own words, "Search the Scriptures, for these are they which testify of me." Moses wrote of Me — David sang of Me—seers prophesied of Me—evangelists recorded My life—apostles expounded My doctrine—and martyrs have died for My name. "These are they which testify of Me." Yes, Lord! Thy word is precious to our souls, because it reveals to us Thy glory, and tells us of Thy love!

Precious, too, is the Word of God, as containing doctrine, precept, and promise. The doctrines are precious, as affording instruction to the mind, and establishment to the faith of the child of God. There can be no real, stable building up in God's truth when the great doctrines of grace are faintly believed and loosely held. These doctrines, then, which exalt the Lamb of God, which lay the glory and power and boasting of the creature in the dust, and which exhibit the electing love and sovereign grace of God in his salvation, are most precious to the truth-experienced heart of the believer in Jesus. Not less precious to him is the preceptive teaching of God's Word. When there is a real experience of the power of the doctrines, there will be a love of the precept. You will desire to be sanctified as well as justified—to have your heart purified, and your life moulded by the holiness of the truth. The precept that enjoins separation from the world—that teaches us to deny all ungodliness, and to live soberly, righteously, and godly in this present evil world—that bids us take up our daily cross and follow a crucified Saviour, and realising our resurrection life in Him, thus to seek those things that are above, where Christ sitteth at the right hand of God—must be precious, inconceivably precious, to a Christ-loving heart. The rebukes, too, of God's Word, humbling though they are, yet are welcome to the believer. The Word that gently chides your backslidings, unvails your follies, checks your inconsistencies, lays your pride, self-seeking, and self-boasting in the dust, is precious to your soul. The Christian feels, that "all Scripture is given by inspiration of God, and is profitable for doctrine, for reproof, for correction, for instruction in righteousness, that the man of God may be perfect, thoroughly furnished unto all good works," and therefore he welcomes all. Beloved, count not less dear to your heart, or as less the tender unfolding of God's love, those parts of His truth which reprove, humble, empty, and lay you low. The rebukes and reproofs of God's Word are as valuable and precious in themselves as the promises, since both equally seek the sanctification of the believer, and both emanate from the same Divine mind, and flow from the same loving heart.

As a source of Divine consolation how many will testify to the preciousness of God's Word! The Bible, while it is a proclamation of mercy to the vilest sinner, is equally the book of the afflicted. As a system of consolation Christianity has no equal. No other religion in the wide world touches the hidden springs of the soul, or reaches the lowest depths of human sorrow, but the religion of Christ. Saints of the living God! suffering members of a suffering Head! we cite you as witnesses to this truth. When your hearts have been overwhelmed, when adversity has wrapped you within its gloomy pall, when the broken billows of grief have swollen and surged around your soul, how have you fled to the Scriptures of truth for succour and support, for guidance and comfort! Nor have you repaired to them in vain. "The God of all comfort" is He who speaks in this Word, and there is no word of comfort like that which He speaks. The adaptation of His truth to the varied, the peculiar and personal trials and sorrows of His

Church, is one of the strongest proofs of its divinity. Take to the Word of God what sorrow you may, — go with what mental beclouding, with what spirit-sadness, with what heart-grief — be its character, its complexion, its depth unsurpassed in the history of human sorrow, — there is consolation and support in the Word of God for your mind. There is in these sacred pages a voice of sympathy and soothing chiming with your grief; and thus "by the comfort of the Scriptures you have hope" that God will not leave you in trouble, but will sustain you in it, will bring you out of, and sanctify you by it, to the endless glory and praise of His great and precious name. O ye sons of God whose faith has been strengthened by the histories of the Old Testament saints — whose minds have been instructed by the dealings of God with His Church in the wilderness — whose hearts have been comforted by the rich experience of David in the Psalms — whose views of God's kingdom prophets have enlarged — whose knowledge of Christ's history evangelists have deepened — whose souls apostles have established in the faith, we cite you as witnesses to the divinity and preciousness of God's Word. "Ye are my witnesses, saith the Lord." Testify to an infidel world what the Bible is, and to the saints what you have experienced it to be. Tell how its revealed truths have established you, how its illustrious examples of piety, faith, and love have animated you, how its exceeding great and precious promises have comforted you, and how the glorious hope of heaven which the gospel unvails has inspired you to run with patience the race set before you, looking unto Jesus. Tell how this precious Word of God has made clear many a perplexity, has illumined many a dark road, has cheered many a lonesome way, has soothed many a deep sorrow, has guided and upheld many a faltering step, and has crowned with victory many a feat of arms in the great battle with Satan, the world, and sin. May we not say of the Bible, as David said of Saul's sword, "There is none like it." Christian mourner, let me once more direct your eye — too dimmed perhaps by tears to behold the precious truth — to this divine source of true, unfailing comfort. God's Word is the book of the afflicted. Written to unfold the wondrous history of the "Man of Sorrows," it would seem to have been equally written for you, O child of grief! God speaks to your sad and sorrowing heart from every page of this sacred volume, with words of comfort, loving gentle, and persuasive as a mother's. "As one whom his mother comforteth, so will I comfort you." The Bible is the opening of the heart of God. It is God's heart unvailed, each throb inviting the mourner in Zion — the poor in spirit, — the widow, — the fatherless, — the bereaved, — the persecuted, — the sufferer, — yea, every form and child of affliction and grief — to the asylum and sympathy, the protection and soothing of His heart. Oh, thank God for the comfort and consolation of the Scripture! Open it with what sorrow and burden and perplexity you may, — be it the guilt of sin, the pressure of trial, or the corrodings of sorrow, — it speaks to the heart such words of comfort as God only could speak. Have you ever borne your grief to God's Word, — especially to the experimental Psalms of David, — and not felt that it was written for that particular sorrow? You have found your grief more accurately portrayed, your state of mind more truly described, and your case more exactly and fully met, probably in a single history, chapter, or verse, than in all the human treatises that the pen of man ever wrote. What a proof that the Bible is the Word of God! We verily believe that no Christian is thoroughly versed in the evidences of the truth of the Bible, or is in a right position to understand its divine contents, until he is afflicted. Luther remarks that he never understood the Psalms until God afflicted him. Fly to the Word of God, then, in every sorrow. You will know more of the mind and heart of God than you, perhaps, ever learned in all the schools before. We must be experimental Christians, if Christians at all. A bare notionalist, a mere theorist, an empty professor of religion, is a fearful deception. Study to know God's Word from a heartfelt experience of its quickening, sanctifying, comforting power. Sit not at the feet of men, but at the feet of Jesus. His Word can alone instruct you in these sacred and precious truths. You must learn in Christ's school, and be taught by the Holy Spirit. And if you are truly converted, spiritually regenerated, a real believer in the Lord Jesus, think not that some strange thing has happened to you when the Lord causes you to pass under the rod of discipline, brings you into trial, and makes you to partake of what may seem to you a soul-diet anything but healthful and nutritious,—"the bread of adversity, and the water of affliction." (Isa. xxx. 20.) But affliction is one of the Lord's moulds for shaping you into an experimental Christian. And to be an experimental Christian His Word must be inwrought into bur soul. What can we know of the promises, the succourings, the sympathy of God's Word,—its perfect adaptation to the crushed and sorrowful condition of our humanity,—but for trial? Thus, more than one-half of the Bible is a "garden inclosed, a spring shut up, a fountain sealed," until the Lord lays sorrow upon our hearts, and brings us into circumstances of adversity. Then this garden unvails its beauty, and this spring pours forth its refreshment, and this fountain overflows with its rich and varied supply. Oh, with what power, depth, and sweetness does the Word of God unfold to us then! It is as though a new book had been composed,—another constellation in the spiritual hemisphere had burst upon the telescope of faith,—another Arcadia had floated into view,—a new world had been discovered! "Blessed is the man whom Thou chastenest, O Lord, and teachest him out of Thy law." "Unless Thy law had been my delight, I should then have perished in my affliction." Draw, then, O child of sorrow, your consolation from God's Word. Put it not away as if it were for others, and not for you. There is not a promise in the Bible, of pardon, of grace, of help, of sympathy, but it is yours, because you are Christ's, "in whom are all the promises of God, and in Him are Yea and Amen to the glory of God the Father." Oh, clasp this precious Word of comfort to your sorrowful heart, and exclaim, "It is mine! The Jesus of whom it speaks is mine,—the salvation it reveals is mine,—the promises it contains are mine,—the heaven it unvails is mine,—and all the consolation, comfort, and sympathy which wells up from these hidden springs, is—mine."

"Laden with guilt, and full of fears,
I fly to Thee, my Lord,
And not a glimpse of hope appears
But in Thy written Word.

"The volume of my Father's grace

Does all my grief assuage;
There I behold my Saviour's face
Almost in every page.

"I'll read the histories of Thy love,
And keep Thy laws in sight,
While through Thy promises I rove
With ever fresh delight.

"'Tis a broad land of wealth unknown,
Where springs of life arise,
Seeds of immortal bliss are sown,
And hidden glory lies.

"The best relief that mourners have,
It makes our sorrow bless'd;
Our fairest hope beyond the grave,
And our eternal rest."

The Word of God is equally valuable and precious to the believer, because of its quickening power. There is a divine vitality in the Word, which, like Ezekiel's vision of the waters, conveys life wherever it comes in "the power and demonstration of the Spirit." As the instrument of regeneration and of sanctification, the Bible is beyond all price. The statements touching these two points are many and conclusive. We quote but a few:—"The law of the Lord is perfect, converting the soul, making wise the simple, rejoicing the heart, enlightening the eyes." (Ps. xix. 7, 8.) See how David extols its quickening power:—"This is my comfort in my affliction: for Thy word hath quickened me." "I will never forget Thy precepts: for with them Thou hast quickened me." As the instrument of the new birth, thus does the Holy Ghost speak of it:—"Being born again, not of corruptible seed, but of incorruptible, by the Word of God, which liveth and abideth for ever." (1 Peter i. 23.) "The Word of God is quick, and powerful, and sharper than any two-edged sword, piercing even to the dividing asunder of soul and spirit, and of the joints and marrow, and is a discerner of the thoughts and intents of the heart." (Heb. iv. 12.) And alluding to it equally as the appointed instrument of holiness, our Lord prays to His Father, "Sanctify them through Thy truth." And to the disciples He employs similar language:—"Now ye are clean through the word which I have spoken unto you." Employing the same argument, the apostle thus exhorts the saints:—"Seeing ye have purified your souls in obeying the truth through the Spirit unto unfeigned love of the brethren, see that ye love one another with a pure heart fervently." Clearly, then, is God's Word an instrument of spiritual life and of gospel holiness, and as such commends itself to the deepest reverence, the warmest love, and the most diligent study of the believer. Suffer, beloved reader, a few words of exhortation bearing upon this subject.

Study the Scriptures of truth with a heart in prayerful uplifting for the accompanying power, light, and anointing of the Holy Ghost. The Word is but a dead letter, unattended by the Spirit. The Word of God is a "sword," but the sword is effectual only as it is wielded by the power of the Spirit. "The sword of the Spirit, which is the Word of God." Expect, then, this Word to be powerful in your own souls, as in the souls of those upon whom you bring it to bear, only as it is clothed with the divine and irresistible might and energy of the Holy Ghost. Then it will quicken, enlighten, and convince; then it will convert, comfort, and sanctify. Ever remember that the Divine Author of the Bible is at your side—invisible and noiseless—when you sit down to read it. Graciously and benignantly He is bending over you, prepared to explain what is difficult, to harmonise what is contradictory, and to shed a flood of light upon each page, causing Heaven's glory to dart into your soul from the diamond spark of a single passage! Such, beloved, are the effects of the gospel, when clothed with the authority and power of God the Holy Ghost. In the quaint but terse language of an old writer, be exhorted "to attend upon the Word with an eye to God. Look not for the new birth only from the Word. It was the folly of the Jews to think to find life in the Scriptures without Christ; life in the letter without the Original of life. (John v. 19, 40.) 'Except the Lord build the house (that is, the temple), they labour in vain that build it.' Without God, all endeavours to build a spiritual temple, are like the strivings to wash a blackamoor white. No believing in the Word, though preached a thousand times, without God's revealing arm. (Isaiah liii. 1.) It is not the file that makes the watch, but the artist by it. No instrument can act without the virtue of some superior agent. It is the altar that sanctifies the gold, and Christ that sanctifies the ordinance. Paul may plant by his doctrine and miracles, Apollos may water by his affectionate eloquence, but God alone can give the increase by His almighty breath. Man sows the seed, but God only can make it fructify....Then have your eyes fixed upon God. It is the Word of His lips, not of man's, whereby any are snatched out of the paths of the destroyer, as well as kept from them. Man's teachings direct us to Christ; God's teachings bring us to Christ. Man brings the gospel at most to the heart; the Spirit only brings the gospel into the heart. Man puts the key to the lock; God only turns it, and opens the heart by it. 'Tis God only can knock off the fetters of spiritual death, and open the gates that the King of Glory may enter with spiritual life. If any, therefore, will regard the Word more than as an instrument, or a partner with God in His operations, He may justly leave you to the weakness of this, and deny the influx of His own strength."

Cultivate a profound reverence for God's Word. Nothing is more grievous to the Holy Spirit than a trifling with revelation. The words of Scripture are divinely inspired. "Holy men of God spake as they were moved by the Holy Ghost." "Which things also we speak, not in the words which man's wisdom teacheth, but which the Holy Ghost teacheth." Stand in awe of this Holy Book! Beware of referring to it doubtfully, or of quoting it with levity. To adopt the words of Scripture irreverently,—to speak of any of its parts with suspicion,—or to employ its phraseology flippantly, is to cast discredit upon inspiration, to press it into the service of the flesh, and to make the Word of God the jest-book of the profane. This is awful trifling with the thoughts and words of the Holy Ghost. God says, "I will look to him...that trembleth at my Word." This was David's holy reverence—"My heart standeth in awe of Thy Word." And this his prayer—"Order my steps in Thy Word, and let not any iniquity have dominion over me."

This profound conviction of the divinity and authority of God's Word will constrain you to bring the state of your soul, your doctrinal sentiments, and your daily life, to its unerring test. The only divine and sure standard is the Word. "To the law and to the testimony," should be our constant rule. Regard, in all matters of faith and practice, the Word of God as authoritative in its teaching, paramount in its voice, and final in its decision. Whatever doctrine or practice squares not with this standard, that will not stand the searching test of this divine touchstone, reject as unworthy your belief and adoption. Let this be your daily practical acknowledgment, "Thy Word is a lamp unto my feet, and a light unto my path." Taking into your hands this lamp, and guiding your steps by this light, your feet will never slide. Cling to the Word of God the more firmly, as others attempt to sap the foundations of its divinity. Be "valiant for the truth on the earth," and "contend earnestly for the faith once delivered to the saints." "Let the Word of Christ dwell richly in you in all wisdom," hiding it in your heart, that you sin not against Him. Read it with prayer for the teaching of the Holy Spirit, comparing scripture with scripture, spiritual things with spiritual. Search it to know more of Christ, more of His atoning work, more of His mediatorial suitability to meet your every state of mind and heart. Study it to know the will of God, the love of your heavenly Father. Take every doubt, perplexity, and sorrow to the Word of God. And before you unfold its sacred leaves, lift your heart in prayer to the Eternal Spirit to guide your reading, to open your understanding, and to unvail your eye to this divine well-spring of life. This is the only rule we suggest for the spiritual and practical reading of God's Word. Human helps may aid you in the study of the sacred literature of the Bible; but to read it with a view to the feeding and nourishing of the divine life in your soul,—that you may grow in knowledge, faith, and holiness,—that you may be instructed, comforted, and armed for the holy war,—you need but rely upon the teaching of the Holy Ghost, who is promised to guide you into all the truth as it is in Jesus. Beware of studying the Bible as a lover of history, of science, of poetry. Study it as a sinner, anxious to know how you may be saved. Read it to ascertain how God can pardon, justify, and take you to heaven when you die. Lay aside your cavilling, debating, and speculating, and approach the Bible as a little child, as a sincere inquirer, as a humble learner, desirous of knowing the Scriptures, that are able to make you wise unto eternal life. In a research so momentous, lay aside all other books, and be the student of this one—the Book of God. Salvation is its one, its grand and absorbing theme—and this is all you need to know as a sinner bound for the judgment-seat of Christ. A notional, speculative reception of the Bible prepares an uneasy pillow for a dying hour; and it is marvellous and solemn to reflect how every subject, every theme, every question growing out of the history, philology, or destiny of God's Word, gives place in that awful moment to the one momentous, sublime salvation therein revealed, by which the soul may escape from hell and soar to heaven. Who then desires to listen to learned disquisitions upon the literature, the eloquence, the poetry, or the sublimity of the Bible? Who, when nature is dissolving, earth is receding, eternity is opening, is in a condition to weigh, examine, and sift the evidences of the divinity of the Scriptures?

The earnest, imploring language of such a one, alive to a conviction of sin and danger, is, "Is there pardon, is there salvation, is there hope for such a sinner as I am? Does the Word of God tell me how I may be saved? Read to me of Christ. Tell me of the Saviour. Point me to the Lamb of God. Direct my eye to the cross, and let me behold Him whose blood cleanseth from all sin. Read to me, speak to me, tell me only of Jesus." Precious Book, that fully meets a crisis of our being, and an awakened, alarmed state of mind, so tremendously solemn as this!

We close this chapter with an earnest appeal to your judgment, conscience, and heart in favour of the Word of God. Whatever you neglect, neglect not the Bible. If a professed believer, beware how you blend in your reading the chaff of human fiction and story with the wheat of God's Word. It is utterly impossible, reason as you may, that you can cultivate a spiritual and devout taste and desire for the truth of God and the fiction of man. The Bible and the novel can never stand side by side. As a Christian, guard against the light, frivolous, frothy literature of the day. It will lessen your conviction of what is true, it will depreciate the value of what is divine, it will impair your taste for what is spiritual, and it will bring poverty, barrenness, and death into your soul. "God speaks to you from every paragraph and sentence of this Holy Book. It is His voice that we hear, His signature that we behold, His ineffable glory, which, the more it is viewed in this bright mirror, may the more powerfully command our wonder and praise. When we approach these divine oracles, and hear the voice of God sometimes speaking out of the midst of the fire, but more often from the blood of sprinkling which speaketh better things than the blood of Abel, we may well bend our knee, and take the shoes from off our feet, for the ground on which we stand is holy. Oh that power might come down upon us from the Spirit of truth and grace, and beams from the Sun of righteousness break in upon our minds as we contemplate the intrinsic glories of the Bible! Let the truth and weight of these revelations sink deep into your ears. As men of this world merely,—as creatures of time,—more especially as the proprietors of immortality, you have a thousand-fold deeper interest in the Bible than in any other, or all other books. It is just as important that you who have the opportunity should become acquainted with the Scriptures, and believe, and love, and obey them, as it is that you should be saved. This Book offers to you that which most you want,—that which is infinitely more to you than all other things,—glory, honour, immortality, and eternal life. We cannot but look upon the prevailing indifference with which the Word of God is regarded, as one of the evils over which we are loudly called to mourn. You send the Bible to the ignorant and destitute,—you carry it to every cottage and waft it to every clime,—and thanks to God that you do so; but to what extent is it studied in your churches, read in your families, taught to your children? There is no surer evidence of living without God in the world than living without intimate communion with the Bible. Who that does not mean to remain in impenetrable obduracy,—who that does not form the deliberate resolve to close every avenue to the divine influence, that is not prepared to plunge the dagger of the second death into his own bosom,—can live in the neglect of these Scriptures of God? And if you believe them, and understand them, will you refuse them the submission of your heart and your everlasting obedience? Do you accredit the stupendous truths contained in this volume, and shall they waken no deep interest, and urge you to no solemn preparation for your last account? There is not one among them that will not prove a savour of life unto life, or of death unto death."[7] What can we add more to this searching, solemn appeal to you who are living in a wilful neglect of that Book which tells you of life in this world, and out of which you will be judged in the world which is to come? Disbelieve, or neglect the Word of God, and you reject the only chart to eternity.

It may not be out of place, in a chapter devoted to the preciousness of God's Word, and may form a suitable close, to submit to the serious attention of the reader a few observations bearing upon the character of the received English version of the Bible; and to enter our solemn caveat against a proposition which has obtained, having for its object the disturbance and displacement of the present translation, by the substitution of an emended or new translation of the Sacred Scriptures. Our views and feelings upon this subject are as decided and strong as they are devoutly and maturely considered. We cannot but look upon each a proposition as not only uncalled for by the unanimous voice of the Christian Church, and not required by the events of her history or the state of the world, but as likely to prove most disastrous to the interests of pure, evangelical religion. That the present version of the Bible, as a human production, is perfect, we affirm not. There are passages the meaning of which other renderings might more clearly elucidate—words that are obsolete—expressions that are obscure—phrases that may chime somewhat harshly upon a refined ear; be it so—the Bible, as a translation, is the work of man! and what work of man ever issued from his hands complete? Any version of the Scriptures offered to us as a substitute for the present, must not only necessarily be an imperfect production, but would, doubtless, from the circumstances in which it would be prepared, contain renderings yet more erroneous, phrases yet more objectionable, defects and blemishes yet more palpable and glaring than the one which we now possess. We need but refer, in proof of this, to the specimens already presented. While thus we candidly concede the imperfections of the existing version, we as honestly and strongly claim for it a degree of fidelity of rendering—of dearness in evolving the mind of the Spirit—and of accuracy, beauty, and excellence as a translation, which no man, and which no body of men, the most erudite and pious in the present age, advanced and intelligent as it is, could equal, much less surpass. The translators of the English Bible were among the most learned and holy men the world ever saw. More ripe scholars and profound theologians the Church of God never produced. Of one of them, William Bedwell, the learned Lightfoot remarks, "Industrious, and thrice learned, to whom I would rather be a scholar, than take on me to teach others." Of another, Dr John Rainolds, the man who suggested to the King the idea of the present translation, Bishop Hall remarks, "The memory and reading of that man were near to a miracle; and all Europe at the time could not have produced three men superior to Rainolds, Jewel, and Ussher." They would all of them, as philologists and divines, be giants in any age. If James I. were in some respects a weak

---

7   Spring.

man, yet, as the pupil of George Buchanan, he was a ripe scholar, and possessed of no mean attainments in divinity. He had the intellectual sagacity, not to say the spiritual discernment, to choose the men who were in all respects, both as to learning and piety, equal to the undertaking. Their advantages for the accomplishment of the work were great. With access at the time to the most ancient manuscripts, — with the versions, ready at their hands, of Tindal, Coverdale, and Matthew, of Cranmer, Geneva, and the Bishops' Bible, — and with a revived study of the Greek language, at that time culminating to its highest point, it would seem as if the God of the Bible, in His wonder-working providence, had provided an especial and befitting scaffolding for the uprearing of this glorious and imperishable structure of learning, piety, and truth—the good old English Bible. To quote the words of an able writer—

"The art of translation cannot in its whole history boast a greater miracle than the English Bible. No less happy and less skilful feat of religious scholarship could have succeeded in winding one book so thoroughly round the hearts of Englishmen, domesticating its characters and scenes in the imagination, and imparting to everything in it a genius loci, an old welcome, familiar air, as if it belonged, upon the Platonic theory, to some distant horizon of the reader's own recollection, some acquaintance with a former world. The sacred homeliness of the language gives to all the conversations and all the dramatic life and action of the inspired volume the authenticity and characteristic tone of a true original. A fragrance from an old world haunts us, the genuine fresh breeze, which has crossed over an ocean of time to visit us on this shore of modern life and society, and inspire a belief in and a communion with the past. Everything that carries us back to the sacred original of man, all the images of primitive life that still remain around us, and remind us of the first rudiments of our social state, the parental and filial relations, husband and wife, master and servant, the household, even spreading corn-fields and patriarchal furrows, the very instruments of agriculture, — everything that appeals to nature or to the past, has something in it akin to the language of our translated Bible." To disturb, then, this excellent version, — the sword which fought so well and successfully the battle of the Reformation, and which again and again has confounded atheism, infidelity, and Romanism, — a version which all sections of the Christian Church consent to receive, and which, by a thousand associations and memories the most hallowed, precious, and undying, is endeared to our hearts, our homes, and our sanctuaries, would seem to be as impolitic as impious. Who would think of altering the text of Homer or of Shakespeare, without a serious violation of good taste, and committing a species of sacrilege and wrong against which a nation would rise. With reverence and awe, infinitely more profound, must we approach the Bible. While it challenges the most searching investigation, and demands the most implicit belief, it forbids the touch of a reckless innovation. The general fidelity of the work as a translation, — its "pure well of English undefiled," — its Anglo-Saxon terseness, — the crystal clearness, distinctness, and beauty with which the fundamental verities of our faith—the great essential doctrines of the gospel—are presented to the mind of the most simple and unlearned, are so many demonstrations in its favour, clustering like sentinels around the most magnificent and stupendous monument of our language which the world possesses. We have remarked, that to supplant this ancient and endeared translation by a modern and strange one, would be hazardous. Much would be risked, little would be gained. A door would at once be opened, through which would rush a tide of innovation and error, sweeping away the ancient and sacred landmarks of learning, and truth, and godliness. The Church of God, standing before her foes with the humiliating acknowledgment that for ages she had been battling with a corrupt and frail instrument, — confronting error with error, wielding a weapon of spurious and uncertain temper, — would be shorn of her strength, and tarnished of her glory. The enemies of the Bible, ever watching for our halting, would exult at the confession, and employ their triumph in engrafting upon its holy pages their preconceived opinions and favourite heresies; and thus playing into the hands of the infidel and the Romanist, the pantheist and the materialist, we should be found fraternising with the Hegels, the Strausses, the Newmans, the Maurices of our day. For these reasons, and others as weighty, we solemnly and earnestly protest against a new or revised version of the English Bible, preferring it, with all its faults, as it is. Possessing an edition, containing the marginal readings on the text, and with the aids afforded by such works of reference as are constantly issuing from the press — philological and exegetical — the spiritual and unlettered student of the Word of God needs no better, — and no better could be constructed, — than the good old English Bible of our hearts, our memories, and our homes, with which we can part but with life itself. Esto perpetua!

> "Hail, sacred Volume of eternal truth!
> Thou staff of age! thou guide of wandering youth!
> Thou art the race which all that run shall win —
> Thou the sole shield against the darts of sin:
> Thou givest the weary rest, the poor man wealth,
> Strength to the weak, and to the lazar health.
> Send me, my King, my Saviour, and my God,
> Through all these paths Thy sainted servants trod;
> Lead me Thy twofold nature to explore,
> Copy the human, the Divine adore;
> To mark through life the profit and the loss,
> And trace Thee from the manger to the cross.
> Give me to know the medium of the wise,
> When to embrace the world, and when despise —
> To wait with patience, to abound with fear,
> And walk between presumption and despair.
> Then shall Thy blood wash out the stain of guilt,
> And not in vain, for me, Thy blood be spilt."[8]

We would venture upon one or two words of needed and solemn caution. There exists in the present day a marvellous fondness for questioning the divine authenticity of certain parts of the Bible. Individuals professing a love to, and reverence for, God's Word, think it not wrong freely to

---

8   Lines composed between one and two centuries ago.

canvass the claims of particular books, chapters, or verses to our full and unhesitating belief, in the presence of their families and households. This evil is a serious and great one. Such persons are not, probably, aware how far they are encouraging in others that natural enmity of the human heart to godliness, which would gladly avail itself of the pretext of an alleged particular interpolation, in order to a general disbelief and rejection of the whole Bible. Breathe not a sentence in the presence of the unconverted calculated to shake their confidence in, or lower their reverence for, the Word of the living God. God will not hold him guiltless who thus casts doubt and discredit upon the volume which is a revelation of His mind and will, and which, when heaven and earth shall have passed away, will exist a glorious and eternal memorial of His love, grace, and truth. To this remark, permit us to add another. You may safely question your sound-ness in the faith, if your principles, your creed, or your life, will not allow of a full reception of every part of the Word of God, whether relating to doctrine, privilege, or duty. If the natural tendencies of your system be to create a distrust or shyness of any part of the Bible, you may be sure that either your creed or your life is in the wrong. We must beware of the un-safe and often false tests of human standards, and feel that we are walking in the "old paths" of truth and righteousness, trodden by patriarchs and prophets, by apostles, evangelists, and martyrs, only as we have for our guide and warrant a "Thus saith the Lord."

Believer in Jesus! endeavour to experience more and more the pre-ciousness of the Word of the Lord. It was precious in the days of Eli—days of evil and of affliction, days of judgment and of death. Surely these are days in which the Word of the Lord should be especially precious to our souls! Bind it closer and firmer to your hearts. Let it dwell richly in you in all wisdom. Believe in it firmly, receive it fully, study it prayerfully, quote it reverently, follow it implicitly, defend it valiantly, disseminate it wide-ly; and in a little while, guided by its counsels and sanctified by its truths, it will conduct you to those realms of glory where, in full splendour, you will behold the Saviour whose salvation it revealed, whose beauty it un-vailed, and of whose love it spake to you while upon earth,—purpling many a cloudy picture, gleaming brightness upon many a dreary path, soothing and cheering many a sad and lonely stage of your earthly pil-grimage,—"and so shall you be ever with the Lord."

> "I love the sacred Book of God;
> No other can its place supply:
> It points me to the saints' abode,
> It gives me wings, and bids me fly.
>
> "Sweet Book! in thee my eyes discern
> The image of my absent Lord:
> From thine instructive page I learn
> The joys His presence will afford.
>
> "Then shall I need thy light no more,
> For nothing shall be then conceal'd;
> When I have reach'd the heavenly shore,

The Lord himself will stand reveal'd.

"When 'midst the throng celestial placed.
The bright Original I see,
From which thy sacred page was traced,
Sweet Book! I've no more need of thee!

"But while I'm here, thou shalt supply
His place, and tell me of His love;
I'll read with faith's discerning eye,
And thus partake of joys above."[9]

---

9   Kelly.

Chapter X.

THE PRECIOUSNESS OF PRAYER.

"Golden vials, full of odours, which are the prayers of saints."—
Revelation v. 8.

If there be an argument which establishes beyond all dispute the doctrine of the fall, and the necessity of a restored and regenerated nature, it is the fact, that from it nothing that is holy, spiritual, or good emanates. The moral soil is so utterly degenerate, that even the flowers which adorn it— the natural virtues still clinging to our humanity—are, in the sight of a holy God, but as noxious weeds, destined finally and utterly to perish. Such was the complete wreck, such the entire paralysis of our nature. "In my flesh," says the apostle, "dwelleth no good thing." If, then, in the midst of this utter and universal corruption, there should be found springing any bud, or blossom, or fruit of real holiness—anything truly gracious, spiritual, heavenly—it must be the product of a divine principle, of a new nature implanted within us by God the Holy Ghost. A striking proof and illustration of this is presented in the subject of this chapter. There exists not a more undoubted evidence of a renewed nature than—Prayer. The absence of it is the unmistakeable evidence of—death; its existence a palpable and positive evidence of—life. Prayer is the most vital, spiritual, and pure emanation of the indwelling of the Spirit in the soul. If, in a case of suspended animation, we marked the slightest symptom of life—the gentlest heaving of the heart—the faintest moisture breathed upon the surface of a mirror—we should certainly hail it as proof of the existence of the vital principle. We should not ask for strong spasmodic action, and postpone all efforts to rouse the dormant pulse, before we pronounced the individual alive. We should be satisfied that the spark still glowed, and this would reassure our hope, and animate our labour. Prayer is the spiritual life of the renewed soul. There may be the absence of profound religious knowledge, great depth of Christian experience, fiery zeal and gigantic energy—nevertheless, if of one thus apparently dormant it is said, "Behold he prayeth!"—if, in the secret walk, all deeply vailed from human eye, there is fellowship with God, communion with the Invisible,—there is life—life divine, life spiritual, life eternal. To change the figure—here is a plant of righteousness growing in a corrupt soil, here is a flower of holiness blooming and exhaling amidst sin, corruption, and death! Surely this cannot be indigenous to our fallen humanity, but must be a seedling, a germ, a graft from the paradise of God. Among the most precious things of

God is this—the principle and spirit, the power and sweetness of—Prayer.

We select the idea from a scene in the Apocalyptic drama which passed before the eye of John. In this vision, among other sublime revelations, he beheld "four beasts and four and twenty elders fall down before the Lamb, having every one of them harps, and golden vials full of odours, which are the prayers of saints." That these elders belonged not to any order of angelic intelligence, is conclusive from the subsequent verse, in which they are represented as acknowledging themselves to be "redeemed to God by the blood of the Lamb." It is clear, then, that they formed a part of the Church redeemed from amongst men. The whole vision is designed to present the fact, that the Church of God is a praying Church; and that the prayers of the Lord's people append before Jehovah as precious incense, holy, fragrant, and acceptable, through the infinite and atoning merits of Jesus Christ. The preciousness of Prayer, then, is our theme, and the following is the order in which we propose to present it:—The sacred incense,—the "golden vials," from whence the incense ascends,—and the preciousness and acceptance of the incense to God. "Golden vials full of odours, which are the prayers of saints."

But observe, in the outset, whose prayers are these:—"The prayers of saints" "Odours (or incense), which are the prayers of saints." What saints? Not the glorified saints. The saints in heaven have done with prayer. The service and the employment, which before was to them the most precious and hallowed, has now ceased for ever. That which is perfect is come, and that which was but in part is done away. Prayer and supplication, which on earth was the source of their sweetest solace and their richest comfort—the vital atmosphere in which they lived—is exchanged for praise. Adoration, thanksgiving, and worship fill every soul, attune every heart, and employ every tongue, in this world of blessedness. Beloved, there is no prayer in heaven, save that of the Great Interceding High Priest. It is a remarkable fact—and it stands in direct refutation of the dogma held by the idolatrous communion of Rome—that there is recorded in the Bible but a single appeal from creatures on earth to the saints in heaven—but one instance of supplication addressed to the glorified spirits—and that was denied! We refer to the appeal of Dives to Abraham. Thus the Romish idea of the invocation of saints is directly opposed to the Word of God. There is but one recognised Intercessor in heaven, the Lord Jesus Christ, who "by His own blood entered once into the holy place," and "ever liveth to make intercession for us." With such a Mediator before the throne, whom the Father heareth alway, why invoke the aid, the sympathy, the prayers of creatures—angel or saint? The Great High Priest is in heaven—will not that suffice? With Him the Father is well pleased—is not this enough? His intercession never fails—what more can you desire? Begirt with His ephod, and wearing His breast-plate, He bears the burdens and participates the sorrows of His Church below. By no avenue but His bleeding heart can they enter,—up no ladder but His cross can they ascend,—and with no name may they entwine their supplications but the one name which transcends every name, the name of—Jesus. Who can fully unfold the blessedness of this truth to the saints of God? Do we not, beloved, rob our souls of the peculiar blessing—the succour, the comfort, the grace—bound up in the intercessory work of our

Immanuel within the vail? What can be more encouraging and animating than to know that Christ remembers us, prays for us, and upholds us in heaven?—that he thinks of us with a Friends affection, compassionates us with a Brother's sympathy, prays for and succours us with a Saviour's meritorious intercession? See you Him not, by faith, standing before the golden altar in glory, presenting the sacred incense of His merits, the temple all filled with its perfume? Think not that the Church below hath no tokens, unmistakeable and precious, of her Great High Priests intercession within the vail of glory. Has the type of this truth no significance? A part of Aaron's vestment was "a golden bell upon the hem of the robe round about." And the Divine instruction was, "It shall be upon Aaron to minister; and his sound shall be heard when he goeth in unto the holy place before the Lord." (Exod. xxviii. 34, 35.) How expressive and how sweet must that sound have been to the waiting congregation without! It was to them an evidence and a token that the priest was within the vail, ministering before the altar, bearing them upon his breast-plate, presenting their sacrifices, and securing by his intercession their acceptance and God's response. Beloved, our Great High Priest has passed within the vail, and appears in the presence of God for us. Hear you not the music of His bells? How entrancing their melody! How precious their significance! Every covenant blessing sent down from God—every gracious answer to prayer returned—every pure beam of love darting into your soul—every spring of joy, and peace, and hope welling up in your heart—every burden sustained—every grief soothed—every temptation broken, is the chiming of these bells upon the robe of Jesus as He ministers before the throne of God in glory. How sweet, how precious, how soothing their melody! Child of God!—

> "Lift up your eyes to th' heavenly seat.
> Where your Redeemer stays;
> Kind Intercessor! there He sits,
> And loves, and pleads, and prays.
>
> "Petitions now and praise may rise,
> And saints their offering bring;
> The Priest, with His own sacrifice
> Presents them to the King.
>
> "Jesus alone shall bear my cries
> Up to His Father's throne;
> He, dearest Lord! perfumes my sigh,
> And sweetens every groan."

"The prayers of saints." If prayer be the breathing of the indwelling Spirit in the soul—if the expression of deeply-felt want—if the language of a child—and if the incense of the heart wafted to heaven through faith in Christ, then the saints of God are the only individuals who offer true prayer. Prayer is too holy and spiritual an exercise for any but the holy ones. None prostrate themselves at the mercy-seat but the poor in spirit—the self-abhorring—Christ-desiring! To them this spot is the dearest in the universe. Here is attraction which, find them where it may, irresistibly draws and indissolubly binds them. All may be gloom beyond—all is sunshine here. The saint in audience with Jehovah is the most morally sublime spectacle in the universe. Angelic spirits must look down upon it with an emotion of blended awe and delight Such is the privilege of a—Saint. Let the world deride the name, and trample in the dust him who wears it, yet is it the most honoured and sacred appellation God ever conferred upon mortal. "Called to be saints"—what a high calling, beloved, is this! Made lower than angels by sin, we are made higher than angels by grace. Redemption has exalted our humanity above every other nature but the Divine. To be clothed upon with the "righteousness of God," is to occupy a position of dignity and glory to which no other creature can aspire. Angels stand in the aphelion, saints in the centre, of the Sun of Righteousness. Lord! let the infidel deny the character, and the worldling scorn the name, number me among thy saints everlasting, upon whom is conferred the privilege of fellowship and nearness with Thee here, and glory, honour, and immortality with Thee hereafter!

But what is the incense?—"the prayers of saints." The emblem is exquisitely beautiful and expressive. It is one of the highest conceptions of poetry, in one of its most sacred forms. Prayer is holy incense. The margin of the passage so renders it, and David so employs the expression in connexion with prayer: "Let my prayer come before Thee as incense, and the lifting up of my hands as the evening sacrifice." We have but glanced at the truth that the saints of God are a praying people—that intercourse with the Triune Jehovah is an essential characteristic. The thought is so important, we propose in a few pages to amplify it. We have said that devotion is a symptom of life, an evidence of true piety, a characteristic of a saint of God. This remark holds good in its universal application. True prayer is that one vital principle that animates, energises, and sanctifies the universal family of God. Whatever their differences of ecclesiastical polity, discipline, or worship—whatever their varied gifts, attainments, or position in society, prayer is the moral atmosphere of the one Church of God. "Moses and Aaron among His priests, and Samuel among them that call upon His name; they called upon the Lord, and He answered them." No man is a saint of God who is not a praying man; and a praying man, find him where you may, is a saint of God. He may prefer the place and the mode of prayer which his conscience best approves; and whether that place be a cathedral or a barn, and the mode be liturgical or free, is of no essential moment. If, penetrating within the inner and hidden shrine, he waves before its altar the censer of a truly contrite, believing, adoring heart, drawing near to God in the name of Jesus, and holding fellowship with the Invisible, that man is a man of prayer, is a recognised saint of the Most High, and as such we should recognise and commune with him as a Christian brother beloved.

But not only is prayer essential to the character of a saint of God, his whole history implies that he is a man of prayer. Your Christian life, beloved reader, necessitates this walking with God in all its minute detail. If it be a divine precept, as it is a precious privilege, to "acknowledge the Lord in all our ways," then this habit of recognising the being and government of God, His love and care for us, His providential guidance of our every step, must keep us in constant and close contact with our Father and Friend. And when to this we add the more spiritual part of our history,—the Christian conflict we wage, the constant discoveries of sin we make, the seductions by which we are assailed, the daily trials, sorrows, and disappointments to which we are subjected,—surely Prayer must be the living, enshrouding atmosphere of a saint of God. Not one moment could we live without it. Prayer—either breathed from the believer's heart on earth, or from the lips of the Great Intercessor in heaven—sustains each moment the life of God in the soul of man. Ah, beloved! whither could you go with those burdens, those wants, those chafings, those backslidings, those shortcomings, those sorrows, which compose so large a part of daily life, but to the throne of grace? Where could you resort for mercy, for strength, for fortitude, for patience, for comfort and soothing, but where the God of love and power meets you and talks with you through Jesus, as man communeth with his friend? It is in this light we come to regard prayer, not merely as a divine command, or as a Christian duty, but as the holiest, sweetest, and most precious privilege God has vouchsafed to us on earth. Look at its grandeur—a mortal, a sinful mortal, in audience with the God of heaven! And when we consider that mortal in the light of a child, and that God in the character of a Father, the spectacle becomes one of unsurpassed beauty and tenderness. But look at its preciousness. It comprehends all the minutiae of our daily life, "Casting all your care upon Him." "Be careful for nothing; but in everything, by prayer and supplication with thanksgiving, let your requests be made known unto God." What a tender, loving rebuke is this of that restraining of prayer, and limiting of God, which restricts our petitions to the major concerns of life, while it leaves unprovided for the minor ones. And yet, beloved, God is as deeply interested in your small cares as in your large ones. Those comparatively trivial events, those lesser circumstances of your history, are often those which you feel the most keenly, which chafe the most sorely, and upon which so much that is important and momentous in your life depends. Learn, then, the blessedness, and appreciate the privilege, of hallowing with prayer the minute details of daily life. Infinite as Jehovah is, He stoops to our little trials, little cares, little wants, little sorrows. Nothing is too small for God that concerns you, His loved child. Study the life of Jesus when on earth. Was there a circumstance, or a want, or a temptation in the history of His disciples too mean or unimportant for His notice? He who, by similitude so significant and impressive, could vindicate and explain the particular providence of God in the affairs of His people, assuring them that the very hairs of their head were all numbered, was not likely to pass unnoticed and unmet the fasting and languor of His disciples, when on one occasion He said unto them, "Come ye yourselves apart into a desert place, and rest awhile." He who created the minute things of nature, alike regards the minute things in providence, and despises not the "day of small things" in grace. God made the atoms that form the pyramids, the mote that dances in the sunbeam, the insect that swims in the ocean drop. Think you, then, that He can be indifferent to, or regard as beneath His notice, the smallest care, the most delicate sorrow, the meanest want, the lowest interest, that relates to you? Impossible! Learn, then, to entwine with your petitions the small cares, the trifling sorrows, the little wants of daily life.

Whatever affects you—be it a changed look, an altered tone, an unkind word, a slight, a wrong, a wound, a demand you cannot meet, a charge you cannot notice, a sorrow you cannot disclose—turn it into prayer, and send it up to God. Disclosures you may not make to man you can make to the Lord. Man may be too little for your great matters, God is not too great for your small ones. Only give yourself to prayer, whatever be the occasion that calls for it. Send up your heart unto God just as it is. Send up a whole heart, and He will return it a broken heart. Send up a broken heart, and He will return it a healed heart. Send up a cold heart, and He will return it a loving heart. Send up an empty heart, and He will return it a full heart. Send up a praying heart, and He will return it a praising heart. Only send up your heart to heaven, whatever its frame or condition, its desires or wants, and your Heavenly Father's loving, gracious heart will descend and meet it when its pinions have scarce left the earth to sweep in faith and prayer the skies. "Trust in Him at all times. Ye people, pour out your heart before Him. God is a refuge for us." "And it shall come to pass that before they call, I will answer: and while they are yet speaking, I will hear." Wonderful encouragement to prayer!

Having thus spoken of the sacred incense, it is meet that we now advert to the censer, You will observe these "odours" are described as ascending from "golden vials." "Golden vials (or bowls) full of odours, which are the prayers of saints." These "golden vials," or bowls—as some critics more literally render the word φιάλη—are the censers of the saints. It is, then, an interesting and important question, What are the censers which the saints of God wave before the altar? In other words, to speak less figuratively, From whence does true prayer spring? It is not, beloved reader, every man who bends the knee before God who offers prayer from a golden censer. There is no religious duty so little understood, or more generally abused, as prayer. How much passes current for prayer with man, which is not prayer with God! It is like mistaking the artificial convulsions of galvanism for the actual breathing of life—the contortions of nature for the actings of grace. An individual may offer to God "strange fire" from an earthly censer. God says, "I cannot away with it." Beloved, true incense floats from a golden censer—what is it?

Shall we begin with the censer of a broken and contrite heart? Here is a censer of the purest gold! Take not man's estimate of it—he, in his blindness, is constantly mistaking the spurious for the true, the precious for the vile. The world holds lightly a broken heart for sin. But take God's estimate,—"Thus saith the high and lofty One that inhabiteth eternity, whose name is Holy; I dwell in the high and holy place, with him also that is of a contrite and humble spirit." A broken heart for sin is God's dwelling! Again,—"To this man will I look, even to him that is poor and of a contrite spirit." God will look at him—He will not look at a proud, self-sufficient, self-justifying heart—for "the proud He knoweth afar off;" but His eye— His eye of love, His eye of delight, His eye of approval—will rest upon the humble, broken, and contrite heart. Despised by the worldly, scorned by the proud, overlooked often by the saints, yet how beautiful, how costly, how precious to Christ is this golden vial! True, it is a contrite heart,—true, it is an empty heart,—true, it is a self-abased heart; but there waves not a censer in heaven, save the Great High Priest's, more beauteous, more costly, more precious than it. This "golden vial" is of heavenly construction. A Divine Artificer made and formed it. God the Holy Ghost alone wrought this penitence, inspired this contrition, awakened this conviction of sin. He it was who abased that pride, laid low that loftiness, stained that glory, and smote that stricken, smitten heart in the dust. His the power that wakes that more than melody from those pale, trembling lips—"God be merciful to me a sinner!" Melody! Oh, angels' harps breathe not sweeter music than this! And God, when He hears it, looks down and sees on earth no spectacle of interest or grandeur to surpass it—one more precious to His heart Bruised and broken though that spirit be, clad in the habiliments of woe and grief, filled with self-loathing and sin-abhorrence, it is in God's eye a golden censer, wafting to His throne earth's sweetest, holiest, richest incense. "The sacrifices of God are a broken spirit: a broken and a contrite heart, O God, Thou wilt not despise."

The believing heart is a golden censer, from which the holy incense of the prayer of faith ascends to God. A heart that humbly believes in the Lord Jesus,—that accepts without demur or hesitation, and as His free gift, His finished salvation,—that rests child-like and wholly upon the one offering by which Jesus hath perfected for ever the salvation of His people is a "golden vial." All real prayer is the prayer of faith. It is offered in faith in God's word—His promise—and in what He is Himself as God,—able and willing to answer prayer. The prayer of faith is but taking God at His word:—"If ye who are evil know how to give good gifts unto your children, how much more shall your heavenly Father give good things (even the Holy Spirit) to them that ask Him?" Now, the prayer of faith is the pleading of this promise with God, thus taking Him at His word. The Lord Jesus here places a blank card in the hands of His saints, and bids them inscribe upon it just what they want. It is a note of hand which He bids them fill up to any amount or character of blessing they require, and He will grant it. "Ask what you will." Beloved reader, the Lord gives you this promise, and bids you send it up to Him for fulfilment with the prayer of faith, trusting Him to make it good. There is much wisdom and love of our heavenly Father displayed in giving us this general promise that we might give it a particular application. Faith in God's promise is not so much a belief that a particular request will be granted—for that request is not named in the promise. But the stipulation is to grant any good asked, anything supplicated, any petition preferred, if only asked in faith—faith in God's faithfulness and power to make good His word, and to obtain the blessing asked. It is a general promise connected with a particular application. The Lord Jesus says, "If ye shall seek anything in my name, it shall be granted you." Therefore do not hang back and say, "My particular need is not mentioned in the promise; my especial case is not provided for in the Word." It is, beloved, if you will but take hold of the general promise of God, and plead it with the prayer of faith. No particular temporal good may be mentioned,—no especial spiritual blessing may be promised,—no single case may be specified; but if the censer of a believing heart waft the incense of the prayer of faith to God, God will grant that particular temporal good, or bestow that especial spiritual blessing, or meet that peculiar and urgent case. It was thus that Jacob prayed. "Thou saidst, I will surely do thee good." What good? Any good, all good! There was the pleading by faith of God's general promise in a particular case of urgency. And when he met the Angel of the Covenant at Peniel, he exclaimed, "I will not let Thee go except Thou bless me…And He blessed him there." The prayer of the Syrophenician woman was the prayer of faith. "Call me a dog, tread me down beneath Thy feet—only grant me my request, and come and heal my child." Her faith had a general apprehension of Christs power to eject the demon from her daughter, and then she flung her particular sorrow upon that heart that never was known to reject a plea, or cast a sorrow back again. Such is the power which the prayer of faith has with God! It is irresistible. No unworthiness, no sinfulness, no backsliding, no unfaithfulness, no depth of want, or peculiarity of case shall prevail with God to turn a deaf ear to the cry of faith. Faith in His word of promise, in His illimitable power, in His boundless resources, in His beloved Son, is so honouring to His nature and glorifying to His name, that the faintest incense which the censer of a lowly, believing heart ever sent up to heaven, reaches the Majesty on high, and brings back the blessing in a gracious and loving response—more than we either asked or thought of. We have to do not only with a prayer-answering, but also with a prayer-exceeding God—a God who always bestows more than we supplicated, because He delights to give, not according to our stinted desires, and measured requests, but according to the infinite merits of His beloved Son and His own wondrous love and power. Ask this faith of prayer at the hands of Jesus. He is not only its Object and its Medium, but He is also its Author and its Giver. Beseech Him to infuse this precious faith into your feeble, stammering petitions. Implore Him to intensify and energise your faint and faltering supplications with this divine heaven-descending and heaven-ascending principle. "Lord, increase my faith! Let me ask in faith, nothing doubting. Nerve my poor, faltering arm, so ready to hang down; stay my fluttering heart upon Thee, so prone to swerve; and help my soul to cast itself upon Thy precious promise to save to the uttermost, and I shall be saved. Lord, I believe; help Thou mine unbelief." Or, is your faith faltering faith—tempted faith—tried faith—sinking faith? Listen to the words of Jesus, once addressed to a doubting believer, and new addressed to you. "O thou of little faith, wherefore didst thou doubt?" "Gracious Saviour! dost Thou acknowledge my 'little faith?' Then my 'little faith' shall acknowledge Thee! I will come to Thee,—I will confide in Thee,—I will look to Thee; come what will, sink or swim, live or die, saved or perish, I will cleave and cling, dear Lord, to Thee! Thou art and Thou shalt be my All in all." Wave this censer before the altar of sacrifice, and your prayer of faith shall be accepted. "This is the confidence that we have in Him, that, if we ask anything according to His will, He heareth us. And if we know that He hear us, whatsoever we ask, we know that we have the petitions that we desired of Him." (1 John v. 14, 15.) The prayer of faith will pardon sin,—the prayer of faith will heal the sick,—the prayer of faith will open heaven,—the prayer of faith will move the Arm that upholds the universe! Ask in faith, nothing doubting, and you shall have the petitions you desire of Him.

A Christ-loving heart is also a "golden vial" full of precious incense—the incense of love. And such is the heart of all who are renewed by the Spirit, and are in a state of reconciliation and peace with God. There may be fluctuation in this holy affection,—it may ebb and flow,—it may be tried, tempted, grieved,—yet a heart in which glows a solitary, glimmering spark of divine love, a heart which can say, "Lord, Thou knowest all things, Thou knowest that I love Thee," is a golden censer, wafting its grateful incense to God. But let us not be satisfied with a dubious or imperfect love to God. Let our return of affection be worthy the Object that inspires it. There are no changes in the tide of Christ's love to us—it is always a flow, never an ebb. What may to our short ken appear an ebb, is in reality not so. It is not that the tide of God's love recedes from us, it is that we recede from the tide of God's love. We quit the depths of this infinite and never-receding ocean, and repair to the shallows of creature good, of human affection, of worldly enjoyment; and then, chilled, disappointed, perchance wounded, we marvel that our love to God has so soon congealed, ceasing to flow in its wonted warm and undivided current. We wonder that the Bible has not the same interest, the means of grace the same attraction, prayer the same sweetness, and the ministry of the word the same power. Alas I the change is in our humanised divine affections, in our lessened spirituality, in our lessened tone of heavenliness, in our truant affections, our undecided heart. We have allowed the idolatry of the creature, the love of the world, or the too eager pursuit of its calling, or the too earnest desire to please and stand well with its friends, to insinuate itself into our heart, and steal away its affections from Christ. But let us retrace our steps,—the door of return is yet open,—and come back to Christ. Repairing afresh the altar where His sacrifice was offered, let us from its holy fire replenish our cold censer with living embers, and once more send up the holy, precious, fragrant incense of a restored, loving, surrendered heart to God.

Not less precious to the Lord is the censer of a praiseful heart. Alas that the elements of thanksgiving and praise should be so wanting in our religion! Yet so it is. We speak of prayer-meetings, but seldom of praise-meetings,—of gatherings for humiliation; confession, and supplication, but how rarely do we assemble to give thanks to God, and to render to Him the praise due unto His great Name. When the pressure is upon us, we are eager to draw in the Divine goodness by prayer; when the pressure is removed, how slow to breathe out the acknowledgment by praise! And yet for our encouragement God has said, "Whoso offereth praise glorifieth me." Since the Lord's government of His people is a government of love, it follows that, whatever the decision of that government may be, it is in love He deals with them. "Whom I love, I rebuke and chasten." If this be so, there is nothing in the dealings of God that may not prompt you to wave before Him the golden censer of a thankful heart. Oh, precious the cloud thus ascending, filling heaven with its odour! In heaven all is adoration, thanksgiving, and praise. And when we offerpraise to God, we approach in our worship on earth the nearest to the worship of the glorified in heaven. Oh, let us, then, not be slow to wave this golden censer, and offer Him the precious incense! We will praise Him for electing love—praise Him for Jesus—praise Him for a divine righteousness—praise Him for a free-grace salvation—-praise Him for a full pardon—praise Him for a throne of grace—praise Him for the Rock that towers above our head, sheltering us with its shadow, and refreshing us with its streams—praise

Him for the blessing given, for the blessing withheld—praise Him for the restorings, for the upholdings, for the chastenings, for the rebukes, for the wounds,—for the darkness of sorrow, for the brightness of joy,—for the retrospect of grief, for the prospective of bliss,—yea, for all that is past, that is present, and that is to come;—for all, all flows from one Divine source—the everlasting and unchangeable love of God in Christ Jesus our Lord.

One point of deep interest yet remains to be considered—the preciousness of the incense: "golden vials, full of odours." Be the incense that is offered to God through Christ what it may—prayer—confession of sin—supplication—praise, yet ascending from the heart, oh, how full of sacred odour is the vessel! It may be a sinful, and yet a contrite heart,—a wandering, and yet a sincere heart,—a changeful, and yet a loving heart; still, in God's eye, it is a "golden vial," and the Lord smelleth a sweet savour in the incense wafted from it to His throne.

Prayer must be precious incense to God, because, in the first place, it is the fruit of the Holy Ghost in the soul. All true prayer—be it but a desire, a groan, a tear, a sigh—is the inspiration of the Spirit. "The Spirit also helpeth our infirmities: for we know not what we should pray for as we ought: but the Spirit maketh intercession for us with groanings which cannot be uttered." It is this truth that stamps a value upon the weakest prayer the saints of God ever breathed, and which imparts to that weak prayer a richer fragrance to God than earth's choicest perfume. We but faintly conceive the costliness and beauty of the lowest work of the Holy Ghost in the soul. It is nothing less than the begetting of the Divine nature in man: the erection and upbuilding of a structure of righteousness that shall outlive all material grandeur, and be radiant with the glory and resound with the praises of Jehovah to all eternity. That must be the power of God the Holy Ghost that can extract incense so sweet, so fragrant, so precious, from hearts so sinful, so vile, so worthless as ours! Such are the prayers breathing from your heart, dear reader. They may be mixed with much of the earthliness of the channel through which they flow,—you may complain of coldness, formality, wandering thoughts, the intrusion of things foreign to your feelings, desires, and enjoyments,—yet, pouring out your heart to God in the most retired, lonely, feeble way, your Father in heaven recognises it as the voice of a child, and "accepts you with your sweet savour." Oh, see, then, that the prayer that breathes from your lips, whether from the pulpit or the closet, whether in public or in private, be the breathing of the Holy Ghost! Seek to be filled with the Spirit. Rest not short of His vital power, and sanctifying influence, and fragrant anointing in your soul. Then, although your prayers may be mixed with tears, and groans, and confessions,—though with a stammering tongue and quivering lip you address the Majesty of heaven and earth, God will descry the voice of His Spirit in your prayers, and will speedily and graciously respond.

But that which imparts the richest fragrance to the prayers of the saints is the atoning merit of Christ's obedience and death, through the medium of whose mediatorship they are offered, and on the ground of whose merits they are accepted. The apostle beautifully propounds this truth:—"Christ also hath loved us, and hath given Himself for us an offering and a sacrifice to God for a sweet-smelling savour." This sacrifice it is—divine in its dignity, expiatory in its character, complete in its offering, and accepted by God—that invests with a cloud of divine incense, most fragrant and precious, every broken petition, every penitential confession, every believing supplication wafted to God from the heart of a saint on earth. The sacrifice of Christ on earth opened a door by which the believer approaches God in heaven. The intercession of Christ, which is the presentation of His merits before the golden altar, secures, the acceptance of his petitions in glory. We marvel not now that these "golden vials" should be "filled with odours, which are the prayers of saints." The Holy Ghost fills the censer, and then Jesus the obedient One, Jesus the crucified One, Jesus the risen One, Jesus the ascended, glorified, interceding One, throws the divine fragrance of His offering around the prayers of His people, and thus they find favour with God. What an encouragement is this to draw near to God in prayer! Who that approaches, though with taint, and fear, and imperfection in his petitions, yet with sincerity, penitence, and faith, shall fail of finding acceptance both of his person and his offering, seeing that the Lord Jesus Christ imparts His merits, employs His advocacy, and blends with the much incense of His sacrifice every humble suit, every heaven-directed petition? "We are many times dejected at the remembrance of our prayers; but the concern that Christ hath in them is a ground to raise us. We have an Advocate that knows how to separate the impertinences and follies which fall from the mouths of His clients; He knows how to rectify and purify our bills of requests, and present them otherwise than we do. How happy a thing is it to have One to offer up our prayers in His golden censer, and perfume our weak performances by applying His merit to them! Satan distracts our prayers, but cannot blemish Christ's intercession. When we cannot present our own case, by reason of diseases and indispositions, we have One to present our cause for us, that can never be distempered, who is more quick to present our groans than we are to utter them. Besides, all prayers put up in His name shall be successful. (John xvi. 23.) The arguments we use from Christ's merits are the same fundamentally upon which the plea of Christ in heaven is grounded, and if God should deny us it, it were to deny His Son, and cast off that delight He Himself has in the merits of His death; but God loves that mediation of His Son, and that this work of His should be honoured and acknowledged. And though we have no promise to have our prayers heard, yet there is no doubt but He will hear the prayers of Christ for us, for Him He hears always. (John xi. 42.)

In another part of the Apocalypse we have a beautiful unfolding of this truth,—the mediation of Christ in connexion with the saints' prayers:—"And another angel came and stood at the altar, having a golden censer; and there was given unto him much incense, that he should offer it with the prayers of all saints upon the golden altar which was before the throne." (Rev. viii. 3.) This "angel" was Jesus, the Angel of the everlasting Covenant, who now stands before the golden altar, waving the golden censer, blending the precious incense of His own divine and atoning merits with the prayers of all His saints. Oh, how powerful, then, with God must be the prayers of His people, entwined and blended with the much incense of such a sacrifice! How can we doubt the success of every petition sent up to the court of Heaven, with such an Advocate to present and plead it? Let us, then, "draw near;" let us come boldly to the throne of grace and ask what we will. Is it pardon? ask it. Is it acceptance? ask it. Is it grace? ask it. Is it some temporal good needed? ask it. The petitioner may be unworthy, and the petition imperfect—there may be much sinfulness in the one, and many flaws in the other; but Christ's merit puts it all right. Upon the ground of that merit, God says to you—"I will accept you with your sweet savour." The person first finds favour, and then the offering. Our persons, "accepted in the Beloved," secure the gracious acceptance of our prayers. Tell me not, then, that there is so much sinful taint marring the fragrance of your prayers—such coldness of spirit—such vagrancy of mind—such intrusion of sinful imaginations and desires—such formality, unbelief, and insincerity—such a lack of power, life, and unction,—in a word, so much unpraying prayer; still, approaching as a true penitent, with some yearnings of spirit after God—some Christ-thirsting, Christ-longing in your soul, and asking in His name, and pleading His blood, there shall be a gracious acceptance of your person, and a prompt answer to your prayers, secured by the cloud of incense which goes up moment by moment from the golden censer which the Angel of the everlasting Covenant waves to and fro before the golden altar in heaven. One touch of that censer, one breath of that incense, annihilates in a moment and for ever all the sinful faults and human imperfections adhering to your prayers. "The prayers of all saints." Sweet and encouraging declaration! No one excluded; the weak, the trembling, the fearful, the unbelieving, those of but shallow knowledge, of little grace, and of tried circumstances, who write themselves "less than the least of all saints,"—even their prayers, presented in the name of Jesus, and offered with the much incense that floats from the golden censer, cover the mercy-seat of heaven with their cloud, and fill heaven with their fragrance. Poor trembling soul! doubt no more the full acceptance of your prayers.

How precious, then, is prayer! Prove its preciousness by personal experience, beloved reader. Are you afflicted?—give yourself to prayer. Are you burdened with sin?—give yourself to prayer. Are you oppressed with sorrow?—give yourself to prayer. Are you bereaved of those you loved?—give yourself to prayer. Does God hide the light of His countenance from your soul?—does Jesus suspend the visits of His love, the gracious manifestations of His presence?—give yourself to prayer. Does Satan tempt—does the world persecute—do the saints wound?—give yourself to prayer. Does loneliness depress—does disease invade—does sickness lay low?—give yourself to prayer. Or, are you approaching the valley of the shadow of death—the solemn moment nearing of your spirit's entrance into the eternal world—the grave unvailing its bosom to receive the lifeless tenement?—Give yourself to prayer. Listen to the gentle voice, the kind invitation of thy covenant God and Father,—"Come, my people, enter into thy chambers, and shut thy doors about thee; hide thyself as it were for a little moment, until the indignation be overpast." These "chambers" of repose and security are many and precious. They include the everlasting love of God,—the cross of Jesus,—the covenant of grace,—the mercy-seat,—the promises of Jehovah,—the full and free invitation of the gospel,—the pavilion of Christ's grace,—the clift of the

Rock; yea, to sum all up in one, "the secret place of the Most High," which is the very heart of God's heart,—hidden, enshrined in which, no evil shall touch thee. "For in the time of trouble, He shall hide me in His pavilion; in the secret of His tabernacle shall He hide me." Oh, the charm, the soothing, sanctifying power of prayer! "Prayer is an all-efficient panoply, a treasure undiminished, a mine which never is exhausted, a sky unobscured by clouds, a haven unruffled by storms; it is the root, the fountain, and the mother of a thousand blessings. I speak not of the prayer which is cold, and feeble, and devoid of energy; I speak of that which is the child of a contrite spirit, the offspring of a soul converted, born in a blaze of unutterable inspiration, and winged like lightning for the skies. The potency of prayer hath subdued the strength of fire; it hath bridled the rage of lions, hushed anarchy to rest, extinguished the wars, appeased the elements, expelled demons, burst the chains of death, expanded the gates of heaven, assuaged diseases, repelled frauds, rescued cities from destruction; it hath stayed the sun in its course, and arrested the progress of the thunderbolt: in a word, it hath destroyed whatever is an enemy to man. I again repeat, that I speak not of the prayer engendered by the lips, but of that which ascends from the recesses of the heart. Assuredly, there is nothing more potent than prayer; yea, there is nothing comparable to it. A monarch vested in gorgeous habiliments is far less illustrious than a kneeling suppliant, ennobled and adorned by communion with his God. Consider how august a privilege it is, when angels are present, and archangels throng around; when cherubim and seraphim encircle with their blaze the throne; that a mortal may approach with unrestrained confidence, and converse with heaven's dread Sovereign! Oh, what honour was ever conferred like this! When a Christian stretches forth his hands, and invokes his God, in that moment he leaves behind him all terrestrial pursuits, and traverses on the wings of intellect the realms of life; he contemplates celestial objects only, and knows not of the present state of things during the period of his prayer, provided that prayer be breathed with fervency. Could we but pray with fervency; could we pray with a soul resuscitated, a mind awakened, an understanding quickened, then, were Satan to appear, he would instantaneously fly; were the gates of hell to yawn upon us, they would close again.

"Prayer is a haven to the shipwrecked mariner, an anchor unto them that are sinking in the waves, a staff to the limbs that totter, a mine of jewels to the poor, a security to the rich, a healer of disease, and a guardian of health. Prayer at once secures the continuance of our blessings, and dissipates the cloud of our calamities. O Prayer! O blessed Prayer! thou art the unwearied conqueror of human woes, the firm foundation of human happiness, the source of ever-during joy, the mother of philosophy! The man who can pray truly, though languishing in extremest indigence, is richer than all besides; whilst the being who never bends the knee, though proudly seated as a monarch of nations, is of all men most destitute. Let us, then, direct our thoughts to Him that was poor, yet rich; rich, because He was poor. Let us overlook the enjoyments of the present, and desire the blessings of the future; for so shall we obtain the blessings both of the present and the future. Oh, may we all obtain them through the grace of Christ our Lord, to whom, with the Father and the Holy Spirit, be ascribed all glory, now and for evermore! Amen."[10]

Prayer is one of the essential elements of the hidden and sequestered walk of the believer with God. It is an engagement so sacred,—often blended with an unfolding of the heart so confidential and hallowed,—it would seem as if this were the soul's most suitable and loved companion in solitude. There can be no painful sense of loneliness when the believer is in converse with God. All places are peopled, and all space is filled when occupied by Him. Complain not that the world is a solitude, while Jesus treads its lone and shaded paths by your side. Mourn not that no responses of love and sympathy wake its stillness—that no echoes break upon your ear but those of your moaning spirit, when Christ talks with you by the way, your Friend and Brother. Oh no, you cannot be alone,—without love, without friendship, without sympathy, without society,—when your spirit is absorbed in God, who is all life, all love, all presence. The affecting sentiments of one whose solitude was hallowed and whose loneliness was cheered with holy converse with God, have sublimely expressed these pensive feelings of the heart:—

> "Like the low murmur of the secret stream,
> Which through dark alders winds its shaded way,
> My suppliant voice is heard,—ah, do not deem
> That on vain toys I throw my hours away!
>
> "In the recesses of the forest vale,
> On the wild mountain, on the verdant sod,
> Where the fresh breezes of the morn prevail,
> I wander lonely, communing with God.
>
> "When the faint sickness of a wounded heart
> Creeps in cold shudd'rings through my sinking frame,
> I turn to Thee,—that holy peace impart,
> Which soothes the invokers of Thy awful name.
>
> "O all-pervading Spirit! Sacred beam!
> Parent of life and light! Eternal Power!
> Grant me through obvious clouds one transient gleam
> Of Thy bright essence in my dying hour!"

Prayer is so spiritual an exercise, it behoves us to be cautious how we confound the gift with the grace of prayer. There may exist in some the gift apart from the grace, and in others the grace apart from the gift. It is of great moment that those especially who are to plead with God in behalf of others keep this distinction in view; and while seeking from God the gift, may be yet more assiduous and intense in their seekings of the grace of prayer. Alas, what spiritual deadness, what perfunctory formality may invade our pulpit devotions! What empty censers may we wave in public, and before our God! There may be the beauty of thought, the elegance of diction, the copiousness of language, without, alas! the reality and power of prayer. Oh for the effusion of the Spirit of prayer upon the pulpits of our

---

10   Chrysostom.

land! But not here alone may be traced the deadening influence of a spirit of formality—the existence of the gift apart from the grace of prayer—but the domestic altar and the closet may witness to this separation. How may we know the difference? We think by the following marks. The gift without the grace of prayer is more wont to vent itself in public; but the grace of prayer most seeks the privacy of communion, and loves to pour itself out when none but God and the conscience are the listeners. The gift of prayer alone inflates the soul with pride; the grace of prayer lays it low in its own eyes, and the greater its enlargement and power, the profounder its humiliation before God. The gift of prayer, working alone, inspires the soul with the fond conceit of its own strength; the grace of prayer constrains it to take hold of the strength of Christ. The gift of prayer, apart from the Spirit, is satisfied with the applause of man; the grace of prayer waits in lowliness upon God, seeking no response save the still small voice of the Spirit in the soul. The gift of prayer contents itself with cold, intellectual, rational views of God, His character and works; but the grace of prayer deals closely with the crucified Saviour, is pervaded with the atoning blood, and is mixed with contrition of spirit, confession of sin, filial love, thanksgiving, and adoration. What need have we, then, to look well to our prayers,—honestly to examine our hearts, and ascertain whether our souls have been baptized with the "Spirit of grace and supplication," and if, when we present ourselves before God either in public or in private, we can in some measure adopt the language of Paul, and say, "Truly our fellowship is with the Father, and with His Son Jesus Christ!" Those who restrict themselves to a Formulary of devotion have need to be doubly watchful of the prayerful state of their souls, lest the constant repetition of a "form of sound words" be a substitute for the inward and spiritual grace of prayer. There are many who read prayers—how few who pray them! We can see no serious objection to a prearranged formulary of devotion, provided the heart accompanies the sentiments and words expressed. The form of supplication taught His disciples by our Lord—which indeed, as we have elsewhere observed, is more properly the disciples' prayer—was intended doubtless as a model rather than a mould. We can see no reasonable argument in favour of its rejection; on the contrary, much that pleads for its employment as a summary of great and important petitions needed by the Christian, the Church, and the world. And yet, while thus conceding the lawfulness of a formulary of devotion, we must still keep in mind the essential element of all true prayer,—the spiritual state of the heart with God.

Our subject is suggestive of close self-examination. Prayer is the moral barometer of the soul,—it proves the existence, and tests the tone of our spiritual life. As a man is in his walk with God, so is he as a man of God. As vital religion is from God, so to God it returns, and with God it deals. It is more solicitous what God thinks, how God approves, and to what degree it lives for God, than it is to commend itself to man. The religion that so shapes its course as to stand well with the world,—that can accommodate itself to the world's opinions, blend with the world's pleasures, win the world's smile,—that thinks as the world thinks, acts as the world acts, temporising, compromising, assimilating,—that is not the religion of God and of the Bible. It may clothe itself in a sanctimonious garb—it may multiply its religious forms and ceremonies, keep its saints' days, its matins and vespers, and yet possess not an element of real godliness. O God, search and try us, and vouchsafe to us grace to search and try ourselves, lest there be found in us any false principles, anything untrue and unsound in our religion, any element fatal to our salvation, anything that interposes between us and Christ's finished, atoning work! Now here, beloved reader, is a divine and certain test—the existence and power of prayer in our souls. Prayer restrained, prayer cold, prayer totally neglected, is symptomatic of a low and lifeless state. Reverse this, and you have the clear and unmistakeable indices of a vital, healthy, and spiritual action of the soul. Let us, then, bring our hearts honestly, frequently, and closely to this test. What is the state of your soul's barometer? Unlike that which indicates the natural atmosphere, the mercury of the soul rises when the moral atmosphere lowers. When clouds are gathering thickly and darkly, when storms are rising, and tempests are sweeping, then it often is that prayer is the most vigorous, the most powerful, the most ascending to God. The seasons of adversity, trial, and sorrow, are the most praying seasons with God's people. Prayer often languishes in prosperity. The spiritual barometer is the most depressed when the sky is the most cerulean, and the atmosphere the most serene, and the sun the most brilliant. Ah! how difficult to maintain a humble, watchful, honest walk with God, when the star of temporal good is in the ascendant. We lose sight then of the Star of Bethlehem—of Him whose birth was mean, whose condition was poor, whose life was wreathed with storms, and whose life closed in humiliation, agony, and blood. But seasons of adversity, of sorrow, of suffering, of need,—when the earthly star is fading and sinking,—are halcyon seasons in the history of the child of God. Then it is that spiritual prayer is in the ascendant, that the sun of the soul attains its meridian. Then we turn to God, betake ourselves to the throne of grace, take the low place, humbled, chastened, child-like, and dependent—the will subdued, the heart prayerful, the spirit praiseful, the soul ascending. Look, then, often and closely to the barometer of your soul. This suggests another thought.

Study to maintain an aptitude of soul for prayer. This, we imagine, is the meaning of the divine precept, "Pray without ceasing." Literally this may not be. It would be impossible for you to be incessantly in the act, or breathing out the expressions of prayer. Nor is this necessary. The bird is not always on the wing. There are moments of repose, when it smooths its ruffled plumage, and its pinions gather strength. But it is ever ready for its flight; and at the first pressure of hunger, or the first note of alarm, it expands its wings and soars. So let us cultivate the spirit of prayer— the heart attuned to the holy duty; the mind sitting so loose to earthly employments and cares, as that at any moment of danger or need it may come into the awful presence of God with devout and solemn reverence. This is to "pray without ceasing." We are to relax no season or habit of prayer—but in the closet, in the family, in the social circle, and in the public sanctuary, call upon the name of the Lord. "We are to maintain an uninterrupted and constant spirit of prayer. We are to be in such a frame of mind as to be ready to pray publicly if requested; and when alone, to improve every moment of leisure which we may have when we feel ourselves strongly inclined to pray. That Christian is in a bad state who has suffered himself, by attention to worldly cares, or by light conversation, or by gaiety and vanity, or by reading an improper book, or by eating and drinking too much, or by late hours at night among the thoughtless and the vain, to be brought into such a condition that he cannot engage in prayer with proper feelings. There has been evil done to the soul, if it is not prepared for communion with God at all times, and if it would not find pleasure in approaching His holy throne."[11] Prayer is to the believer what wings are to the bird—it assists his soul heavenward; and when the rude winds of adversity blow, and the seductions of the world would enchain him to earth,—then, resorting to prayer, the believer soars as on eagle's wings to a purer atmosphere and sunnier skies. Such is the Divine promise,—"They that wait upon the Lord shall renew their strength; they shall mount up with wings as eagles; they shall run, and not be weary; and they shall walk, and not faint." See, then, O child of God! that the pinions of thy soul are ever ready for their heavenly flight. Sit so loose to carnal good, hold the creature, however dear, by a band so slight, and creature-blessings by a tie so slender, that at any moment, and in any place, your heart may turn to God, and exclaim,—"Whom have I in heaven but Thee? and there is none upon earth that I desire beside Thee." And as the bird requires no preparation for its flight, save only its instincts of danger or of need, so your soul needs no preparation ere it draws near to God, ere it betakes itself to the throne of grace, save the deep conviction of your poverty and want, your heart's thirst for holiness, your spirit's yearning for Christ. Alas! how many restrain prayer before God because of their low frames! They find their minds are so earthly, their hearts so cold, their spirits so depressed, so strong and unconquerable a distaste and disinclination for prayer, that, yielding to their feelings, they relinquish this, the most quickening and reviving, as it is the most precious and comforting, of all spiritual privileges. But, beloved, the Lord demands of you, ere you approach Him in prayer, no self-fitness, no previous preparation, but that you, a poor, sinful, unworthy soul, needing Christ, coming empty to Christ, bringing all your sins and backslidings, and sorrows and wants to Christ, may "receive out of His fulness grace for grace." Approach Jesus as you are—come with elevated frames, or with depressed frames; with the language of praise, or with the utterance of want; with the gloom of despondency, or with the aspiration of hope,—only fall prostrate at the feet of Jesus, and receive the blessing He is able, and is willing, to bestow—the blessing found only there.

> "All the fitness He requires
> Is to feel your need of Him."

This suggests another thought There is great danger of a wilful quenching in our minds the spirit of prayer. If when the Holy Ghost prompts us to pray—if, when we feel the soft, silent, gentle stirrings of our heart to rise to God, we suppress the emotion, unheed the voice, or postpone the act, we quench the Spirit's influence, and withdrawing, He

---

11 Barnes.

leaves us to a cold and smokeless censer—a heart from whose altar no real prayer ascends. Oh, it is a serious and solemn thing not to have an ear quick to catch the voice of the Spirit—a heart ready to respond to the call of Christ. With more than oriental poetry has the inspired penman, in his graphic description of the Church, portrayed this state:—"I sleep, but my heart waketh: it is the voice of my beloved that knocketh, saying, Open to me, my sister, my love, my dove, my undefiled: for my head is filled with dew, and my locks with the drops of the night. I have put off my coat; how shall I put it on? I have washed my feet; how shall I defile them? My beloved put in his hand by the hole of the door, and my bowels were moved for him. I rose up to open to my beloved; and my hands dropped with myrrh, and my fingers with sweet-smelling myrrh, upon the handles of the lock. I opened to my beloved; but my beloved had withdrawn himself, and was gone: my soul failed when he spake: I sought him, but I could not find him; I called him, but he gave me no answer." (Song of Sol. v. 2-6.) She heeded not the monition of the Spirit,—she responded not to the voice of Jesus,—she quenched the spirit of prayer in her soul; and when she arose to meet her Lord—lo! He was gone! Cultivate then, beloved, a holy aptitude for prayer, an earnest, watchful heeding of its earliest and gentlest call. Then prayer will not be a strange employment or an irksome task. In your closet, in your counting-house, in your morning or evening rambles, amidst domestic cares or professional engagements, your heart will feel the attraction of heaven, and prayer, like a pillar of incense ascending from the altar, will rise wafted to the throne of God.

There is an important view of prayer we must not overlook. Are we not great losers from not cherishing a watchful spirit unto prayer? We ask, we petition, we invoke, but how little expectation is there of God's response; how little patient waiting for the Lord's answer, how little watching for the blessing! Verily, this is an essential and serious defect in our Christianity which must be remedied. But what is the Divine precept touching this point? "Praying always with all prayer and supplication in the Spirit, and watching thereunto with all perseverance and supplication for all saints." (Eph. vi. 18.) "Watching thereunto with all perseverance." The same idea is presented in other words:—"Blessed is the man that heareth me, watching daily at my gates, waiting at the posts of my doors." (Prov. viii. 34.) The allusion here is to the position of the priest, waiting at the door of the tabernacle of the congregation where the Lord had promised to speak unto him, in holy expectation of the Lord's answer; it depicts also the expectant attitude of the congregation itself, watching the opening of the temple-gate, whence the priest would come, bearing in his hands the blessing his intercession had procured. Such must be our watching and waiting for the answer of our prayers. Expect God will answer you, and He will answer. Look for the blessing you have craved, and you shall receive it. To petition, and expect no response,—to ask, and look for no reply,—to pray, and care for no answer,—to implore a boon, and turn away in indifference and unbelief, is to cast the deepest dishonour on a prayer-hearing and a prayer-answering God. Marvel not that God answers neither by fire, nor by dew, nor by the still small voice—you are not waiting at the door of the tabernacle, nor watching at the temple-gate in holy, earnest, sincere desire for, and expectation of, the blessing! This was the Psalmist's position—"I will direct my prayer unto Thee, and will look up." Oh, be this our holy attitude!—looking up above all human improbabilities and impossibilities,—looking above all our sinfulness and unworthiness,—looking above all the dark, depressing, painful circumstances of our position,—looking above creature help, sympathy, and succour,—looking up to God alone! The more we look up to God, the less we shall find it necessary to look down to man. The more we look up to God, the more thoroughly we shall be schooled in the holy art of looking up. David looked up when he had breathed his prayer to God. The disciples looked up when Christ ascended into heaven, and a cloud received Him out of their sight. Stephen looked up amidst the agonies of his martyrdom, and saw Jesus standing at the right hand of God. My soul! do thou look up above thy broken cisterns, thy dark clouds, thy difficulties and thy sorrows, and behold thy God waiting to be gracious, ready to answer. "Why art thou cast down, O my soul? and why art thou disquieted within me? hope in God; for I shall yet praise Him, who is the health of my countenance, and my God." (Ps. xliii. 5.) Be you found, then, beloved, honouring God by a holy, believing expectation. He will regard your cry, and the answer will come. "For the vision is yet for an appointed time, but at the end it shall speak, and not lie: though it tarry, wait for it; because it will surely come, it will not tarry." (Hab. ii. 3.) Oh, for stronger confidence in Jehovah touching prayer! Lord, increase our faith! Is there a suppliant Thou wilt reject? a case Thou wilt despise? a blessing Thou wilt withhold? a want Thou canst not meet? a sinner Thou refusest to comfort? a sin Thou wilt not pardon? or a poor humble penitent Thou wilt not accept? No, not one. Then, Lord, I come, and will wait and watch, nor let Thee go until Thou bless me! Arise, my soul! He calleth thee. Behold, Lord, I come! I come!

With such encouragements to prayer—the Spirit inditing, Christ endorsing, the Father responding—let us draw near and ask large blessings. Already, in answer to prayer, the Church of God in America, in Ireland, in Scotland, and in some parts of our own land, is receiving the baptism of the Spirit. As the tidings reach us of thousands pressing into the kingdom of God in connexion with a work too scriptural in its character, too supernatural in its power, and too decided in its results to be mistaken for the work of man, we exclaim with the wondering and grateful feelings of the Psalmist, "Thou, O God, didst send (marg. shake out) a plentiful rain (marg. a shower of liberalities), whereby Thou didst confirm Thine inheritance, when it was weary." (Ps. lxviii. 9.) The "signs of the times," the spiritual and intelligent study of which we too much overlook, are mighty and impressive in their significance. Christ is about to do great things in behalf of His Church—to "shake out showers of liberalities." The Holy Spirit is on His march through the land, travelling in the greatness of His strength and in the marvels of His grace. The moral barometer of the world indicates the approach of showers of blessings—"the former and the latter rain abundantly." The cloud, now larger than a man's hand, is stretching across continents, oceans, and islands, freighted with life, light, and love to a lost world. "Thy kingdom come," has long been the prayer of the Church. His kingdom has, in measure, come; but it is destined to come in the full triumph of its grace, and in the final acclaim of its glory.

It is yet to come with a power, a victory, and a majesty such as the world never yet has beheld. Jesus is to take to Him His great power and reign. What are these extraordinary movements of the Spirit but a preparing the way for the personal coming and reign of the Lord? Before that great and glorious advent, "this gospel of the kingdom is to be preached in all the world for a witness to all nations, and then shall the end come." In view of this great and predicted fact, we look upon religious Revivals as the ordained and surest pioneers of Christian missions. The baptism of the Holy Ghost in this and other nations is but the arising and girding of the Church of God to go up and possess the land which His Providence has made ready for the "feet of Him that bringeth good tidings, that publisheth peace." The uprootings and overturnings of the nations of the earth are but the usherings in of the kingdom of Jesus. The strongholds of error and of despotism upon the continent of Europe, impaired by time and shaken by revolution, are preparing to yield to truth and liberty. The chains of idolatry, superstition, and caste in heathendom, smitten by rebellion and loosened by mutiny, are ready to fall from the myriads they have for centuries enslaved. India and China, Turkey and Japan, with well-nigh the entire world, for ages hermetically closed to Christ's gospel, are throwing wide their gates to admit and even welcome the messenger and the almoner of Christ's Church. What encouragement this to united, believing, persevering prayer! "Thus saith the Lord, the Holy One of Israel, and his Maker, Ask me of things to come concerning my sons; and concerning the work of my hands command ye me." (Isa. xlv. 11.) Infinite condescension!—worthy of Him who "made Himself of no reputation, and took upon Him the form of a servant, and was made in the likeness of men." Lord, behold us at Thy feet, wrestling with Thy word of promise—"Command ye me!" "Drop down, ye heavens, from above, and let the skies pour down righteousness; let the earth open, and let them bring forth salvation, and let righteousness spring up together."

Let us not be hindered and straitened in our prayers for this precious blessing—the outpouring of the Spirit upon ourselves, upon our families, upon the Church of God, and upon the world—by the idea that the Spirit is already in the Christian Church, the promise and gift of her Lord, a present and inalienable blessing, and that therefore we are not warranted to pray for and expect a fresh outpouring of the Holy Ghost. That the Holy Spirit is the Indweller of the Church of God, abiding with her for ever, and that the renewing and sanctifying of the saints is by Him, we fully and gratefully acknowledge. No declaration of our Lord could be more unmistakeable when He says, "I will pray [to] the Father, and He shall give you another Comforter, that He may abide with you for ever; even the Spirit of truth." But the presence of the Holy Spirit in the Church, and the gracious and especial manifestation of the power of the Spirit in the Conversion of sinners, are two different things—the one not a denial or a contradiction of the other. How cold, how deathlike, how unscriptural that teaching which tells us that because the Spirit is already the Indweller of the Church of God, all prayer and supplication for the expression of His convincing, life-giving, and sanctifying power is a work of supererogation! The outpouring of the Spirit, the Word of God warrants us to look for in these last days. Peter thus quotes the prophecy of Joel:—"And it shall come to pass in the last days, saith God, I will pour out of my Spirit upon all flesh." The effusion of the Spirit on the day of Pentecost was but the commencement of a series of Revivals—the first instalment of the blessing—that were to trace and signalise the gospel and final dispensation. We do not regard these especial baptisms as the giving of another Spirit; it is the same Holy Spirit who converted the three thousand on the day of Pentecost whom we now invoke, and who, in response to these invocations, is graciously pleased to visit the Church with "times of refreshing from the presence of the Lord." We have our Lords own warrant to ask in faith the bestowment of the Spirit—"If ye, then, being evil, know how to give good gifts unto your children, how much more shall your heavenly Father give the Holy Spirit to them that ask Him." This promise and this warrant touching supplication for the manifestation and outpouring of the Holy Spirit was designed to prompt the desire, and guide the prayers, and feed the faith, and inspire the hopes of the Church of Christ to her latest age. And sad will it be for us when we shall cease to offer unto our ascended and glorified High Priest that incense of believing and importunate prayer, which shall enclose the Church and the world within the descending, all-enfolding cloud of a quickening and sanctifying Spirit! "The time is coming, and prophecy has foretold it, when in every land there shall be offered to God a peace-offering—when from the closet and the sanctuary, from the hill-top, the field, the forest-side, where the children of God shall, like Isaac, walk forth at eventide to meditate—the voice of pious supplication shall ascend in one continuous stream; until our globe, as it rolls along its orbit, shall seem but a censer revolving in the hand of the Great High Priest, and pouring out at every aperture a cloud, dense and rich, of incense, fragrant and grateful to God."

> "Come, then, and added to Thy many crowns,
> Receive yet one; the crown of all the earth,
> Thou who alone art worthy!—
> The very spirit of the world is tired
> Of its own taunting questions, ask'd so long—
> 'Where is the promise of your Lord's approach?'
> Come, then, and added to Thy many crowns,
> Receive yet one, as radiant as the rest,
> Due to Thy last and most effectual work—
> Thy word fulfill'd, the conquest of a world."[12]

---

12   William R. Williams, D.D.

Chapter XI.

THE PRECIOUSNESS OF CHRIST'S SYMPATHY WITH OUR INFIRMITIES.

"Himself took our infirmities, and bare our sicknesses."—
Matthew viii. 17.

Our Lord's union with our nature—the essentially divine in coalescence with the perfectly human—was not, as the Doecetae, a branch of the Gnostics, heretically taught, a mere appearance of humanity, a fiction, and illusion;—it was an actual and personal, a living and tangible humanity,—a mysterious and profound, but not less true and visible, manifestation of God in the flesh! It was, probably, in part to refute this early heresy that the Apostle John wrote his Epistle, in which he thus condemns the errorist while he affirms the truth:—"Every spirit that confesseth that Jesus Christ is come in the flesh is of God: and every spirit that confesseth not that Jesus Christ is come in the flesh is not of God: and this is that spirit of antichrist, whereof ye have heard that it should come; and even now already is it in the world." (1 John iv. 2, 3.) It is not, then, less a doctrine essential to the Christian system, or less an evidence of a true Christian, and of a sound Christian teacher, than it is a source of the richest consolation and soothing to the Christian Church, that the Son of God became, by a mysterious union of the two extremes of being, the Son of Man; and as such—"Himself bearing our infirmities, and carrying our sicknesses"— becomes at once a fount of sympathy and love, its soothing and its healing spreading like a sea over our sin and sorrow stricken humanity. In this point of light, the truth of Christ's sympathy with our infirmities—which furnishes the theme of the present chapter—presents itself with an actuality and vividness the most realising and personal. The proper discussion of our subject suggests, in their order, the consideration of the infirmities which appertain to our humanity—our Lord's personal participation in those infirmities—and the preciousness of His sympathy with the varied infirmities of His people.

The existence of physical infirmity in the saints of God is a fact so self-evident as to require no laboured argument. It is the natural effect of sin—a part of the curse under which our humanity came in consequence of the fall. To assert that we were "conceived in sin, and born in iniquity"—as the Bible most distinctly and emphatically does—is to claim for our whole being—physical, moral, and intellectual—the existence of weakness, imperfection, and decay, which no surviving and still lingering emblems of our original stateliness and grandeur can possibly annihilate or conceal. How true a picture of the animate and the inanimate world has the pen of inspiration drawn, when it describes "the whole creation as groaning and travailing in pain together until now!" In this paralysed and convulsed condition the saints of God are equally involved. Our humanity is essentially the same as that from which the electing love and sovereign grace of God has rescued and separated us. We are "by nature children of wrath, even as others." Our humanity differs, from the most enslaved and degraded of our species only as Jesus has borne its sins, removed its curse, and, by the Spirit's renewing and indwelling, has made it the temple of God. Before we enter more fully upon this subject, let us remark, that the bodily infirmities under which the children of God labour are to be regarded rather as the consequences of sin than as in themselves sinful. For the want of clearly observing this distinction, many of the Lord's people walk in bondage. Sin is the cause, infirmity the effect. In all the instances in which the word is employed in the Bible, this idea would seem prominent. Thus, for example, physical deficiencies, bodily weaknesses, or actual sickness, are described as infirmities of our nature. We read of "a certain woman which had been healed of a spirit of infirmity." Her spinal cord was contracted, and she was bowed down and could in no wise lift up herself. We also read that many came to Christ "to be healed of their infirmities;" and that, "in that hour He cured many of their infirmities." And when Paul enjoined upon Timothy the use of a little wine, the plea upon which he enforced the duty was his "often infirmities." And when, in the lowly spirit of the Gospel, he abjures all self-glorying, laying his mouth in the dust, and esteeming himself the chief of sinners and the least of saints, he exclaims, "If I must needs glory, I will glory in the things which concern mine infirmities." And in another place he says, "Therefore I take pleasure in infirmities, in reproaches, in necessities, in persecutions, in distresses, for Christ's sake: for when I am weak, then am I strong." Let it then be distinctly remembered that sin is not an essential adjunct, a necessary concomitant of our nature—it is rather an accident of our being. Our nature was created sinless, reflecting, without a line to deface its beauty, or a shadow to becloud its lustre, the intellectual and moral image of God. This curious and magnificent mechanism, as it came from the hands of the Divine Artificer, was pronounced by Him to be "very good." What a glorious creature was man! No shade of care upon the brow, no hectic flush upon the cheek, no paralysis benumbed the limb, no trembling agitated the nerve, no heart flutter, nor convulsions, nor pain, nor restlessness— nothing, in a word, to shade, deform, or depress his humanity,—he was without sin, and consequently without suffering. We may therefore infer, and the inference is replete with comfort to the holy and spiritual mind, that our bodily infirmities are not sins, and are only to be viewed in that light as, through our unprayerfulness and unwatchfulness, they become causes or occasions of sin. But let us take a more comprehensive view of this subject, seeing that Christ's sympathy extends to all the infirmities to which His people are subject—this it is which makes that sympathy so precious.

Chief and prominent we must place the inbeing of sin—the believer's great infirmity, and the source and parent of all others. Sin is a word easily spoken, soon written—a mere monosyllable—but of what mighty and solemn import! Sin is the cause of all evil, the source of all sorrow, the spring of all suffering—its guilt, tyranny, and condemnation only met, cancelled, and removed by the incarnation and sacrifice of the Son of God. What must be the nature, the magnitude, the terribleness of sin, to demand on the part of God's moral government such an expedient! Now, it is this in-being of sin in the believer that forms the baneful root of all infirmity, and is to his holy mind the greatest of them all. Listen to the inspired language which, in all ages and dispensations, has been but the one cry of the Christian Church—"O wretched man that I am! who shall deliver me from this body of this death?" A deep truth is unfolded here—the principle or body of sin in the believer, as constituting the ground of his profoundest humiliation and sorrow. It is not the dark speck, here and there, as indicating the existence and process of the moral gangrene that produces the painful anxiety of the apostle—it is the corrupt body itself. We come short of just views of sin if we only estimate its enormity by its outbreak here and there—the spots upon the surface. The evil lies deeper and is concealed. We speak of the principle of sin, from which all sin originates. We do not ask you, reader, if you confess and mourn over sin in its external and overt acts,—this, doubtless, you often do with deep self-abasement. But the deepest sorrow for sin is that which springs from the conviction and consciousness of its indwelling principle and power—this should be our profoundest humiliation before God. To think of the depraved nature, the evil heart, the corrupt mind, the empoisoned and impure fountain, the body of sin and death constantly borne about with us—lying down and rising up with us—carried into our most sacred places, and with us in our most hallowed engagements—constantly, inseparably, ever prompting to evil—oh, this is our humiliation, and this should be our sorrow. Beloved, count not yourself to have arrived at any proper or adequate view of the burden and sinfulness of sin, until you have been brought to embody in your daily acknowledgments, humiliation, and sorrow, the sin that dwelleth in you. Then shall we be set upon the great work of mortification—and only then. No longer seeking merely the moral filtration of the impure streams, we shall task our utmost energies to the work of purifying the fountain. And who seeth not that, this done—the source of evil met, the heart seasoned with grace—we shall then the more cheerfully and successfully address ourselves to the work of "cleansing ourselves from all filthiness of the flesh and spirit, perfecting holiness in the fear of God?"

There are other infirmities which may be classed as constitutional. Our spiritual and mental constitutions, like our physical, vary. As each individual has a natural constitution peculiar to himself, so has he a moral and intellectual one. Our constitutional infirmities are not all alike. The temperament of some is warm, excitable, impetuous; they have ardent, impulsive feelings; their affections are fervent, their sensibilities strong, their emotional nature intense—they can sympathise, can weep, can love. The temperament of others is cold, phlegmatic, immovable; they have but little of the emotional, the susceptible, the sympathizing, and it requires a great calamity often to rouse them to feeling. There are yet others, whose mental characteristics are those of depression, despondency, and gloom. Overlooking the bright and cheerful tints of life's landscape, they love to ruminate upon its dark and somber hues,—always gazing upon the gloomiest aspect of the picture, and dwelling with morbid pleasure upon the most unpromising and hopeless. Others, again are of a sanguine and hopeful temperament; they live in a world of illusion and romance; without adequate premises they leap to conclusions, and without proper data they assume facts; credulous, unsuspecting, and confiding, they take for granted what some minds accept only upon demonstration. Now, all these are, doubtless, constitutional infirmities. It is an infirmity to be too feeling; it is an infirmity to be too cold. It is an infirmity to be too trusting; it is equally an infirmity to be too suspicious. It is an infirmity to be totally fascinated by the sunny, golden, and mellow tints of the picture, and equally so to be mentally absorbed and depressed by its shaded and gloomy colouring. "This is my infirmity," may be the exclamation, as each one passes in review. Yes, they are infirmities: levity, gravity; the sanguine, the desponding; the feeling, the phlegmatic; the confiding, the distrusting; the sensitive, the impassable; the ardent, the frigid; the liberal, the parsimonious; the credulity that believes anything, the scepticism that believes nothing;—all these—and a thousand more constitutional characteristics that might be adduced—in consequence of the sin that dwelleth in us, are infirmities clinging to our fallen humanity, the source and the occasion frequently of our deepest and bitterest sorrows.

And then there are infirmities purely of a physical nature. We embody and bear about with us the seeds and germs of all disease and decay, which, in any climate, in any place, and at any moment, may develop itself, and which, indeed, are gradually and imperceptibly, but most surely, conducting us to the grave. Who can behold the frailty of some, the nervousness of others, the incessant suffering of others more, —of multitudes who know not a day's perfect health, an hour's freedom from pain, a night's unbroken sleep—and not be convinced that the Church of God is "compassed with infirmity?"

Under this head of infirmity may be classed, too, the sufferings and persecutions, the privations, trials, and temptations, to which the saints are constantly exposed, and by which they are frequently assailed. The soul has its infirmities as well as the body; there are spiritual and mental, as well as natural and physical, weaknesses and frailties. Sin, and the curse which followed in its wake, have sown man's path, from his cradle to his tomb, with mingled seed. At each step, and each bend, there springs up a multitude of various ills, and woes, and sorrows. The tare grows side by side with the wheat; the thistle with the rose; the nightshade with the myrtle; the cypress with the laurel;—joy and sorrow, laughter and tears, hope and despondency, the marriage and the tolling bell, all, all blend together in our march to eternity. The woof of our humanity is of many colours; the stones that pave our pathway to the grave are of variegated hues. Such are the varied and dissimilar conditions of God's people. It is the infirmity of one believer that his faith is always faltering; of another, that his courage is always failing: of one, that he is of a desponding tendency of mind, taking but little of the comfort and hope of the gospel; and of another, that he confides too implicitly in himself, and looks too exclusively to his ever-varying and fluctuating experience for the strength and evidence of his Christianity. The experience of Asaph is, doubtless, that of many;—"Will the Lord cast off for ever? and will He be favourable no more? Is His mercy clean gone for ever? doth His promise fail for evermore? Hath God forgotten to be gracious? hath He in anger shut up His tender mercies? And I said, This is my infirmity" (Ps. lxxvii. 7-10.)

It must always, too, be considered one of the infirmities of our spiritual condition, that we look so much to the dark providences of God in our history, rather than to His power, faithfulness, and love in the providence. God must be in all His providential dispensations. They are the chariots in which He rides. "He maketh the clouds His chariot." When, then, we are absorbed in a fearful, unbelieving view of the chariot that comes near to us, and overlook Him who sits in it—the God of love, our Father, our Friend—it is no marvel that, with good old Jacob, we exclaim, "All these things are against me." Beloved, there is nothing that is really against you if you are in union with Christ Jesus. There is no enchantment, no divination. It is a "curse causeless!" It may be a tedious way, a narrow way, a thorny way, a self-denying way, a way bedewed with your tears, vocal with your sighs, perhaps tinted with the oozings of your heart's blood—nevertheless it is a right way by which Jesus is leading you, step by step, home to God. You will see that it was all right when you arrive there; and then with the countless minstrelsy of heaven redeemed like you by precious blood, and who with you have come out of great tribulation, you will exclaim, "He hath done all things well."

There is a tendency, too, through the infirmity of our faith, to hesitate and falter when summoned to walk in some path of duty. It is seldom that God so leads us but at the sacrifice of some creature good, the surrender of some, cherished idol. It is a part of that moral discipline that imparts symmetry and completeness to our Christian character. The call of duty is always the call of God. And yet how we hesitate and demur! How we linger upon the loved spot we are to leave—how we cling to the precious ties we are to sunder—how we grasp the sacred enjoyments we must perhaps for ever relinquish! But the path of duty is onward—and onward must be our course. Then we learn how great is the infirmity of our grace. We once thought we could do anything for Christ—now that His glory and our interests clash, we pause, we weep, we reason. But it is only our infirmity, and the Lord knoweth that it is so. And as sure as He enables us by His grace to take the first step in the path of duty—fearful, trembling, hesitating though it be—He comes and helps each succeeding one by the sympathy of His love, and by the succourings of His grace; and we exclaim, "I can do all things through Christ who strengtheneth me." In this way of duty, in which there is so severe and lingering a crucifixion of self, lessons in the divine life are learned, and truths in God's Word are experienced, such as, probably, would not be in any other way. In the world there are schools for different branches of knowledge and science, where the principles and systems peculiar to each one are alone taught. Christ has different schools for His disciples:—there is the school of correction, the school of trial, the school of sorrow, the school of temptation, the school of self-denial, the school of active service, the school of patient endurance—in one or all of these schools Jesus is instructing the disciples on earth, and training them for heaven, teaching them the peculiar lessons, and bringing them into the experience of the peculiar truths found in no other way. There are two natures in the believer, the active and the passive—both of which the Lord will unfold and discipline, and both shall alike honour and glorify Him. Peradventure you have reasoned thus—that, because the infirmities of the body or of the mind prevent you from the active service of Christ, you are therefore but a dry tree, a useless member of the body, a cumberer of the ground. Ah! my reader, the Lord has wisely chosen for you another and a different school—that of passive submission to the Divine will—the school of suffering, which is the school of God. Your duty, strength, and service for Christ is to sit still, to cultivate in your soul the passive graces of the Holy Spirit; and so by meekness, quietness, and silence, glorify your Father in heaven.

"They also serve, who only stand and wait."

But it is possible the Lord sees fit to train you for glory in the school of active and laborious employ. He may summon you to a post of labour at home which, perhaps, your judgment would the last have selected, or from which your taste, feelings, and inclinations recoil. Or, it may be, He sends you to the far heathen, severing the fond and sacred endearments of home, and sundering the ties that bound you by associations so precious to the land of your birth. Well, beloved, it is Christ's school, in the which He is teaching, disciplining, and training you for heaven. By nature, by providence, and by grace He has fitted you for active service in the Church, and into His vineyard He condescendingly sends you. While others are learning the same lesson, and are being taught the same truth—the lesson of their own poverty and nothingness, and the truth of Jesus' all-sufficiency and unspeakable preciousness—amid scenes of trial and sickness, of suffering and want, you are being taught by the Master in the school of toil, of hardship, and of self-denial. Be it so, beloved. Each line from the circumference leads to the one centre—Jesus; and Jesus will ere long bring both the active and the passive disciple He has trained for glory on earth, to rejoice together in the same happy and eternal home in heaven.

We have now reached an essential and touching part of our subject—Christ's personal participation with the infirmities of His people. "Himself took our infirmities, and bare our sicknesses." "Himself" did it. It was a personal act. He confided the task to, and He imposed the burden upon, no other. Nor would He admit a partner in the transaction. None should share it with Him. Not a sin, not a sorrow, not a pang, not an infirmity, not a tear, not a sigh would He divide with another. He would tread the path alone, and of the people there should be none with Him. "Himself took our infirmities." Oh, in what a touching light this places the love of our Jesus—the all-concentrating, all-absorbing, all-engrossing love of our Emmanuel—for His people! He so loved us that He would do all for us Himself, nor share the work, nor divide the glory, nor participate the love of another being in the universe. Himself did it, and did it alone. The question then arises—In what way may we regard our Lord as taking our infirmities and bearing our sicknesses? We think the answer will be supplied by the following considerations:—

First, by His assumption of our humanity. He could only come under the obligation to participate in our circumstances by taking up into union with the Godhead the nature that sin and the curse had bowed to the earth. The human nature to which His Godhead stooped was as free from the taint and pollution of sin as His divinity, and yet was it real humanity. "A body hast thou prepared me." "He was made sin" (or an offering for sin) "for us who knew no sin." He was "holy, harmless, undefiled, and separate from sinners." Keep firm hold of this doctrine of your faith, O believer! The shadow of a shade of sin in the human nature of the Son of God would have been eternal destruction to His elect Church—fatal to the accomplishment of His sacrifice, and the salvation of His people. We have said that it was real, true, actual humanity. Its mysterious and close union with the Godhead did not alter it, even as there was no essential change in the Godhead when it took up into union the manhood. There was a union—a personal and inseparable union—of the two natures, but no change in either—both retained their peculiar and essential properties. The humanity was blest by its union with the Deity, but not changed, in the least degree, into the essentially divine. It was filled and enriched with excellent gifts—even the Holy Spirit without measure—but was not in the least degree elevated into an equality with the Divine nature—it retained its own property intact. In taking upon Him the form of a servant, Christ did not abdicate the form of God. He, indeed, emptied Himself and made Himself of no reputation, and was reputed a man, and a very poor and de-spised man, too; yet He never ceased to be God. The glory of His Godhead was indeed enshrouded, but not extinguished; it was obscured, but not lost. Our infirmities shaded the lustre of the Sun, but the Sun behind those infirmities shone with undimmed and undiminishable splendour. "He could not have been a sufficient Mediator had He ceased to be God, and He had ceased to be God had He lost any one perfection proper to the Di-vine nature; and losing none, He lost not this of unchangeableness, which is none of the meanest belonging to the Deity. Why by this union with the Divine nature should He lose this any more than He lost His omniscience, which He discovered by His knowledge of the thoughts of men; or His mercy, which He manifested to the height in the time of His suffering? That is truly a change when a thing ceaseth to be what it was before. This was not in Christ. He assumed our nature without laying aside His own. When the soul is united to the body, doth it lose any of those perfections that are proper to its nature? Is there any change either in the substance or qualities of it? No; but it makes a change in the body, and of a dull lump it makes it a living mass, conveys vigour and strength to it, and by its power quickens it to sense and motion. So did the Divine nature and the human remain entire; there was no change of the one into the other, as Christ by a miracle changed water into wine, or men by art change sand or ashes into glass. And when He prays for the glory He had with God before the world was, He prays that a glory He had in His Deity might shine forth in His person as Mediator, and be evidenced in that height and splendour suit-able to His dignity, which had been so lately darkened by His abasement; that as He had appeared to be the Son of man in the infirmity of the flesh, He might appear to be the Son of God in the glory of His person, that He might appear to be the Son of God and the Son of man in one person."[13]

But His assumption of our humanity—"the Word made flesh"—was only a part of His participation with our infirmities—the physical infirmities of our nature. The body He took was but the vehicle by which He acted. He approached yet closer to the actual bearing when he was made under the curse, and took upon Him our sins. As sin and the curse which followed are the sources of all our infirmities—mental, moral, and physical—so, by becoming a sin-offering for the one, and coming under the other, He "Himself took our infirmities, and bare our sicknesses." By this act of bearing our sins, He more truly and strictly took our infirmities than though He had actually sinned as we have sinned. Our great, our grand, our chief infirmity is—sin! This is the parent, and root, and spring of all infirmity. Jesus took our sins: "He bare our sins in His own body on the tree;" "He was wounded for our transgressions, He was bruised for our iniquities." Could language be stronger? Not merely the punishment for sin, but sin itself was laid upon Him!—yet was He "without sin." And thus it was our blessed Lord "took our infirmities, and bare our sicknesses." And now trace His own actual, personal participation in our infirmities. Jesus knew what it was to be weary—to hunger and thirst—to be homeless and friendless—to be maligned, traduced, slandered—to be wounded by, foes—to be deserted by friends—to be taunted by men—to be tempted by Satan—to be forsaken by God. Was not this a taking upon Him our infirmities? Did not this include them all? What is thine infirmity, O child of God? Is it sin?—Jesus bore it. Is it sickness?—Jesus carried it. Is it a weak, infirm, frail body?—Jesus assumed it. Is it loneliness?—Jesus lived much in solitude. Is it irritability, impatience, fretfulness, nervousness?—Jesus bore the sin and curse from whence this springs. Is it wounded love, betrayed confidence, disappointed friendship?—Jesus trod this shaded path before you. Is it poverty, straitened circumstances, humiliating dependence?—Jesus too was poor, and, succoured by the charities of those who ministered of their substance to His wants, was subjected to this humiliation. Are you bereaved?—keenly did Jesus feel this sorrow, when His tears fell fast and thick upon the grave of His friend at Bethany. Tell me, then, have you an infirmity which your Lord did not bear before you? "Himself took our infirmities, and bare our sicknesses." How illustriously did Christ exhibit this assumption of, and sympathy with, our infirmities when He was on earth! Take a general survey. He healed the sick—restored sight to the blind—made the lame to walk—the deaf to hear—and lifted up those that were bowed down. Nor this only. He restored reason to its throne—ejected demons from their usurped dominion of the soul—chased the cloud of sadness from the spirit, and made the widow's heart to sing for joy. How beautiful and artless the narrative—how graphic and lifelike the description!—"When even was come, they brought unto Him many that were possessed with devils: and He cast out the spirits with His word, and healed all that were sick: that it might be fulfilled which was spoken by Esaias the prophet, saying, Himself took our infirmities, and bare our sicknesses." Pause, and contemplate the scene—it is full of poetry and power. It is twilight—or, as Mark narrates, "at even when the

---

13   Charnock.

sun did set" All nature is in harmony with the touching spectacle. The sun has almost finished his daily course, his burning wheels reposing upon the utmost verge of the sky. The last smile of day yet lingers, gilding with liquid gold the lofty dome of the Temple, and tipping with streaming silver the mountain's brow and the leafy spires of the grove. All is hushed, as if Nature itself were dead. The confused din of the tumultuous city has ceased, and the toil-worn labourer rests from his employ. The weary winds forget to blow—the gentle gales have fanned themselves to rest— not a wavelet breaks the smooth surface of the lake. The aspen ceases to quiver, and echo herself slumbers. This is the hour and this the scene Jesus has chosen for His works of benevolence and power. Holy and precious the instruction! Is it, beloved, the twilight of life with those on whose behalf we would implore the compassion and help of the Saviour? Is the sun of human existence just setting, his last, his latest rays falling upon the world's gray landscape, now receding into the deep shades of night? Hear you their plaintive cry, "Woe unto us! for the day goeth away, for the shadows of evening are stretched out?" Take heart, my brother! The sun has not yet gone down—night's darkness has not yet come; it is not too late to bring in faith and hope the objects of your sympathy and love to Jesus. It was "at even, when the sun did set, they brought unto Him all that were diseased, and He healed them." What Jesus then was He is now, "the same yesterday, today, and for ever." Despair not, then, of their salvation. Lay them down at His feet, cast them upon His heart, take hold of His robe, nor let Him go until He speaks the word, and lo! "at evening-time it shall be light." Blessed Saviour! The world's din is hushed—the thick shades of evening are gathering over life's landscape—the sun of human probation touches the horizon—the long, dark night of eternity approaches—the all-important crisis has arrived—one look, one word, one touch from Thee, and there shall be healing, there shall be light, there shall be life!

How precious, then, the sympathy of Christ with human infirmity! His fitness thus to sympathise is portrayed by the apostle as inspiration alone could depict it—"We have not an high priest which cannot be touched with the feeling of our infirmities; but was in all points tempted like as we are, yet without sin. Let us therefore come boldly unto the throne of grace, that we may obtain mercy, and find grace to help in time need. For every high priest, taken from among men, is ordained for men in things pertaining to God, that he may offer both gifts and sacrifices for sins: who can have compassion on the ignorant, and on them that are out of the way; for that he himself also is compassed with infirmity." Behold your Lord's fitness to share and sympathise with all your infirmities! He was "encompassed with infirmity." He knew what hunger and thirst were—He knew what labour and fatigue were—He knew what languor and sleeplessness were—He knew what pain and suffering were—He knew what spiritual depression and mental darkness were—He knew what the fiery darts of temptation were—He knew what the weight, and curse, and sorrow of sin were—He knew what the assaults of the world, the malignity of foes, the fickleness of friends, the distrust and woundings of brethren were—He knew what it was to be denied by one disciple, to be betrayed by another, and to be forsaken by all! Child of God! what more shall Christ endure, what ruder path shall He tread, what deeper sorrow shall He experience, what bitterer cup shall He drink, what darker cloud shall He penetrate, what infirmities more human, more severe, more humiliating, shall He take, in order to be touched with the feeling of yours? Will not this suffice to wake your heart to love, to win your mind to confidence, to inspire your soul with hope, to replenish your spirit with joy, and tune your lips with praise—that Christ's sympathy, so human yet divine, all so tender, all so clinging, all so personal, entwines around your every infirmity— bodily, mental, spiritual—and makes it all His own? "Touched with the feeling of our infirmities."

"And dost thou weep in sorrow, brother?
Think not thou hast a lonely lot;
The very pang now thine, Another
Endured for thee, and murmur'd not.

"To consecrate the path of sorrow,
He left the glory of the skies;
And deign'd our suffering flesh to borrow,
That He with grief might sympathise.

"Dost mourn beneath the fierce temptation?
On Him the tempter's shafts were cast.
Are thine the waves of tribulation?
Oft o'er His soul those waters pass'd.

"Each suffering that enthrones thy pillow,
Is felt within thy Saviour's heart;
His hand will hold thee o'er each billow,
For He hath felt thy every smart.

"He who stood by the sisters weeping,
Their brother raised, and dropt the tear,
Marks all thy tears with eye unsleeping,
When grief bends o'er the recent bier.

"Though far removed from mortal vision,
His heart still beats with sympathy;
The sufferings of His earthly mission
Have left deep scars, which plead for thee.

"In all thy sufferings, think not, brother,
Thine is a lone, unfriended lot;
Look up, and feel there is Another,
In sympathy who ceaseth not."[14]

"And bare our sicknesses." You inquire, How could this be, since Christ knew not bodily disease? But it was not necessary, in order to constitute a perfect sympathy in Christ with our physical infirmities, that He

---

14   Rev. W. J. Brook, M.A.

should know in His own person what sickness was. He bare our sicknesses when He bare our sins, and by His atonement put them for ever away. If He bore the cause of all our sorrows and infirmities, surely He is fitted to sympathise with its effects—and sickness is one. And when Jesus ministers at our sickbed, imparting succour and soothing, alleviation and recovery,—when He approaches and vouchsafes patience of spirit, and strength of endurance, and submission to the Divine will, giving gracious manifestations of Himself by day, and songs of praise and thanksgiving in the night season, and then raises you up again to health, to duty and service—surely, then, He may be said, in a most emphatic sense, to bear our sicknesses. Sick believer! you are not alone—Christ is with you. He knows all your weakness, infirmity, and pain. He understands perfectly the mysterious relation of mind and body, and can enter into all those delicate shades and subtile distinctions in the mutual operation of the one upon the other, which escape the eye even of the most skilful and vigilant. What is purely mental, what is simply physical in your case, and how they sympathise and often seem to blend, is to Him who bear our sicknesses when He took our sins, and who rebukes and heals all our diseases now, an object of the intensest interest. Suffering one! Christ is bearing that suffering with you. The burning fever, the writhing pain, the faintness, the languor, the sinking—all is known to Him. The difficulty of concentrated and consecutive thought, your inability to meditate, to read, to pray, the absence of spiritual enjoyment, the dimmed evidences, the beclouded hope, the fears and tremblings—all, allare entwined with your Redeemer's sympathy. His "grace shall be sufficient for you," His "strength shall be made perfect in your weakness;" and thus you shall be enabled to "glory in your infirmities, that the power of Christ may rest upon you."

With the infirmity of prayer we may especially invoke and expect the aid of Christ's precious sympathy. That there is a close relation between the two, is clear from the passages we have already quoted, and, for our argument, will quote again. The reasoning of the apostle is, "We have not an High Priest which cannot be touched with the feeling of our infirmities; but was in all points tempted like as we are, yet without sin." Then follows the exhortation—"Let us therefore come boldly unto the throne of grace, that we may obtain mercy, and find grace to help in time of need." The connexion of our infirmity in prayer, and the tender, succouring sympathy of Christ with that particular infirmity, is adduced as an encouragement to pray. And who is not sensible of infirmity in prayer? In no spiritual duty, perhaps, is our earthliness, weakness, and failure more manifest. In proportion to the elevation, spirituality, and solemnity of the engagement, is our frailty and shortcoming. It is your infirmity that you feel such a reluctance to pray and that when you rouse yourself to the privilege, it is to you a burden and a task. It is your infirmity that, at the Mercy-Seat, your mind is so wandering, your thoughts are so vagrant, your heart is so divided , that, in spite of your endeavours to concentrate the mind on the great business of converse with God, it starts off like a broken bow; and the feelings, that ought to dissolve and flow forth in one ardent current of affection, congeal as into icicles around the Mercy-Seat, bathed in the very sunbeams of Divine love. The deep consciousness, too, of your sinfulness operates often as dissuasive to prayer. You cannot imagine how one so unworthy may be permitted—yea, invited—to approach; and when you approach, the suspicion haunts your breast that such petitions as yours can never find acceptance with God. But we have not an High Priest who cannot be touched with the feeling of this infirmity. What a provision has His mediatorial work made for it in the unceasing sympathy of the Holy Spirit. Thus reasons the apostle—"Likewise the Spirit also helpeth our infirmities: for we know not what we should pray for as we ought; but the Spirit itself maketh intercession for us with groanings which cannot be uttered." (Rom. viii. 26.) To this intercession of the Spirit He adds the merits of His own oblation. Blending, as we have shewn in the preceding chapter, the incense of His merits with the incense of our prayers, and tenderly commiserating the feebleness and frailty of a nature which, "when it would do good, finds evil present with it," He graciously purifies and perfumes each petition, and then presents it with acceptance to God. Come boldly, then, to the throne, ye timid, trembling souls!—ye whom sins distress, whom guilt burdens, whom sorrow bows, whom infirmity disheartens,—for you have a "High Priest who can be touched with the feeling of your infirmity," and who invites you to draw near and ask what you will in His name.

If Christ patiently bears and tenderly sympathises with your infirmities, be you as patient and sympathising towards the infirmities of your fellow-Christians. In this respect "let the mind be in you which was also in Christ Jesus." Our brethren are encompassed with infirmity—each having his own and peculiar cross to carry, his burden to bear. Learn to be like Christ—gentle, patient, charitable, and sympathising. The sympathy which the Gospel inculcates in the disciples of Christ towards our fellow-disciples is large and comprehensive in its nature. The precept is—"Rejoice with them that do rejoice, and weep with them that weep." The exhortation is—"We then that are strong ought to bear the infirmities of the weak, and not to please ourselves." Now, the feeling implied in these words is something more than sympathy, or at least as commonly understood,—it is sympathy in its strict, literal, and legitimate import,—something far exceeding ordinary pity or commiseration. The family of God is one household, one brotherhood. And the essential unity of this one family is in nothing more truly and touchingly exhibited than in the oneness of sorrow and of joy which pervades alike each member of the sacred household. But, as if the Holy Spirit would define yet more clearly the nature of true sympathy, the Church of God is presented under the similitude, not of a family only, but of a body. Alas! we find not always in a family the mutual affection and confidence, the sympathy and intercourse which ought to distinguish and hallow an institution so sacred and precious as the domestic. But if we pass from the similitude of the family to that of the body, we think we shall have a more vivid conception of the nature of that sympathy which ought to animate the Church of Christ. "Now ye are the body of Christ, and members in particular." The sympathetic union of the body—each part with the other, and all with the whole—is of so close, tender, and inseparable a nature as not to be surpassed nor equalled. The sympathy which a sound member of the body has with a suffering member, is a sympathy which makes that suffering its own. The network of nerve, so fine and universal, which extends from the censorium to the furthest extremity, indicates to the remotest member the existence of suffering in any one part of the body, and instantly awakens a responsive sympathy, which amounts, in fact, to a corresponding uneasiness and suffering. There may be said to be actual pain in one member when there is sympathy with positive pain in another. So should it be in the Church of God, which is "the body of Christ." In virtue of our individual membership, we are to make a brothers or a sister's affliction, sorrow, and infirmity as much ours as if it were our own. If one brother is wronged, wounded, slandered—or another is bereaved, afflicted, tried— or yet another is borne down by some heavy, clinging infirmity;—I am to make that brother s wound, that brothers affliction, that brother's infirmity my own. That blow is to be upon me as well as upon him, and that wound is to penetrate my heart as it penetrates his:—"That there should be no schism in the body; but that the members should have the same care one for another. And whether one member suffer, all the members suffer with it; or one member be honoured, all the members rejoice with it." (1 Cor. xii. 25, 26.) "Bear ye one another's burdens, and so fulfil the law of Christ." Such is the sympathy of our great and glorious Head. "In all their afflictions He was afflicted." And the trials, and sorrows, and infirmities which still adhere to His Church on earth, the Holy Ghost denominates the "afflictions of Christ." In behalf, then, of Christ's infirm and suffering body, we bespeak your patience, gentleness, and sympathy. Speak gently, or, rather, speak not at all, of a brother's failing; unveil not a sister's weakness to another eye. Act towards that infirm or erring one as though that infirmity and that error were your own. Imitate your Lord and Master. "For even Christ pleased not Himself; but, as it is written, The reproaches of them that reproached thee fell on Me." Guided by this principle, actuated by this spirit, and imitating this example, you will be gentle towards those who are "weak in the faith," will participate in "the infirmities of the weak," and, "if a man be overtaken in a fault, ye which are spiritual will restore such an one in the spirit of meekness: considering thyself, lest thou also be tempted." Think not, beloved, that we are exacting too much from you in requiring that you should thus identify yourself with the Christian sufferer, and act as though that sufferer were yourself. Your common Christianity demands it, and your exemplification of the sympathy is one of the surest tests of your membership. And our identification with a brother's infirmity is nothing more than the practical recognition of our being "members one of another;" and nothing less was meant by the apostle when he enjoined on believers, that they should "remember those who were in bonds," not merely as pitying and commiserating, but as actually "bound with them." Lamb of God! mould us to Thy truth, and make us like Thyself!

> "Lord, leave us not to wander lonely
> Through this dark world, unloved by Thee;
> All other friends are helpless only,
> Though full of love as friends may be.
> Drear are the fondest homes around us,
> Sad, like our hearts, when Thou art far;
> When Thou hast sought us, heard us, freed us,

How sweet Thy consolations are!
Hear us, cheer us,
Lord, and leave us not!

"Leave us not when pride and anger
In the heart would dare rebel;
Claim us in our utmost danger,
Calm us at the mouth of hell.
Leave us not till we inherit
Charity that works no ill,
And we hear Thy gentle Spirit
Truly whisper—'Peace, be still!'
Hear us, cheer us,
Lord, and leave us not!

"Leave us not in days of trial;
Let us act at duty's call,
Though it lead to self-denial,
Though we have to give up all.
Raised on high, or humbled lowly,
Praised or scorn'd from land to land,
Bear us up, our Father holy,
Bear our burdens in Thy hand.
Hear us, cheer us,
Lord, and leave us not!

"When of friends death has bereft us,
Let us still in Thee rejoice:
Near us when in doubt, to guide us;
Near us when we faint, to cheer;
Near in battle's hour, to hide us;
Nearer ever, and more dear.
Hear us, cheer us,
Lord, and leave us not!

"Leave us not when foes come nigher,
Cheer us when the grave looks cold;
Lead us onward, upward, higher,
Forward to the gates of gold.
Leave us not when ailing, failing,
Sore depress'd, and bending low;
Be Thy love then most availing,
Then to aid us be not slow.
Hear us, cheer us,
Lord, and leave us not!

"Leave us not till Thou hast brought us
To the holy, wealthy place,
There to see Thee who hast bought us,
Fought our fight, and won our race:
There to hear no more the shouting,

And the thunder of our foes;
Danger past, and past all doubting,
And the grave's austere repose.
Hear us, cheer us,
Lord, and leave us not!"[15]

---

15   Emmet.

Chapter XII.

THE DEATH OF THE SAINTS PRECIOUS.

"Precious in the sight of the Lord is the death of His saints."—
Psalm cxvi. 17.

There are two stand-points from which the believer views death, so widely separated and so totally dissimilar as essentially to change both its character and its appearance. The first is the prospective view—the looking forward to death. From this position the spectacle is one from which even the feelings of the Christian instinctively recoil. Death is a part, a terrible part, of the curse; and no firmness of faith in Christ, or brightness of Christian hope, can entirely disarm the feeling, that it is a momentous thing even for a saint of God to die! In the prospective view of death, it appears in its pure, unmitigated character—an arbitrary sovereign, an armed despot, a relentless foe, a melancholy and inevitable crisis of our being; severing the spirit from the body, the soul from home, the heart from all its loved and cherished ties of earth; and terminating, too, the believer's witness for God, his service for Christ, and his mission to man. In looking forward, then, upon death, we marvel not that, from this standpoint of time, the saints of God should shudder at the prospect.

But the second view of death is the retrospective—the looking back upon death. How different the spectacle! how changed its aspect! It is from the stand-point of glory that "the spirits of just men made perfect" survey death. The dread crisis is passed, the cold river is crossed, the enemy is conquered, the victory is won; and standing among the heavenly minstrelsy, the palm-bearing throng who line the golden sands of the heavenly Canaan, and from thence looking back upon their defeated foe, they raise their paean of triumph yet more expressive and melodious than that which rose in the triumphant song of Israel, "Sing ye to the Lord, for He hath triumphed gloriously; the horse and the rider hath He thrown into the sea." "Death is swallowed up in victory, mortality in life!"

But even the prospective of death is not without its gleams of irradiation to the believer in Jesus. It is not all sadness and gloom, blessed be God! Separating from it all that is of nature and sense, and viewing it in the light of the cross and with the eye of faith, we can see the beauty and feel the force of the words of the epitaph which the Spirit has inscribed upon the tomb of all who sleep in Christ—"Blessed are the dead which die in the Lord from henceforth: yea, saith the Spirit, that they may rest from their labours; and their works do follow them." Believer in Jesus! we are

149

about to present to you the Gospel view of death; and although it is the sad prospective, yet it is not all cypress which climbs around the gloomy portal that conducts you into the dark valley; the laurel is there; the ever-bright, ever-living laurel, entwines with the dreary cypress, and tells of victory and of hope. "Precious in the sight of the Lord is the death of His saints."

In the preceding pages we have portrayed the character, defined the principles and privileges of the saints of God, unfolding, in the progress of our discussion, many great and precious things appertaining to their order. One view yet remains—and this will form an appropriate close to the volume—their departure to glory to be for ever with Christ, and the preciousness of their translation to the Lord. "Precious in the sight of the Lord is the death of His saints."

Until the personal coming of the Lord—to which we may presently advert—to quicken the sleeping saints and to translate the living, death is the inevitable condition of the saints. They die as others die—it is a part of the curse to which all must submit, although, in the experience of the believer, it truly is the "curse causeless." The Lord could, if so it pleased Him, exempt them from the long and painful process of disease and decay, and without their seeing death, without a cloud or a fear, take them to glory. In the case of some He does. In a moment, in the twinkling of an eye, they are absent from the body and they are present with the Lord. This He sometimes does with those whom He early calls by grace and as early calls to glory. It is not that He loves them less, but that He loves them more, that He takes them soonest to be with Himself. "Whom God loves best He takes soonest." The son of Jeroboam, who only of that family had "something good in him toward the Lord God of Israel," came to an early grave. We repeat that God could, if most for His glory, take all His saints to heaven without their tasting the "bitterness of death." But it pleases Him that they should tread the path their Lord and Master trod, who, in all the events of His life, "left us an example that we should follow His steps." But while the saints of God must die, there yet is much in death from which they are exempt. They are exempt from it as a penalty, as a sting, as a condemnation. Death in the case of believers is not a curse, but a blessing; it is not a penalty, but a privilege. Death is one of the precious blessings of the covenant of grace—quite as much so as life. "All things are yours...whether life or death." Death is as much a covenant blessing as is the pardon of our sins, or the justification of our persons. Christ met death, the "king of terrors," clad in all the darkness, and horror, and bitterness of the curse. He grappled with it, tasted it, received its sting, and bowed to its mandate. Having thus passed through its terrible ordeal, as our Surety and Redeemer, He gives it back to us clad in a robe radiant with lustre, holding a broken sceptre in one hand, and a wreath in the other, with which He crowns each believer who succumbs to his momentary power, thus essentially changing its character and appearance, so that now the death of God's own saints is precious. This, beloved, is a pleasant view of death. It is delightful for you who, "through fear of death, are all your lifetime subject to bondage," to contemplate it among the precious things of God.

The death of His saints is precious to the Lord, because their persons are precious to Him. We shall never fully know, though sounding its fathomless depths, and scaling its illimitable heights through eternity, the love of God to His saints. When the finite can compass the Infinite, we may then understand to its extent the "love of Christ which passeth knowledge." So great is this love, it extends not to the persons only, but to all that belongs to a child of God. It separates not between the believer and his minutest interest, there being nothing attaching to an accepted sinner that is not dear to God. Human friendship affords an apt, though necessarily an imperfect, illustration of this. Real affection is undivided and supreme. We cannot love the person of a friend and feel indifferent to his personal interests. His happiness and well-being, his character and usefulness, will ever be closely and inseparably interwoven with our deepest interest and with our warmest love. Entwining him with our sacred affections, we have entwined in the same coil of love all the elements of his being, and all the circumstances of his history. His sorrows becloud, his joys brighten, our spirit; in his depression we are depressed, in his honour we are honoured. The atmosphere in which he lives influences the emotional of our nature, and our sensibilities rise or fall, are elated or depressed by his moral temperature. Of all the definitions of friendship, none can equal the truth and beauty of the inspired—"Thy friend, which is as thine own soul." (Deut. xiii. 6.) Sanctified by the grace of Jesus, what a tender, touching affection is this, linking us to another being, and to all that being's interests, as closely and as faithfully as though they were our own!

"It is the secret sympathy—
The silver link, the silken tie—
Which heart to heart, and mind to mind,
In body and in soul can bind."

There are few gifts of God more rare and precious than such a friendship—a friendship which becomes an inseparable part of our own being. We are, perhaps, but little aware how deeply we are indebted to its moulding, soothing, preserving influence. Who that has felt it finds not a response to the poet's language?—

"Friendship I mysterious cement of the soul!
Sweetener of life, and solder of society!
I owe thee much. Thou hast deserved of me
Far, far beyond what I can ever pay.
Oft have I proved the labours of thy love,
And the warm efforts of thy gentle heart,
Anxious to please."

But the friendship of God transcends all friendship, even as the love of God transcends all love. God loves not only the persons but the interests and concerns of His people. There is nothing, beloved, appertaining to you that Christ does not feel an interest, in. He is concerned in all your sorrows, in all your trials, in all your infirmities, in all your wants, in all your temptations. Think not His is a divided affection. Oh, no! your person precious to His heart, all that relates to you is precious—your life is precious—your death is precious. Can you think of the departure to eternity of one you love with indifference? Can you stand by that dying bed, and mark the ebbing of life from "thy friend, which is as thine own soul," without emotion?—without the feeling that your own existence were passing from you? Oh, no! Think, then, how precious to the Lord must be the death of His saints! It is as if His own life—the life He inspired, the life He ransomed, the life He renewed, the life He kept—were dissolving into immortality, yea, were dissolving into Himself! The life of the believer is the life of God in his soul; and when disembodied, it ascends to glory, it rises to the Divine source from whence it came, and although maintaining a separate and personal existence, becomes, in a measure, absorbed in God, and God, in the fulness of its joy, becomes all in all. Precious, then, to Christ is the death of His saints. When they die, He is with them. He is there to succour with His grace, to soothe with His presence, to brighten with His glory. He is there to nourish the faith that droops, to quench the temptation that assails, to dissipate the cloud that darkens, to remove the guilt that distresses, to quell the fear that agitates, and to cheer the solitude and loneliness of the valley with gracious manifestations of Himself, and to breathe words of kindness, comfort, and love, as the soul,

> "Passes through glory's morning gate,
> And walks in Paradise."

Believers die in reliance upon the atoning sacrifice of Christ, and so their death is precious in His sight. They die without a shred of human righteousness to cover them, without an argument that springs from themselves to plead for them, reposing in simple, childlike faith—the faith of an empty, helpless, believing sinner—upon the finished work of Immanuel. His blood and righteousness, beloved, will be your only hope in death, as in life, and that will be quite enough to meet the awful solemnity of that hour. We have witnessed and have read of the closing scenes of many believers—some eminent as preachers, scholars, and writers—but we never saw or heard of one who, in that solemn hour, derived any evidence, or comfort, or hope from his holiness, his labours, or his usefulness of life,—all exclusively and humbly have relied upon the Redeemer's blood and righteousness, and died clinging as sinners to the Saviour, as the guilty to the Crucified. And must not such a death be inconceivably precious to Jesus?

True believers die in the Lord, and this imparts a character and preciousness to their death delightsome to God. What significance and depth of meaning in these words—"Blessed are the dead who die in the Lord!" The thought of dying out of Christ may well impart to the unbeliever a fearful dread of dying. Such may truly regard death as the most terrible of all terrible things. Unconverted reader! better never to have been born into this world than to pass into the next out of Christ. It is to die as you were born—in sin, in rebellion against God, unconverted, under the curse, and condemned for ever. "He that believeth on the Son hath everlasting life: and he that believeth not the Son shall not see life; but the wrath of God abideth on him." (John iii. 36.) Oh, to confront the "king of terrors" with all your sins upon you, with all your guilt attaching to you, cherishing the enmity against God of your carnal mind, the weapons of rebellion in your hand, the love of sin, and the supremacy of Satan and the slavery of the world in your heart! Oh! is this the proper state in which to stand before a holy and a righteous God? Are you willing to die in this condition? Have you made up your mind to go into eternity without reconciliation, without pardon, without the wedding-garment, without an interest in Christ? Surely you have not seriously and intelligently considered your position, nor have weighed—if, indeed, they can be weighed—the fearful consequences of dying in your sins—unrepentant, unbelieving, unconverted. Think of passing through that dark, mysterious avenue that leads from time into eternity, without the presence of Jesus! Think of finding yourself disembodied in the world of spirits, yourself a spirit, affrighted, agitated, trembling, your escort up to the judgment-seat, lost, condemned spirits like your own! Think of appearing before the tribunal of Infinite Justice without a plea, without an argument, without a Saviour! Think of the trial—think of the scrutiny—think of the unveiling of your whole life—think of the sentence—think of the condemnation—banishment from God, exile from heaven, the loss of the soul, the undying worm, the unquenchable fire, for ever dwelling with the devil and his angels! "Take ye the unprofitable servant, and cast him into outer darkness; there shall be weeping and gnashing of teeth." Awful words to fall from the Lamb of God, who died on Calvary for the greatest of sinners! Have you carefully pondered these things? "What wilt thou say when He shall punish thee?" But there is hope! Death has not yet cited you to Christ's dread bar. Thine adversary has not yet delivered thee to the judge. God yet gives thee space for repentance. Count His long-suffering salvation. Repent! Ground your weapons beneath the Cross! Fall in the dust before God! Cry mightily to Him for mercy! Escape for thy life, and look not behind! Betake you to Christ, and give not sleep to your eyes nor slumber to your eyelids until you have shut yourself within Christ, where not a drop of the wrath of God shall ever touch you. Need we remind you what a Saviour He is,—that He casts out none who come to Him—that He welcomes all poor penitents—heals every broken heart—binds up every wounded spirit—washes in the fountain of His blood the guiltiest, clothes the naked, pardons the vilest, accepts the chief of sinners, and saves to the uttermost all that come to God by Him,—and all this on the ground of His most free, unconditional grace? "How shall we escape if we neglect so great salvation?"

But believers die in Christ. They die interested in Christ, they die shut up in Christ, they die clothed with Christ, they die in a union with Christ from which nothing shall ever separate them. In the fullest, broadest, most emphatic and blessed meaning of the words, they "die in the Lord;" and precious in His sight is their death.

The glory which the death of the saints brings to God must endear to Him their departure. "This spake He, signifying by what death He should glorify God." The Lord is glorified by the death of His saints. Their faith in Him at that solemn hour glorifies Him. The grace that sustains them under their sufferings glorifies Him. Their confidence in His promises, their hope in His salvation, their patient submission to His will, and their longing to depart to see His face, to be perfected in His likeness, and to be with Him for ever, glorifies Him. And think you not that glory surpassing all conception is brought to Christ when the dying saint, in that solemn moment, commits, entrusts, and breathes out his precious soul into the hands of Jesus, exclaiming, "I know whom I have believed, and am persuaded that He is able to keep that which I have committed unto Him against that day?" "Lord, into Thy hands I commit my spirit, for Thou hast redeemed me."

Precious, indeed, must the death of His saints be to the Lord, because then it is that He gathers them to Himself. "Father, I will that they also whom Thou hast given me be with me where I am, that they may behold my glory." Behold how Christ longs to have His saints in heaven with Him! So near and precious are they to His heart, He will not rest until all the travail of His soul, all the sheep of His fold, all the precious gems of His cabinet, encircle His throne, cluster around His person, fill and sparkle in His jewelled diadem. Not one shall be lost. Not a babe of the family, not a lamb of the flock, not a crown-jewel shall be missing in that day. "They shall never perish, neither shall any one pluck them out of my hands." Deity has redeemed them, Deity has preserved them, and, enshrined in the glories of Deity, they spend their happy eternity. Blessed truth! glorious hope! Weak saints shall be there, doubting believers shall be there, restored backsliders shall be there—the hand that but touched the hem shall wave the palm—the eye that but dimly beheld the cross shall drink in all that splendour—the tongue that but lisped, "My Father," shall join the song and swell the chorus. Child of God! trembling believer! doubting, fearful one, to whose heart the Saviour is more precious than life itself! you shall be there. There is a place in that crown, a mansion in that home, a bower in that paradise for you. And when death releases you from the bondage of corruption, and your happy spirit wings its way to heaven, the angels will clap their wings, and all the family above will strike their golden harps and cry, Welcome, welcome home! So precious are you to Jesus—the fruit of His dying agonies, the "pearl of great price," bought with His most precious blood, and kept by His Divine power—He must have you to behold His glory, to see His face, to repose upon His breast, to bask in His smiles, to chant His praises, to serve Him day and night in His temple, to be like Him and with Him for ever. We wonder not, then, that "precious in the sight of the Lord is the death of His saints."

But is it death to die? Approach that chamber where the saint of God is departing. Enter with a hushed footstep, for solemn is that scene, sacred is that spot—it is the verge of glory, it is the expanding gate of heaven. Celestial beings, viewless and noiseless, are there—angels and the spirits of the glorified hover round that bed. The Triune Jehovah is there—the Father watching the child He adopted, the Son upholding the soul He redeemed, the Holy Ghost strengthening the heart He had made His temple. Is this the chamber of death? this the last enemy, the final conflict, the closing scene? Surely this is not dying! What! this mental calmness, this spirit-joy, this soul-sunshine, this victory of faith, this stupendous, glorious triumph of the immortal over the mortal—is this death? Hark! What angel sounds are those? Whence this melody? It is the voice of the departing one. Listen to the strains—

"Jordan's stream shall ne'er o'erflow me

While my Saviour's by my side;
Canaan, Canaan lies before me,
Soon I'll cross the swelling tide.

"See the happy spirits waiting
On the bank beyond the stream,
Sweet responses still repeating,
Jesus, Jesus is their theme."

And then all is still! The "silver chord is loosed," and the panting spirit, borne on the wing of song, has swept upwards into the beaming presence of God, and rests in the embrace of Christ. Call not this death—it is life! Call it not destruction—it is the rejuvenescence of the soul, the moment when it renews its youth and expatiates amidst the wonders, glories, and sublimities of its new-born creation. All this triumph, all this glory, all this joy, we owe to Jesus' death and resurrection. In the faith of the atonement—

"It is not death to die—
To leave this weary load,
And, 'midst the brotherhood on high.
To be at home with God.

"It is not death to bear
The wrench that sets us free
From dungeon chains, to breathe the air
Of boundless liberty.

"It is not death to fling
Aside this sinful dust,
And rise, on strong exulting wing;
To live among the just.

"Jesus, thou Prince of Life!
Thy chosen cannot die;
Like Thee, they conquer in the strife,
To reign with Thee on high."

Precious, too, because death is the end of all their sorrows and sufferings, their infirmities, sicknesses, and sins. It is the termination of all evil, the birthday of all good. Oh, precious death, that dissolves the last link that binds me to corruption, that breaks the last fetter of sin, stifles the last groan, hushes the last sigh, dries the last tear, and introduces me to the sinless, sorrowless companionship of those who are before the throne of God and the Lamb "without fault!" Oh, who with but the lowliest hope in Christ longs not, wearies not, sighs not to be there? How the contrast intensifies this yearning! Here is earth—there is heaven. Here is sin—there is purity. Here is toil—there, is rest. Here is continual sorrow—there is fulness of joy. Here is exile—there is home. Here are imperfect saints—there, the "spirits of just men made perfect." Here are partings and changes—there, eternity restores the holy loves of earth, sanctifies and fixes them for ever! Oh, pants not your spirit for the eagle's flight that you may be there?

"Earth—with all its sin and sadness,
Pain and sickness, grief and care;
Heaven—with its unspoken gladness,
Light and love, and all that's fair;
How the two contrasted stand—
This dark world, and that bright land.

"Here the eye grows dim with weeping,
Here the cheek is wan with woe,
For the loved ones who are sleeping,
For the hopes that are laid low.
In the light of heaven's ray,
Tears of earth are wiped away.

"Here our toilsome way pursuing,
Compass'd round with many foes,
Pleasures are not worth the wooing,
Thorns are found with every rose;
There—the sorrowful are blest,
There—the weary are at rest.

"Here a lonely watch we 're keeping
On the battle-plain of life,
Lest the foe should find us sleeping,
And unfitted for the strife;
There the war and conflict cease,
Heaven's atmosphere is peace.

"Here the songs of praise we're singing
Often languish as they rise;
Fetter'd is the spirit's winging,
Cold and dead its harmonies;
In the chorus of the sky
Hallelujahs never die.

"Here our painful cross we're bearing,
Where our Master leads the way;
Here the shame and grief we're sharing
That for us upon Him lay;
There, we lay our burden down,
Change the cross into the crown.

"Here the parting word is spoken,
Where our hearts the closest cling;
And upon the spirit broken,
Like a knell its accents ring;
There—before the Saviour's throne
Parting is a word unknown.

"Here—we long to be like Jesus,
Here—we taste His matchless grace;
But whene'er from earth He frees us,
We shall shall see His blessed face;
With His saints for ever stand,
In our glorious fatherland."[16]

But while thus, beloved, we have concentrated your meditation for a time upon the death, the preciousness of the death, of all who believe in Jesus, we by no means would have you infer that this is the subject which should the most preeminently, earnestly, and exclusively arrest and fix the thoughts and expectations of your soul. The coming of the Lord, and not the death of the saints, is the grand theme, the "blessed hope," which the Holy Ghost proposes for our meditation, and presents to our faith. The great motive to watchfulness and prayer, to separation from the world, holiness of life, and readiness of habit to meet the Lord, is drawn, not from our going to Christ by death, but from Christ's coming to us in personal glory. Death is a part, and a fearful, gloomy, repulsive part, of the curse. View it in its most pleasant and attractive light, it is a humiliation. It is a conquest—it is a separation—it is a change—it is a decay—it is a solemn, a fearful plunge of the spirit into a world mysterious, invisible, unknown! But turn your thoughts to the coming of the Lord. How different the spectacle! It is a glory—it is a triumph—it is a reunion—it is the advent of a Conqueror—it is the appearing of a Saviour—it is as the coming of a Friend. Not, then, by the approach of death—precious though to Christ that death may be—but by the yet more powerful, yet more precious, yet more persuasive, lovely, and soothing prospect of the coming of Jesus, does the Holy Ghost seek to awaken, sanctify, and comfort the saints. How impressive is the language—"Waiting for the coming of the Lord Jesus"—"To the end He may establish your hearts unblameable in holiness before God, even our Father, at the coming of our Lord Jesus Christ with all His saints"—"I pray God your whole spirit, and soul, and body be preserved blameless unto the coming of our Lord Jesus Christ"—"We beseech you by the coming of our Lord Jesus Christ, and by our gathering together unto Him"—"Be patient, therefore, brethren, unto the coming of the Lord"—"For the coming of the Lord draweth nigh"—"Looking for the blessed hope, and the glorious appearing of the great God and our Saviour Jesus Christ"—"To all them that love His appearing"—"I will come again and receive ye unto myself, that where I am there ye may be also"—"He which testifieth these things saith, Surely I come quickly. Amen. Even so, come, Lord Jesus." Is not this a prospect worthy the study, the hope, the longing, the future, the destiny of the Church? Dwell upon the scene—a master's hand has sketched it. "In the first place, it presents to the expectation of the saints all that is to be loved and desired in the person of the Lord Jesus Christ, by whom he hath been redeemed, and upon whom he hath been nourished and sustained, not in His humility, as heretofore, but travelling in the greatness of His strength; not as a servant, but as a sovereign, uniting in Himself all the tender intercessions of the priest

---

16 Willis.

and the powerful majesty of the king, a priest upon his throne for ever. We shall behold Him whom, not having seen, we loved; we shall see Him as He is, in whom, while yet we saw Him not, we rejoiced with joy unspeakable, and full of glory. We shall see all the glorious attributes of God made manifest in manhood: the son of Mary glorified into the Son of God, and clothed with the all-sustaining power of the Word of God. In the next place, we shall behold all enemies put under His feet; Satan, the accuser of the brethren, cast out of the earth, and with him all his evil angels which dwell in the natural man, and rule the world. And we shall see the prison doors of death unbarred, and the grave yield up her dead; and then shall come to pass that saying of the prophet, 'Death shall be swallowed up in victory.' In the next place, we shall be gathered with all the saints of God since the world was, who shall all stand in their lot in the latter day, and in their flesh shall see God — the general assembly of the first-born, whose names are written in heaven; the Church of the living God, the patriarchs, the prophets, the apostles, the glorious army of the martyrs, the whole host of the redeemed, whom He shall bring with Him; and we, who remain till His coming, shall be caught up with Him into the air, and shall be for ever with the Lord. This is not a cheerless parting, but a joyful meeting and eternal union of those who are spiritually dear to one another; and, as touching natural affections, let it be remembered, that the natural man is then no more, the spiritual man alone is, and his affections alone remain. Then our father and mother, brother and sister, are they who have fulfilled the will of our heavenly Father. In the next place, this body of wickedness, this body of sin and death, shall be exchanged for the likeness of Christ's glorious body; for sinful flesh and blood shall not inherit that kingdom, nor corruption incorruption; mortality shall be swallowed up of life; it is sown a natural, it is raised a spiritual body; it is sown in dishonour, it is raised in honour; it is sown in weakness, it is raised in power. So that all shall be strength, harmony, and union within us; the perfect man, the holy man, complete in all things, and wanting nothing. In the next place, we shall be for ever with the Lord, partakers of His throne, partakers of His crown, and partakers of His government; His assessors in judgment, His deputies in power, ruling over the cities of His dominion, and judging the tribes of the sojourners of the earth. For though I inquire not into the mode or manner of our being, yet this I am not ashamed to declare, that we shall be like the Lord who ascended up from earth as easily as He descended; who after His resurrection, and even before it, passed to and fro without let or impediment of matter, and governed the elements with a sovereign control. And so shall we, in the exercise of that government and sovereignty which we shall then be permitted to hold of the earth, be as Adam, a king in his majesty, whom the elements of nature and all living, moving creatures upon the earth harmed not, but delighted to obey. Finally, we shall behold the earth and all the sojourners therein living in peace and blessedness, under the government of the Lord Jesus Christ; nature repossessed of all her original beauty, and society of all its proper blessedness; peace, gentleness, and meekness restored on every hand; all men blessed in Jesus, and calling Him blessed: 'nothing to corrupt or to destroy in my holy mountain, saith the Lord; for the earth shall be full of the knowledge of the glory of the Lord, as the waters cover the channels of the deep.'"

Look, then, on this picture and on that, and say which is the most pleasant, and attractive, and hopeful—which the best calculated to soothe in grief, to sustain in trial, to fortify in assault, to nerve in conflict, to animate in service, to stimulate to holiness, and to throw over all the future of the soul the glory and radiance of Christian expectation and hope—the dread approach of the grim king of terrors, or the glorious appearing of the great God our Saviour? For His coming, then, let us be looking—for it let us be prepared. Gird up the trailing robe, trim the waning lamp, nerve the trembling arm, and rouse the drooping heart. Our Lord is coming to bring us to Himself. All things betoken His near approach. Soon we shall behold His chariot, hear His voice, see His face, and fall in love and ecstacy upon the bosom that sorrowed, and sighed, and bled for us on the cross. "Let your loins be girded about, and your lights burning; and ye yourselves like unto men that wait for their lord, when he will return from the wedding; that when he cometh and knocketh, they may open to him immediately. Blessed are those servants whom the lord, when he cometh, shall find watching."

And now, my beloved reader, we part! We have spent many a sacred hour, have travelled many a pleasant path, and have discoursed upon many a hallowed theme together as we have roamed through these pages. Have we the experience of these "precious things of God" in our souls?—their preciousness in our hearts?—their sanctifying power and influence in our lives? Then, though now we separate, each to his toil, his care, his conflict, in a little while and we shall meet again, to part no more for ever! Then, beloved, you will not need the human tongue to tell the preciousness, nor the human hand to portray the beauty, nor the human imagination to unveil the glory of our Immanuel, for we shall "see Him as He is," and be with God for ever. Oh, look to Jesus—cling to Jesus— live, labour, die for Jesus! Ten thousand lives, ten thousand deaths—spent in exile, endured in martyrdom—were little, indeed, for such a Saviour! Build your hope of heaven solely, exclusively, upon this "precious Cornerstone." Sweep from its surface all the wood, hay, and stubble of human merit and creature trust,—all the chaff, rubbish, and dust of sacramental grace and religious ceremonial,—and plant your foot of faith, hope, and love, firm upon the bare, the naked Rock—the "Rock that is higher than you." Never, never will you perish, if upon this Divine Foundation—this "chief Cornerstone, elect, precious"—you lay your many sins, rest your weary soul, lean your dying head, and rear your hope of glory. Then, "when He shall come to be glorified in His saints, and to be admired in all them that believe," you will rise from the dust, enter into joy, and revel amidst the precious things of God in endless blessedness. Amen, and amen.

> "Our Jesus is the Cornerstone
> Jehovah built His Church upon,
> And never fallen to the ground
> Shall that blest edifice be found.
> The worldly-wise, with boasted sense,
> Count Him a rock of great offence;
> And all who are not newly born

Behold Him with contempt and scorn.
Sufficient goodness of their own
Makes Jesus but a stumbling-stone;
By reason of their blinded eyes,
God's way of saving they despise.
But when, in His appointed hour,
The Holy Spirit comes with power,
And leads the soul to Sinai's mount,
And opens there the black account,
He stands condemn'd, and looks around;
No friend nor helper can be found.
But when the Comforter comes near,
And sweetly whispers in his ear
That Jesus came for him to bleed,
His name is precious then indeed;
Precious as God's appointed way
His own perfections to display.
For what of God is understood
Save through the Lamb's redeeming blood?
He's precious all our journey through,
As when the first believing view
Removed the heavy load of sin,
And brought the peace of God within.
He's precious as our covenant Head,
And precious when, in sinners' stead,
He paid the law's immense demands
Into His righteous Father's hands;
And precious when "Tis done,' he cried,
And bow'd His sacred head, and died.
Then death for ever lost its sting;
The Church may now of victory sing.
Precious when faith beholds Him rise
Victorious to His native skies;
And precious, now in heaven He pleads,
And for His members intercedes.
If varied often be our case,
He's precious then in various ways
When weary, weak, or sore oppress'd,
He's precious as a place of rest.
When clouds of darkness intervene,
And Jesus' beauties can't be seen,
Why do we linger by His cross,
And count all else but dung and dross?
Because He's precious to us still,
Nothing on earth His place can fill.
When under fresh-contracted guilt
Sorrow and heartfelt shame are felt,
The blessed Spirit comes again,
Sprinkles the blood, and heals the pain.
How precious, then, the Son of God,

From whose dear side the fountain flow'd!
With joy we lift our heads again,
And sing the Lamb that once was slain.
Sometimes, lest we should lift our head,
As if the Man of Sin were dead,
We're left to feel a deadly blow,
To humble pride and keep us low.
God shews us some inherent sin,
Which makes us cry, Unclean! unclean!
Yet 'midst the thorns He'll safely keep
The feet of all His helpless sheep.
He but designs from self to wean,
And make us more on Jesus lean.
While trav'lling through a hostile land,
With mighty foes on every hand—
When call'd in battle to engage,
And hot the fight through Satan's rage—
How precious, then, our conquering Lord?
How sweet to hear that cheering word,
'You need not fear, you need not flee,
Stand still, and my salvation see.'
Then shout, ye saints, the battle's won!
Your Captain is to glory gone!
Gone up your places to prepare,
And soon He'll fetch and place you there,
With all the heavenly host to praise
A precious Christ through endless days."[17]

THE END.

---

17 Sturton.